Fodor's Inside

Portland

CONTENTS

ABOUT THIS GUIDE

Inside Portland shows you the city like you've never seen it. Written entirely by locals, it includes features on the city's street art and galleries and plenty of insider tips. The result is a curated compilation infused with authentic Portland flavor, accompanied by easy-to-use maps and transit information.

Whether you're visiting Portland for the first time or a seasoned traveler looking to explore a new neighborhood, this is the guide for you. We've handpicked the top things to do and rated the sights, shopping, dining, and nightlife in the city's most dynamic neighborhoods. Truly exceptional experiences in all categories are marked with a ★.

Restaurants, bars, and coffee shops are a huge part of Portland's appeal, of course, and you'll find plenty to savor in its diverse neighborhoods. We cover cuisines at all price points, with everything from enduring institutions and groundbreaking chefs to the perfect late-night street snack; use the $ to $$$$ price charts below to estimate meal costs. We

cover hotels in the Experience section at the front of this guide. We list adult prices for sights; ask about discounts when purchasing tickets.

Portland is constantly changing. All prices, opening times, and other details in this guide were accurate at press time. Always confirm information when it matters, especially when making a detour to a specific place. Visit Fodors.com for expanded restaurant and hotel reviews, additional recommendations, news, and features.

What It Costs: Restaurants			
$	$$	$$$	$$$$
under $16	$16–$22	$23–$30	over $30

Prices are the average cost of a main course at dinner or, if dinner is not served, at lunch.

Experience
Portland

VANCOUVER, WA

NORTH

NORTHWEST

NORTHEAST

SOUTHWEST

SOUTHEAST

WELCOME TO PORTLAND

What distinguishes Portland, Oregon, from the rest of America's cityscapes? For some, it's the wealth of cultural offerings and never-ending culinary choices; for others, it's the city's proximity to the ocean and mountains, or simply the beauty of having all these attributes in one place. Strolling through Downtown or one of Portland's many diverse and dynamic outlying neighborhoods, there's an unmistakable vibrancy to this city—one that's encouraged by clean air, infinite trees, and an appealing blend of historic and modern architecture. Portland's various nicknames—Rose City, Bridgetown, Beervana—tell its story.

PORTLAND TODAY

Rich cultural offerings, endless recreational activities, and a friendly vibe make Portland universally alluring, but the white-hot food scene is arguably its top visitor attraction, especially its fervent embrace of the locavore movement. The city maintains a strong appreciation for artisan craftsmanship, which encompasses everything from coffee, beer, chocolate, and other edibles (recreational marijuana was legalized in Oregon in 2015) to furniture, jewelry, apparel, and household goods. These touchstones of modern urbanism have made Portland the kind of place that younger creative spirits, tech workers, and artists want to visit and live in.

Indeed, the city's population has risen sharply since 2000, from 529,000 to about 655,000, and so too has the cost of living. It's still cheaper to live here than in other big West Coast cities, but traffic congestion has become a serious menace and higher rents and home prices have altered, for better or for worse, Portland's former reputation as a laid-back, hippie-prevalent place where—according to a famous line in the snarky TV satire *Portlandia*, "young people go to retire."

The city feels increasingly more upscale and its citizens more professionally ambitious. Glassy modern condo and apartment buildings are popping up seemingly everywhere, but with the injection of people and money, there are also more design-driven boutiques, hotels, and restaurants opening. Above all else, Portland is constantly evolving, and mostly in exciting ways.

1840S–1880S

Although the legendary Lewis and Clark Voyage of Discovery navigated past the Columbia River's confluence with the Willamette in 1805, no permanent settlement was attempted here until 1843, when a couple of enterprising pioneers—Asa Lovejoy and William Overton—filed a claim to establish what would become, within 15 years, the largest city in the new Oregon Territory. Overton soon sold his half to Francis Pettygrove, a native of Portland, Maine. The name of this new settlement was determined by a coin toss between Pettygrove and Lovejoy, a Bostonian. Had fate played out differently, you'd be reading a book about Boston, Oregon.

After Oregon was admitted as a U.S. state in 1859, it began to prosper thanks to its strategic position as a deepwater port. In 1888, its population now at around 45,000, the city built the first steel bridge on the West Coast across the Willamette River, connecting Downtown with the East Side, which over the next half century would fill in with mostly residential but also a number of smaller commercial neighborhoods.

1890–WORLD WAR II

With the city's rise as a port city, it also developed an unfortunate reputation as a lawless den of iniquity, especially in what is now the Old Town/Chinatown neighborhood, which from the late 1880s through the first couple of decades of the 20th century teemed with bordellos, gambling halls, and saloons. Although more legitimate businesses began to take foot during the period between the two world wars, Portland started to lose national prominence as Seattle, San Francisco, and Los Angeles grew far more rapidly.

THE POSTWAR ERA

After playing a vital role in the U.S. military's shipbuilding efforts during World War II, the city once again began to earn an infamous reputation throughout the 1950s, this time as a hotbed of organized crime and government corruption. In the 1960s, the countercultural spirit of San Francisco spread north to Portland, which became a hub of social protest.

In 1979, the city implemented an ambitious Urban Growth Boundary to help contain suburban sprawl and maintain urban vitality. This move, along with the implementation of a number of smart design measures—such as building a light-rail transit system, zoning for growth along transportation corridors, and encouraging environmentally sustainable development—helped to launch Portland's reputation as an exemplar of urban planning. By the late 1990s, metro Portland had undergone a tech and population boom, which coincided with its steady ascent—thanks to Nike, Columbia Sportswear, and Under Armour—into a center of sports apparel manufacture. Rapid growth, in part thanks to the city's increasing reputation as a hub of creativity, progressive politics, and entrepreneurism, has continued right through the first two decades of the 21st century.

WHAT'S WHERE IN PORTLAND

Portland is organized into five key sections with directional names: Southwest, Northwest, North, Northeast, and Southeast. Each of these larger districts contains at least a dozen or more smaller neighborhoods, such as Downtown in Southwest, Hawthorne in Southeast, the Pearl District in Northwest, and so on. To help you organize your visit, here's a rundown of the areas we cover in this book. The numbers refer to chapter numbers.

2. DOWNTOWN

At the center of it all, Portland's Downtown boasts the Portland Art Museum, the Portland'5 Centers for the Arts, and the Portland Farmers Market along with a slew of notable restaurants and the bulk of the city's hotels. Nearest to the Pearl District, Downtown's West End has become an increasingly stylish dining and retail area in recent years. Due west of Downtown lies enormous Washington Park, which contains many must-sees, including the Hoyt Arboretum, International Rose Test Garden, Japanese Garden, and Portland Children's Museum.

3. PEARL DISTRICT AND OLD TOWN/CHINATOWN

Bordering Downtown to the north is Portland's trendy and posh Pearl District, which teems with upscale restaurants, bars, and shopping (don't miss Powell's Books), along with pricey condos and artists' lofts. Due east and also bordering part of Downtown, the city's Old Town/

Chinatown neighborhood is home to a fun if sometimes rowdy nightlife scene, Lan Su Chinese Garden, and Portland Saturday Market.

4. NOB HILL AND VICINITY

From offbeat to upscale, Nob Hill and adjacent Slabtown's shopping, restaurants, and bars draw a discerning crowd. Immediately west, Forest Park is the largest forested area within city limits in the nation. Trailheads are easily accessible from Nob Hill as well as from Washington Park, which lies just south.

5. INNER NORTH AND NORTHEAST PORTLAND

Containing the Moda Center basketball and concert arena, the Oregon Convention Center, and the Lloyd Center Mall, as well as some trendy dining, shopping, and bar-hopping along the Burnside Street corridor out to 28th Avenue, the portions of Portland's North and Northeast quadrants closest to Downtown are a hodgepodge of prosaic and intriguing. After Downtown, this area has the largest concentration of centrally located hotels.

6. INNER SOUTHEAST PORTLAND

Vibrant pockets of foodie-minded eateries, craft cocktail bars, and funky indie boutiques make Inner Southeast, especially the formerly industrial Central East Side, a must-visit. You'll also find the funky commercial sections of Hawthorne, Division, and Belmont west of the 30th Avenue in this part of town, as well as the family-popular OMSI science museum and Tilikum Crossing bridge.

7. OUTER NORTH PORTLAND

Known as the "fifth quadrant," North Portland sits on the peninsula formed by the joining of the Willamette River and the Columbia River. North Mississippi and North Williams avenues are see-and-be-seen dining and drinking destinations. Farther out, old-school neighborhoods like Kenton and St. Johns have more affordable, locals-favored businesses that offer a diverse and unpretentious sense of the city's charms.

8. OUTER NORTHEAST PORTLAND

The Outer Northeast area includes one of the city's top neighborhoods for indie retail and dining, the Alberta Arts District, as well as inviting neighborhoods like Hollywood and Beaumont. This huge quadrant extends north to the Columbia River and way out east to the city border, and is home to some intriguing attractions like the Grotto and Rocky Butte.

9. OUTER SOUTHEAST PORTLAND

Another of the city's largest districts, the Outer Southeast area includes the hip sections of Belmont, Hawthorne, and Division east of 30th Avenue as well as beautiful Mt. Tabor Park and up-and-coming Montavilla and Foster-Powell, which is also where you'll find sizable Asian and Latino communities. To the south, the historic and mostly residential neighborhoods of Sellwood and Moreland contain a smattering of notable shops as well as some pretty parks.

10. VANCOUVER, WA

Although very much its own city, Vancouver lies just across the Columbia River from North Portland and has enjoyed a recent resurgence thanks to a stunning new Waterfront redevelopment and a bounty of hip new restaurants, bars, and breweries in its central downtown and Uptown Village neighborhoods. It's become a part of the metro area well worth exploring.

TOP EXPERIENCES IN PORTLAND

In Portland, the "must-sees" aren't always purpose-built attractions and museums. This is a city where the activities you shouldn't miss often revolve around eating, drinking, and—as an effective remedy for indulging in too much of the former—getting outside and enjoying nature.

BIKE THE BRIDGES AND RIVERFRONT

Rent bikes or use the city's bike-share program to venture out on two wheels up and down the riverfront promenades on both sides of the Willamette River, and also to pedal across some of the city's distinctive bridges, such as the historic Hawthorne Bridge and the stunningly contemporary **Tilikum Crossing**.

WATCH THE SUNSET AT MT. TABOR

This leafy and hilly East Side park set atop an extinct volcanic cinder cone is lovely for light hiking and heavy napping all day long, but it's especially dramatic at dusk, when you can picnic or laze on a blanket and watch the sun fall over Downtown and the West Hills.

GO BREWERY HOPPING IN NORTH PORTLAND

There are several Portland neighborhoods where you can walk among three to five excellent craft breweries (the Pearl District and Central East Side leap to mind), but the North Mississippi area has some especially terrific beer venues and is pretty to walk through, too. Top stops in the area include **Ex Novo, LABrewatory, Ecliptic,** and **Stormbreaker.**

EXPLORE THE MILES OF AISLES AT POWELL'S

Set out on a book-buying adventure at this iconic bookstore, one of the largest and most famous in the world. You'll find an exhaustive selection of both new and used books, plus literary-minded gifts, an inviting coffee cafe, and a rare book room that contains an amazing collection of first editions.

STROLL THE JAPANESE AND CHINESE GARDENS

Two of the loveliest green spaces in a city rife with them are devoted to the serene design aesthetics and native plantings of Japan and China. Walk first through the **Japanese Garden** up in **Washington Park,** and then down through the smaller **Lan Su Chinese Garden** in Old Town, where you can end your adventure sipping tea in a traditional pondside teahouse.

FEAST AT A FOOD CART POD

Head to one of the city's famously bustling and reasonably priced food cart pods—such as **Prost! Marketplace,** the **Bite on Belmont,** or **Portland Mercado**—and have a progressive lunch or dinner by sampling dishes from two or three different vendors. The offerings are diverse, and you could easily nosh on a Thai veggie bowl, Texas-style barbecue brisket, and Norwegian smoked salmon rolls at the same cart pod, while also discovering a great selection of craft beer and artisan coffee.

SPEND SATURDAY AT MARKET

Start your Saturday with a tour of the convivial, tree-shaded **Portland Farmers Market** in the South Park Blocks by Portland State University, where you can listen to live music; score local hazelnuts, honeys, chocolates, and berries; and savor delicious breakfast fare from several vendors, including Pine State Biscuits and Verde Cocina. Then walk or hop on MAX light rail a short distance to Old Town, where the legendary open-air **Portland Saturday Market** features the arts and crafts of more than 250 artisans.

HIKE THE HILLS TO PITTOCK MANSION

Just minutes from Downtown, set out on a hike through dense Douglas fir and cedar groves in one of the nation's largest urban forests, **Forest Park.** Stop at the **Portland Audubon Society** to see the wildlife displays, and end at **Pittock Mansion,** a historic hilltop estate that offers self-guided tours and has sweeping views of Mt. Hood and Mt. St. Helens.

ATTEND A FESTIVAL AT TOM MCCALL WATERFRONT PARK

This sweep of green that fringes the Downtown section of the Willamette riverfront hosts fantastic festivals from spring through fall, starting with Cinco de Mayo and continuing with the Rose Festival, Portland Pride, the Waterfront Blues Festival, and the Oregon Brewers Festival. When there's not a festival happening, the **Tom McCall Waterfront Park** and adjoining promenade is lovely for a stroll, jog, or bike ride.

WATCH A MOVIE AT A HISTORIC PUB THEATER

Portland abounds with handsomely restored vintage theaters, many of them from the early 20th century and located in hip, historic neighborhoods—there's the **Bagdad Theater** in Hawthorne, the **Laurelhurst Theater** at 28th and East Burnside, the **Academy Theater** in Montavilla, and the fairest of them all, the ornately designed 1926 **Hollywood Theatre** in Northeast. Some of these show first-run movies on giant screens, some second-run and arthouse films on smaller screens—all

of them serve pub food and a good range of local beers and wines.

STOP AND SMELL THE ROSES AT WASHINGTON PARK

First visit the incredible **International Rose Test Garden** in Washington Park, with its 550 varieties, and then venture over to North Portland's **Peninsula Park & Rose Garden** for more floral exploring, along with, perhaps, a tour of the rose garden in **Ladd's Addition** in Southeast.

SIP SPIRITS ALONG DISTILLERY ROW

Walk through the Central East Side's artisan distillery district, stopping at a few of the city's best spots for finely crafted vodka, gin, whiskey, and liqueurs, many that feature Oregon berries and other local ingredients. To save money on tastings and track your adventures, purchase a Distillery Row Passport for $20.

GET YOUR GALLERY FIX AT A MONTHLY ART WALK

Two of the city's most intriguing neighborhoods—the upscale Pearl District, with its converted warehouses and shiny new condos, and the quirky and low-keyed **Alberta Arts District**—host highly popular evening gallery strolls once a month. It's First Thursdays in the Pearl, and Last Thursdays in Alberta.

ATTEND AN AMAZING PRIX-FIXE MULTI-COURSE DINNER

Many of the most memorable—and talked-about—dining experiences in Portland are reservation-only multicourse feasts held at typically intimate in-the-know venues, such as **Beast, Langbaan, Nodoguro,** and **Farm Spirit.** You usually buy your tickets in advance, can expect to spend $75 to $150 (more if you choose wine pairings) per person, and arrive with a big appetite. And in return, you'll enjoy a locally sourced, seasonally driven culinary experience of a lifetime.

PORTLAND WITH KIDS

Portland abounds with kid-oriented attractions and activities. Just getting around the Rose City—via streetcars and light-rail trains on city streets and bicycles—is fun. For listings of family-oriented concerts, performances by the **Oregon Children's Theatre,** and kid-relevant movies, check the free *Willamette Weekly* newspaper ⊕ *www.wweek.com*.

MUSEUMS AND ATTRACTIONS

The **Oregon Museum of Science and Industry (OMSI)** contains touch-friendly exhibits, a big-screen theater, the state's biggest planetarium, and a 240-foot submarine moored just outside in the Willamette River. Along Portland's leafy Park Blocks, the **Oregon History Museum** and **Portland Art Museum** both have exhibits and programming geared toward kids. In Old Town, kids enjoy walking amid the ornate pagodas and dramatic foliage of the **Lan Su Chinese Garden**. On weekends, visit the **Portland Saturday Market**, where food stalls and musicians keep younger kids entertained, and the cool jewelry, toys, and gifts appeal to teens. And, just up Burnside Street from the market, **Powell's City of Books** contains enormous sections of children's and YA literature.

PARKS

Portland is dotted with verdant parks, many with fields, playgrounds, and picnic areas. Standouts include the **Fields Park** in the Pearl, **Westmoreland Park Nature Playground** near Sellwood, and **Esther Short Park** in Vancouver. The most famous urban oasis in the city, **Forest Park** (along with adjoining Washington Park) offers a wealth of engaging diversions, including the **Oregon Zoo, Portland Children's Museum,** and **World Forestry Discovery Center Museum**. The **International Rose Test Garden**—near which there's an excellent playground—and **Japanese Garden** are fun for kids of all ages.

OUTDOOR ADVENTURES

Tour boats ply the Willamette River, and a couple of marinas near **OMSI** rent kayaks and conduct drag-boat races. Several shops in town rent bikes for use on the city's bike lanes and trails. **Oaks Amusement Park** has rides galore. Within day-tripping distance, **Mt. Hood** has camping, hiking, and biking, and three of the most family-friendly ski resorts in the Northwest. The pick-your-own berry farms and pumpkin patches on **Sauvie Island** make for an engaging afternoon.

FOOD AND DRINK IN PORTLAND

A long growing season, lower costs than other West Coast cities, and a hunger for locally sourced, small-batch food and drink has transformed Portland from a meat-and-potatoes kinda town into a city that's topped many a food critic's "best of" lists over the past 20 years.

FARM-*TO*-TABLE

In this playground of sustainability and creativity, many restaurants change menus weekly—sometimes even daily—depending upon what they can source from local, and often organic, farms and markets, be it fiddlehead ferns or hazelnuts, chanterelle mushrooms or steelhead trout. Restaurants like **Clyde Common, Higgins,** and **Paley's Place** have been sourcing locally since well before this approach became ubiquitous. Many of the top tables in town offer prix-fixe multi-course tasting menus or family-style feasts in addition to their à la carte offerings, and these set meals often provide a delicious way to experience a chef's most creative, seasonally based efforts.

SEAFOOD

With 362 miles of coastline, bays, tidal flats, and estuaries, Oregon has a stunning variety of fish and shellfish. Portland restaurants and locals are attuned to the seasons, from the start of Dungeness season (late fall) to the best months for catching salmon (March and April).

King, or Chinook as it's often called here, is the prize when it comes to salmon, but silvery coho and genetically related steelhead trout are also popular, as is Columbia River sturgeon and ocean-caught rockfish, lingcod, and albacore tuna. Low tide on Oregon's beaches can yield thin razor clams—usually served pan-fried. Mussels grow in clusters along rocky coastal stretches, while oysters are harvested in several spots as well.

GLOBAL CUISINE

There's an excellent variety of ethnic dining here, especially Thai and Vietnamese, the quality of which tends to be stellar whether you're enjoying hearty pho or green curry at a low-frills hole in the wall or supping on elevated regional fare at upscale spots like **Pok Pok** and **Langbaan.** More recently, Portland has seen an influx of notable Japanese restaurants (from izakayas to ramen parlors) as well as purveyors of first-rate Korean, Indian, and Indonesian fare. As Portland's Latino community has grown, so too has its variety of Mexican, Peruvian,

Argentine, and other Latin American offerings. This is also a great town for French, Italian, and Mediterranean cuisine.

WINE, SPIRITS, AND BEER

Diners in Portland often spend as much or even more money and time on decisions about wine, beer, and cocktails than they do on food. Pinot Noir grapes, which thrive in the nearby Willamette Valley, have been the central force of Oregon wine-making since the industry took root in the 1960s, but Pinot Gris and Chardonnay also perform well. In Portland, you can expect to see a wide range of Pacific Northwest wines on menus, so don't assume Pinot Noir is the only, or even the best, local wine to try. In other parts of Oregon, especially warmer southern areas and the Columbia Gorge—and also Washington state—virtually every kind of varietal can thrive, including big-bodied, sun-loving Syrahs, Tempranillos, and Malbecs. Craft brewers proliferate in Portland, and although the region's reputation is for hoppy IPAs, experimentation is the name of the game, and many local producers specialize in sours, saisons, porters, and less-common European beers. Artisan distillers also have a tremendous presence, and many local bars make their own bitters and shrubs and offer highly ambitious cocktail programs. The line between bars and restaurants in Portland is pretty gray—many lounges serve first-rate pub fare, tapas, pizza, and the like. And some of the best drinking spots in town are acclaimed restaurants.

BREAKFAST AND BRUNCH

More than a few self-professed Portlander foodies would name breakfast their favorite meal, and indeed, this city abounds with excellent cafes and diner-style spots that specialize in the morning meal. A few of Portland's top restaurants serve brunch and dinner, rather than lunch, daily. Unfortunately, if there's a meal that's jumped in price more than any other as Portland's "it" factor has risen, it's breakfast and brunch. It's not uncommon for even rather modest spots to charge $12 to $14 for omelets or waffles. On weekends, as you might expect, scoring a table at brunch can also require standing in line.

BAKED GOODS AND DESSERTS

Artisan bakeries are one of Portland's great strengths, and many of the city's top coffeehouses also serve exquisite pastries, cookies, and cakes either baked in-house or sourced from top local purveyors. Gourmet doughnuts have long been a Portland thing (world-famous Voodoo Doughnut is fun, but most snobs of the genre would rank a half-dozen other shops ahead of them). Ice cream is another treat that's skyrocketed in stature, with Salt & Straw, Ruby Jewel, Fifty Licks, and the yogurt shop Eb & Bean turning out fabulous frozen desserts in often daringly imaginative flavors.

WHAT TO WATCH AND READ

Well before Portland became a much-hyped exemplar of urbanism, trendy design, and hip dining, authors like Ken Kesey, Beverly Cleary, and Chuck Palahniuk were writing about Oregon in refreshingly authentic, sometimes unsentimentally raw, terms. More recently, Hollywood has used Portland as a setting for a number of films and TV shows. Here are some of the more memorable depictions of the city and surrounding region.

BEEZUS AND RAMONA
The first book in children's book author Beverly Cleary's Portland-based Ramona Quimby series is one of her most beloved. This title and others in the series are set on Klickitat Street, in the same Northeast Portland neighborhood (near the Hollywood District) that was also the geographical focal point of the earlier Henry Huggins books.

FUGITIVES AND REFUGEES
Fight Club novelist Chuck Palahniuk penned this endearingly strange and sometimes seedy memoir and travelogue as something of a love letter to the weirder aspects of his one-time hometown, Portland.

GEEK LOVE
Katherine Dunn's National Book Award finalist novel from 1989 was inspired by the author's Portland upbringing and follows an Oregon family's strange trials and tribulations as part of a traveling carnival.

THE GOONIES
The beloved Richard Donner–directed teen adventure comedy was filmed entirely on the section of the Oregon Coast that's nearest to Portland, including Cannon Beach and Astoria, which is home to the historic jail in the movie and now serves as the Oregon Film Museum.

LEAVE NO TRACE
The critically acclaimed 2018 movie starring Ben Foster is based on the novel *My Abandonment*—which was inspired by a true story—and follows the plight of a military veteran who lives off the grid in Portland's Forest Park until being found and relocated to a Christmas tree farm in rural Oregon. It was filmed on location in Portland and neighboring Clackamas County.

MY OWN PRIVATE IDAHO
Locally based LGBTQ indie director Gus Van Sant's 1991 drama, led by the poignant performances of Keanu Reeves and River Phoenix, is filmed primarily in Portland, with many

scenes at what is now the posh Sentinel Hotel. It's perhaps the most celebrated of several movies that Van Sant set and shot in Portland, includng *Drugstore Cowboy* and *Paranoid Park*.

THE LATHE OF HEAVEN

The late sci-fi novelist and Portlander Ursula K. Le Guin set this award-winning 1971 novel in a futuristic and dystopian version of Portland (in 2002). There have been two TV movies made about the book.

LEAN ON PETE

The 2017 melodrama (based on a novel of the same name) chronicles the plight of a teen caring for an aging racehorse and is set and filmed in both Portland and the high desert ranching country of eastern Oregon.

PORTLANDIA

Locals are quite used to being asked by curious fans of this satirical sketch TV series just how accurately the city is portrayed in this hit show starring Carrie Brownstein and Fred Armisten, which ran on the IFC channel from 2011 through 2018. Depending on whom you ask, the answer typically ranges from very to not very, but whatever one thinks of the often hilarious series, it undoubtedly helped put Portland on the travel radar of plenty of people around the world who'd never before given it much thought. The show was filmed locally at a number of recognizable spots around town, including the Vera Katz Eastside Esplanade (in the show's opening credits), Prasad restaurant and its adjoining yoga studio, Portland City Hall, Olympia Provisions, Paxton Gate, Caravan–Tiny House Hotel, Land Gallery, and many others.

SOMETIMES A GREAT NOTION

Although renowned Oregon native son Ken Kesey rarely included specific references to Portland in his novels, which include the even more famous *One Flew Over the Cuckoo's Nest* (the movie adaptation of which was filmed just down the road in Salem), his books and films—including this rich depiction of the travails of an Oregon logging family—provide rich insight into the region's personality and history. This was his second novel, and in 1971 it was made into a movie starring Paul Newman and Henry Fonda.

WILD

Cheryl Strayed's 2012 memoir about discovering herself while hiking the Pacific Crest Trail inspired the 2014 Reese Witherspoon film of the same name. And while the book and movie covers her time on the trail in California and Washington, too, most of the movie is filmed in Portland or nearby (such as the Bridge of the Gods, in Cascade Locks).

WILD WILD COUNTRY

Filmed partly in Portland, this spellbinding 2018 Netflix six-part documentary recounts the strange but true story of the Rajneeshpuram religious cult that settled in rural central Oregon in the early 1980s, and how the libertarian-minded and very private residents of the region fought back.

PORTLAND TIMELINE

Although it was one of the West Coast's largest by the late 19th century, Portland is nevertheless a fairly young city. Still, a lot has happened in its 170-year existence. Here are some of the events and important eras that have helped make the city what it is today.

Pre-1800s: The land that is now Portland is inhabited by members of the indigenous Chinook people, primarily the Multnomah and Clackamas tribes.

1805: Meriwether Lewis, William Clark, and their team of intrepid explorers pass through the area via the Columbia River, during their Voyage of Discovery from Missouri to the Oregon Coast.

1843: Entrepreneurs and land speculators Asa Lovejoy and William Overton file a claim to settle land just west of the Willamette River in the Oregon Country, then a disputed parcel of the Northwest under joint U.S. and British control.

1845: The name for the new city is chosen by a coin toss between Lovejoy, who hails from Boston, Massachusetts, and Francis Pettygrove, who comes from Portland, Maine, and to whom Overton had recently sold his half of the land claim.

1846: The signing of the Oregon Treaty establishes the U.S.–British (Canadian) border at the 49th parallel, rendering the Oregon Country part of the United States.

1848: Oregon formally becomes a U.S. territory, and Oregon City—15 miles down the Willamette River from Portland—becomes the capital.

1851: Portland, now with a population of about 800, officially incorporates as a city.

1859: Oregon becomes the 33rd U.S. state, with Salem—45 miles southwest of Portland—its capital. Portland, however, with a population of 2,800 (compared to 900 in Salem and 1,250 in Oregon City) is and will remain the state's largest settlement.

1873: About 20 blocks of downtown burn in a fire.

1877: The Oregon Zoo is founded.

1892: The Portland Art Museum is established, making it the West Coast's oldest art museum.

1905: Portland's popularity—and population—soars following the Lewis and Clark Exposition.

1907: The Rose Festival is established—it remains Portland's most prominent and best-attended annual event.

1910: The city's population reaches 207,000, trailing only San Francisco, Los Angeles, and Seattle in Western U.S. cities.

1930: The population reaches 300,000, and Portland's tawdry reputation as a dangerous and seedy port city finally starts to give way—to a degree—to its prominence as one of the West Coast's most important commercial centers.

1942: Portland establishes the country's first urban assembly center for the purposes of sending Japanese residents to internment camps—it's one of many instances in the city and state's long history of ethnic and racial discrimination.

1942: The development of the Kasier Shipyards and the worker community of Vanport, created to supply military aircraft for the U.S. war efforts, adds about 150,000 workers and their families—including a significant number of African-Americans—to the city's population.

1948: Vanport is wiped out by a massive flood.

1970: The NBA's Portland Trail Blazers becomes the city's first major sports franchise.

1971: Powell's Books opens.

1984: Pioneer Courthouse Square opens and becomes a social hub of Downtown.

1986: The city's TriMet transit system launches MAX light rail service.

1992: The Portland Farmers Market begins operation.

1995: Rose Garden Arena (now the Moda Center) opens.

2009: Sam Adams is elected, making Portland then the largest U.S. city with an openly LGBTQ mayor.

2009: Major League Soccer's Portland Timbers franchise is established.

2011: TV's fictional (but pretty spot-on) satire *Portlandia* debuts.

2015: The nation's first major bridge designed exclusively for public transit and pedestrians, Tilikum Crossing, opens.

2018: The city population reaches 653,000, as Portland's popularity, especially with younger workers, artists, makers, entrepreneurs, and tech workers continues to rise.

BEST PORTLAND EVENTS

Prime event season in Portland is spring through fall, with many gatherings taking place along the Downtown riverfront or in area parks, but an increasing number of artistic and cultural festivals and showcases now take place during those often inclement and dark days of winter.

JANUARY

Fertile Ground Festival of New Work
This grassroots opportunity for the city's creative minds to premier plays and spoken word, stage dance and theatrical performances, and present comedy and film takes place over 10 days and emphasizes boundary-pushing, explorative works. *Late Jan.–early Feb.*

FEBRUARY

Portland Seafood and Wine Festival
Head to the Oregon Convention Center to sample Dungeness crab, albacore, king salmon, and other riches from Northwest waters, along with exceptional wines, plus live music. *Early Feb.*

Portland Winter Light Festival
Begun in 2016, this vibrant, fast-growing event features well over 100 light installations and more than 60 kinetic concerts and performances all around the city. *Early Feb.*

Biamp PDX Jazz Festival
Warm up your cold winter nights by attending some of the fantastic concerts held during this nine-day program created in part to celebrate Black History Month. Past performers have included Dianne Reeves, Ravi Coltrane, and Wayne Shorter. *Late Feb.–early Mar.*

MARCH

Portland Dining Month
Here's your opportunity to enjoy a three-course meal at a reasonable fixed price ($33 currently) at more than 100 of the city's top dining venues. *All month*

Portland International Film Festival
Held at the Portland Museum of Art's acclaimed Northwest Film Center, this world-class event begun in 1977 is the most prestigious and well-attended of the city's many cinematic events. More than 100 screenings take place over two weeks. *Early–mid-Mar.*

APRIL

Design Week Portland
In a city where creativity, technology, and maker culture intersect quite famously, the popularity of this program featuring hundreds of open houses, exhibits, workshops, and lectures continues to skyrocket. *Early–mid-Apr.*

Soul'd Out Music Festival
Soul, R&B, and blues legends like Prince, Diana Krall, Lauryn Hill, and Mos Def performed at some of the city's top venues during this six-day celebration. *Mid-Apr.*

MAY
Cinco de Mayo
Portland's Cinco de Mayo festival celebrates its sister-city relationship with Guadalajara, Mexico, and runs a full weekend in early May. *Nearest weekend to May 5*

Portland Rose Festival
Arguably the most famous event in the state, the festival consists of more than 60 family-friendly events and parties held over two weeks, including a rollicking carnival at Downtown's Waterfront Park, a Starlight Parade, a military Fleet Week exhibition, dragon boat races, the nation's largest rose show, and the Grand Floral Parade. *Late May–early June*

JUNE
Portland Pride Festival
One of the largest LGBTQ festivals on the West Coast, Portland Pride draws thousands to a parade throughout downtown and a massive two-day gathering in Waterfront Park. *Mid-June*

World Naked Bike Ride
The wildly free-spirited (and free-of-charge to participate) World Naked Bike Ride, the largest-such event in the world, features about 10,000 riders—partially or fully undressed—on a 6-mile route through the city. *Late June*

Chamber Music Northwest
One of the most enjoyable and popular chamber music festivals in the country, this series of concerts takes place at Reed College (complete with pre-concert picnics on the campus's beautiful lawn) as well as other venues around town. *Late June–early July*

JULY
Waterfront Blues Festival
Taking place in early July on the Downtown riverfront lawn just south of the Hawthorne Bridge, this venerable blues celebration has featured both established and up-and-coming acts like Cyril Neville's Swamp Funk, Robert Cray, Little Feat, and Macy Gray. Many spectators watch from boats in the Willamette River. *4th of July weekend*

Oregon Brewers Festival
Come to Downtown's Waterfront Park for a long weekend of sampling hoppy IPAs and unusual sour ales, cask-aged limited releases, and other fine ales from more than 80 of the nation's most respected craft brewers. *Late July*

Cathedral Park Jazz Fest
It's free, it takes place in the shadows of North Portland's stunning St. Johns Bridge, and it's been going strong since 1981. This three-day

music gathering draws an always superb list of jazz and blues talents. *Mid-July*

AUGUST

Providence Bridge Pedal

Six of Downtown Portland's scenic and often historic bridges are closed to auto traffic during this well-attended bike ride that's popular with everyone from families to experienced riders. Both 5- and 18-mile routes are available. *Early Aug.*

SEPTEMBER

Art in the Pearl

Visit the leafy North Park Blocks to peruse works in every medium by more than 100 artists at this highly respected, juried art festival that also features great food and live music. *Labor Day weekend*

Time-Based Art (TBA) Festival

Presented over 10 days by the Portland Institute of Contemporary Art, this diverse showcase of often edgy, experimental dance, music, theater, and visual art takes place at a variety of venues around town—from warehouses to theaters. *Early–mid-Sept.*

Feast Portland

Launched in 2012, Feast has rapidly become one of the most talked-about international culinary festivals in the country, with events and meals prepared by both local and national star chefs. Highlights include an open-air "brunch village," a massive barbecue at Fields Park, and the "Big Feast" grand tasting at Waterfront Park. *Mid-Sept.*

OCTOBER

Portland Film Festival

Held over a full week, this show-case geared toward emerging, cutting-edge filmmakers takes place throughout town at a number of Portland's historic neighborhood cinemas. *Mid-Oct.*

NOVEMBER

Wild Arts Festival

At this wonderful Portland Audubon fundraising event, you can meet with and buy from artists and writers exhibiting their wildlife-related works, from wooden birdhouses to landscape paintings to local nature and hiking guidebooks. *Weekend before Thanksgiving*

DECEMBER

Holiday Events and Light Displays

From tree-lightings in the Pearl District to seasonal decorations at Pittock Mansion to festive concerts and musicals at many different venues, Portland abounds with fun gatherings tied to the holidays. Top places to see holiday light displays include the Oregon Zoo, Peacock Lane in Southeast, and the Grotto in Northeast. *All month*

BEST PORTLAND EVENTS

Several great companies offer visitors a distinctive way to experience the city, from brewpub-hopping bike tours to fascinating walks through some of the city's most interesting neighborhoods.

Cycle Portland Bike Tours and Rentals Trust your guide at this well-established outfitter to know Portland's popular and lesser-known spots. Tour themes include Essential Portland, Foodie Field Trip, and Brews Cruise, but you can also customize a tour. The well-stocked on-site bike shop serves beer on tap. ✉ 117 N.W. 2nd Ave., Old Town/Chinatown ☎ 503/902-5035, 844/739-2453 ⊕ www.portlandbicycle-tours.com ✉ From $39.

Lost Plate The evening dinner and drinks, morning coffee and donuts, and afternoon food-cart tours lead by knowledgeable, local guides include all food and booze. These gluttonous adventures hit some truly legit, less-touristy, and memorable establishments, and they're vegetarian-friendly. ✉ Portland ☎ 503/409-5593 ⊕ www.lostplate.com ✉ From $49.

Oregon Helicopters You'll be treated to dazzling aerial views of the city on the short (10-minute) and suprisingly affordable Skyscrapers and Bridges tours offered by this chopper tour company that takes off from Old Town. Longer experiences includes flights over the city's parks, Multnomah Falls, and the Gorge. ✉ 33 N.W. Davis St., Old Town/Chinatown ☎ 503/987-0060 ⊕ www.oregonhelicopters.com ✉ From $49.

Pedal Bike Tours One of the best ways to get a sense of Downtown's history is on the company's colorful Intro to Portland tour, but the decadent Donuts of Portland and Portland Brewery Trail excursions are the most fun. This Old Town outfit also rents bikes and can help you customize your own pedal adventures. ✉ 133 S.W. 2nd Ave., Old Town/Chinatown ☎ 503/243-2453 ⊕ www.pedalbiketours.com ✉ From $49.

Portland Walking Tours A slew of tours are offered by this company, but it's the Beyond Bizarre tour that generates the most buzz. Ghost-hunter wannabes and paranormal junkies make this a popular tour that often sells out. There's also the Underground Portland tour, which highlights the city's sinister history, and a Chocolate Decadence excursion. ✉ 131 N.W. 2nd Ave., Old Town/Chinatown ☎ 503/774-4522 ⊕ www.portland-walkingtours.com ✉ From $19.

BEST BETS

You could easily spend a week in Portland and still not make your way to every one of the top eating, shopping, sightseeing, and cultural experiences in town. To give you at least a fighting chance of getting to as many must-sees as possible, here's a list of our favorites to help you plan. Search the neighborhood chapters for more recommendations.

ACTIVITIES AND SIGHTS

MUSEUMS

Oregon Historical Society Museum Downtown

Oregon Jewish Museum and Center for Holocaust Education Pearl District

Oregon Museum of Science and Industry (OMSI) Inner Southeast

Pittock Mansion Nob Hill and Vicinity

Portland Art Museum Downtown

Fort Vancouver National Historic Site Vancouver, WA

PARKS AND GARDENS

Cathedral Park Outer North

Forest Park Nob Hill and Vicinity

International Rose Test Garden Downtown

Lan Su Chinese Garden Old Town/Chinatown

Mt. Tabor Park Outer Southeast

Portland Japanese Garden Downtown

Powell Butte Nature Park Outer Southeast

Tanner Springs Park Pearl District

Vancouver Waterfront Vancouver, WA

NEIGHBORHOODS

Alberta Arts District Outer Northeast

Central East Side Inner Southeast

Hawthorne District Outer Southeast

North Mississippi Avenue Outer North

SHOPPING

UNIQUE EXPERIENCES

First Thursday Pearl District

Made Here PDX Pearl District

Movie Madness Video Outer Southeast

Paxton Gate Outer North

Pine Street Market Old Town/Chinatown

Portland Farmers Market Downtown

Portland Saturday Market Old Town/Chinatown

Powell's City of Books Pearl District

Serra Dispensary Old Town/Chinatown

CLOTHING, JEWELRY, AND ACCESSORIES

Artifact: Creative Recycle Outer Southeast

Betsy & Iya Nob Hill and Vicinity

Compound Gallery Old Town/Chinatown

Grayling Jewelry Outer Northeast

Halo Shoes Pearl District

Machus Inner Southeast

North of West Downtown

Una Inner Southeast

Wildfang Downtown

HOME GOODS AND LIFESTYLE SHOPS

Beam & Anchor Inner North and Northeast

Crafty Wonderland Outer Northeast

Kiriko Old Town/Chinatown

Pendleton Home Store Old Town/Chinatown

Tender Loving Empire Downtown

Urbanite Inner Southeast

FOOD AND DRINK

Cacao Downtown

Jacobsen Salt Co. Inner Southeast

The Meadow Outer North

Providore Fine Foods Inner North and Northeast

FOOD

BREAKFAST AND BRUNCH

Broder Inner Southeast

Jam on Hawthorne Inner Southeast

Mother's Bistro Downtown

Pepper Box Cafe Inner Southeast

Pine State Biscuits Outer Northeast

Screen Door Inner North and Northeast

Sweedeedee Outer North

Tasty n Alder Downtown

UPSCALE AND FARM-TO-TABLE

Arden Pearl District

Bullard Downtown

Coquine Outer Southeast

Farm Spirit Inner Southeast

Jacqueline Inner Southeast

Olympia Provisions Inner Southeast

Ox Restaurant Inner North and Northeast

Ned Ludd Outer Northeast

Paley's Place Nob Hill and Vicinity

EUROPEAN

Ava Gene's Outer Southeast

Delores Inner Southeast

Kachka Inner Southeast

Le Pigeon Inner Southeast

Mediterranean Exploration Company Pearl District

Navarre Inner North and Northeast

BAR FOOD, BURGERS, AND SANDWICHES

Cheese Bar Outer Southeast

Interurban Outer North

La Moule Inner Southeast

Lardo Inner Southeast

Matt's BBQ Outer North

The Observatory Outer Southeast

Sammich Inner North and Northeast

PIZZA

Apizza Scholls Outer Southeast

Ken's Artisan Pizza Inner Southeast

Lovely's Fifty Fifty Outer North

Montesacro Pinseria Romana Pearl District

Oven and Shaker Pearl District

Pizza Jerk Outer Northeast

Rally Pizza Vancouver, WA

ASIAN FOOD

Afuri Ramen Inner Southeast

Bamboo Sushi Downtown

Bollywood Theater Outer Southeast

Departure Restaurant + Lounge Downtown

Gado Gado Outer Northeast

Han Oak Inner North and Northeast

Hat Yai Outer Northeast

Ha & VL Outer Southeast

Langbaan Inner Southeast

Master Kong Outer Southeast

Nodoguru Inner Southeast

Pok Pok Outer Southeast

LATIN AMERICAN FOOD

Andina Pearl District

Lechon Old Town/Chinatown

Little Conejo Vancouver, WA

Portland Mercado Outer Southeast

Tamale Boy Outer Northeast

Tienda Y Panaderia Santa Cruz Outer North

DESSERTS

Blue Star Donuts Downtown

Eb & Bean Inner North and Northeast

Jinju Patisserie Outer North

Lauretta Jean's Outer Southeast

Pip's Original Doughnuts & Chai Outer Northeast

Ruby Jewel Ice Cream Downtown

Salt & Straw Ice Cream Outer Northeast

DRINKS

COFFEE AND TEA

Coava Coffee Roasters Inner Southeast

Never Coffee Lab Outer Southeast

Proud Mary Outer Northeast

Relevant Coffee Vancouver, WA

Smith Teamaker Nob Hill and Vicinity

Tao of Tea Outer Southeast

Tea Chai Te Outer Southeast

Upper Left Roasters Downtown

Water Avenue Coffee Inner Southeast

CRAFT BEER

Beerded Brothers Brewing Vancouver, WA

Breakside Brewery Nob Hill and Vicinity

Cascade Brewing Inner Southeast

Culmination Brewing Inner North and Northeast

Deschutes Pearl District

Ecliptic Brewing Outer North

Ex Novo Brewing Inner North and Northeast

Gigantic Brewing Outer Southeast

Level Beer Outer Northeast

Loowit Brewing Vancouver, WA

Storm Breaker Brewing Outer North

Von Ebert Brewing Pearl District

WINE BARS

Burnt Bridge Cellars Winery & Bar Vancouver, WA

Coopers Hall Inner Southeast

Enso Winery Inner Southeast

OK Omens Inner Southeast

Oui Wine Bar at SE Wine Collective Outer Southeast

Teutonic Wine Company Outer Southeast

COCKTAILS

Bantam Tavern Nob Hill and Vicinity

Bible Club Outer Southeast

Botanist Pearl District

Driftwood Room Downtown

Expatriate Outer Northeast

Hey Love Inner Southeast

Multnomah Whiskey Library Downtown

Pope House Bourbon Lounge Nob Hill and Vicinity

Scotch Lodge Whiskey Bar Inner Southeast

Expatriate, Outer Northeast

Hey Love, Inner Southeast

Multnomah Whiskey Library, Downtown

Pope House Bourbon Lounge, Nob Hill and Vicinity

Scotch Lodge Whiskey Bar, Inner Southeast

COOL PLACES TO STAY

Portland has an unusually rich variety of distinctive, design-driven boutique hotels, historic properties, and charming B&Bs, and while you'll find the usual mix of budget-oriented, mid-range, and upscale chains here, if you'd rather avoid cookie-cutter brand-name properties, you're in the right city.

DOWNTOWN

Heathman Hotel The choice of countless celebs and dignitaries since it opened in 1927, this wonderfully atmospheric, art-filled hotel has undergone a stylish update. It's still filled with regal touches, including the high-ceilinged tea court lounge and a library of books signed by their authors, but the common spaces and ample guest rooms have a bright, contemporary feel. The snazzy Headwaters restaurant serves some of the best seafood in town. *Rooms from: $239 ⊠ 1001 S.W. Broadway Downtown ☎ 503/241-4100 ⊕ www.heathmanhotel.com.*

Kimpton RiverPlace With textured wall coverings and pillows made of Pendleton wool, this stylish hotel on the banks of the Willamette River captures the look and feel of the Pacific Northwest. More than a quarter of the large, airy guest rooms overlook the water, and bathrobes, coffee and tea, and yoga mats are provided. King Tide Fish & Shell restaurant serves outstanding seafood. *Rooms from: $269 ⊠ 1510 S.W. Harbor Way Downtown ☎ 503/228-3233 ⊕ www.riverplacehotel.com.*

The Nines The top nine floors of a former landmark department store, this swanky Marriott Luxury Collection has the city's poshest accommodations, with luxe decor and two notable resteaurants. Rooms are chic and modern, with a soothing cream-and-blue color scheme, fine bedding, BeeKind bath products, and stunning views of Downtown, the West Hills, and even Mt. Hood from east-facing rooms. *Rooms from: $359 ⊠ 525 S.W. Morrison St. Downtown ☎ 503/222-9996 ⊕ www.thenines.com.*

Sentinel The discerning common areas in this landmark, early-20th-century buildings capture Portland's maker aesthetic, with locally sourced textiles, furnishings, and goods. The design scheme extends to the guest rooms, where you will find rich, hunter-green walls, Pendleton wool blankets, framed Oregon botanicals, and a minibar stocked with Oregon goodies. *Rooms from: $239 ⊠ 614 S.W. 10th Ave. Downtown ☎ 503/224-3400 ⊕ www.sentinelhotel.com.*

The Woodlark The latest offering from the uber-hip Provenance Hotels brand connects a pair of stately early 1900s Downtown buildings that have been outfitted with well-curated local art, mid-century modern furnishings, and a slew of wellness amenities, from a first-rate fitness center to in-room streaming workout videos. The living room–like coffee bar in the lobby is a perfect roost to while away an afternoon, and Bullard restaurant is superb. *Rooms from: $245 ⊠ 813 S.W. Alder St. Downtown ☎ 503/548-2559 ⊕ woodlarkhotel.com.*

PEARL DISTRICT AND OLD TOWN/CHINATOWN

Canopy by Hilton One of the only lodgings in the Pearl District, this sleek, contemporary member of Hilton's new Canopy brand eagerly encourages guests to chill out and relax in the hotel's extensive—and gorgeous—industrial-chic lounge and dining areas, where complimentary evening beer and wine is served. The smartly designed rooms have floor-to-ceiling windows and eco-friendly design elements. *Rooms from: $269 ⊠ 425 N.W. 9th Ave. Pearl District ☎ 971/351-0230 ⊕ www.canopy3.hilton.com.*

The Hoxton London's hipper-than-thou Hoxton brand opened this see-and-be-seen hotel in 2018 on the border between Old Town and Downtown. It has all the requisite features of a trendy lodging, from a cool rooftop bar to a basement speakeasy, and the lobby—with its cushy armchairs and vintage-chic aesthetic—is a charming spot to hang out. The smallest rooms are truly tiny but also well-designed; book a larger one if you're wanting to spread out a bit. *Rooms from: $189 ⊠ 15 N.W. 4th Ave. Old Town/Chinatown ☎ 503/770-0500 ⊕ www.thehoxton.com.*

Society Hotel This quirky, bargain-priced boutique hotel with simple, stylish, and affordable rooms is just steps from Old Town nightlife and Lan Su Chinese Garden and occupies an 1880s former boardinghouse for sailors. Standard rooms with or without private baths have functional blond-wood furniture and white linens. Bargain hunters should consider one of the cozy bunk beds that include an attractive common space with a kitchenette. *Rooms from: $109 ⊠ 203 N.W. 3rd Ave. Old Town/Chinatown ☎ 503/445-0444 ⊕ www.thesocietyhotel.com.*

NOB HILL AND VICINITY

Inn at Northrup Station. Designed originally to be apartments, this contemporary all-suite boutique hotel with bright colors and retro-chic furnishings is right in the heart of Nob Hill and a quick Streetcar ride from the Pearl and Downtown. Accommodations have either patios or balconies as well as kitchenettes or full kitchens, and rates include a generous continental breakfast. *Rooms from: $249 ⊠ 2025 N.W. Northrup St. Nob Hill ☎ 503/224-0543 ⊕ www.northrupstation.com.*

INNER NORTH AND NORTHEAST

Hotel Eastlund This mid-20th-century Lloyd District/Convention Center building has stylish rooms outfitted California king beds, smart-technology gadgetry, and airy bathrooms with smoked-glass walk-in showers. The convivial restaurant, Altabira, has dramatic city skyline views. *Rooms from: $179* ⊠ *1021 N.E. Grand Ave. Lloyd District/Convention Center* ☎ *503/235-2100* ⊕ *www.hoteleastlund.com.*

KEX Portland. Opened in fall 2019, the first U.S. outpost of the hip, design-driven Reykjavík hotel–hostel has been developed expressly with the aim of encouraging travelers and locals to mix and mingle together, whether in the inviting lobby-restaurant or with friends in the cedar sauna. Both private rooms and shared (with 4 to 16 beds) are available, and all guests can relax with a drink from the roofdeck bar and start the morning with a hearty European-style breakfast buffet. The restaurant, Dóttir, serves superb Iceland-meets-Oregon fare. *Rooms from: $115* ⊠ *100 N.E. Martin Luther King Blvd. Central East Side* ☎ *971/346-2992* ⊕ *www.kexhotels.com.*

INNER SOUTHEAST

The Jupiter NEXT Across the street from its sister, the original mod-hip Jupiter Hotel, this futuristic-looking mid-rise offers a more upscale—but still moderately priced—lodging experience, complete with several airy outdoor spaces and a sceney lobby bar and restaurant, Hey Love. The artfully designed rooms have big picture windows, some with Downtown skyline views, and a mid-century–meets–21st-century feel. *Rooms from: $155* ⊠ *910 E. Burnside St. Central East Side* ☎ *503/230-9200* ⊕ *www.jupiterhotel.com.*

OUTER NORTHEAST

Caravan–Tiny House Hotel This cluster of itty-bitty custom-built houses-on-wheels offers visitors the chance to experience Portland's unabashed offbeat side. As the name suggests, the five guest houses—each designed quite differently—are quite small, between about 100 and 170 square feet, but each of these ingeniously designed bungalows has a private bath and top-notch bedding and bathrobes. *Rooms from: $155* ⊠ *5009 N.E. 11th Ave. Alberta Arts District* ☎ *503/288-5225* ⊕ *www.tinyhousehotel.com.*

QUICK SIDE TRIPS

Part of what makes Portland such a special place to live and visit is its proximity to one of the most gorgeous stretches of Pacific shoreline on the West Coast, the dazzling volcanic peaks and soaring ramparts of the Cascade Range and the Columbia Gorge, and the internationally renowned wineries of the Willamette Wine Country. It's possible to visit any of these areas in a day, although if you have a little extra time, consider overnighting—you'll find memorable places to stay in all of these regions. That said, folks visiting from elsewhere are sometimes surprised to learn that Portlanders think nothing of driving 150 to 200 miles round trip in a day to experience the surrounding area's incredible beauty.

THE COLUMBIA RIVER GORGE AND MT. HOOD

Stretching east from Portland, the Columbia River cuts through a dramatic section of the Cascade Range, forming the breathtaking 110-mile-long Columbia Gorge. Towering cliffs on both the Washington and Oregon sides of the river form an eye-popping backdrop, and meandering highways line both banks. Water and wind sports abound, as do countless opportunities for hiking to magnificent vistas and alongside rushing waterfalls, including one of the most iconic photo ops in the Northwest, Multnomah Falls. There's also a rapidly growing wine-making, craft-brewing, and culinary scene in the Gorge, especially in the towns of Hood River and—across river in Washington—White Salmon and Lyle. Just 60 miles east of Portland, the state's highest mountain—11,250-foot Mt. Hood—is the only place in the Lower 48 where you can ski year-round. There are five different facilities, including historic Timberline Lodge, which is also a memorable place for a meal or overnight stay, and during the warmer months, the lower slopes of the mountain are ideal for hiking around crystalline alpine lakes and through wildflower meadows.

Timing: You can easily explore the Columbia Gorge and Mt. Hood as separate day trips, or you combine them in an absolutely magical 160-mile loop drive that takes three hours without stops but is best enjoyed over the course of a full day.

THE WILLAMETTE WINE COUNTRY

About an hour's drive from Portland, this swath of fertile, hilly countryside is home to more than 500 wineries and has earned a reputation as one of the finest producers of Pinot Noir in the world—some say the best outside Burgundy. Winemakers in these parts also produce first-rate Pinot Gris and Chardonnay as well as an increasingly varied portfolio of other varietals, often with grapes sourced from elsewhere in Oregon and Washington.

Timing: From Portland, the closest notable towns for wine-touring—all within a 30-mile to 40-mile drive— are Dundee, McMinnville, Carlton, and Forest Grove. You can also drive a 90-mile loop through these northern Willamette Valley wine towns in about two hours without stops. But, of course, you're going to enjoy a tasting and maybe a tour at a few wineries. Be sure to designate a nondrinking driver for your explorations, especially if you're visiting multiple wineries. Or consider spending a night at some of the wonderful accommodations in the area, including the posh Allison Inn & Spa, the urbane Atticus Hotel, and the retro-hip Vintages Trailer Resort, a sunny compound of restored and stylishly decorated Airstreams and other mid-century trailers.

OREGON'S NORTH COAST

When it's sunny and warm in Portland, locals rush to the Oregon Coast. Interestingly, this is also the case when it's rainy and cool in Portland. Whatever the weather conditions, the rugged, rocky, and windswept Oregon Coast is a joy to explore, whether to watch migrating whales, raging winter storms, or colorful tide pools. From Portland, it's easiest to reach the northern section of the coast, which starts around Tillamook (famed for its cheese and ice cream) and meanders north along scenic U.S. 101 through several picturesque towns, including the upscale gallery village of Cannon Beach, the family-friendly boardwalk town of Seaside, to historic and increasingly hip former salmon-canning town of Astoria, which sits at the mouth of the Columbia River. The whole region abounds with terrific seafood restaurants and offers easy access to sweeping boulder-strewn beaches and soaring headlands laced with hiking trails—Oswald West and Ecola State Parks are two of the best spots for coastal treks.

Timing: From Portland, allow about 90 minutes to two hours drive to Tillamook, Cannon Beach, or Astoria. If you're up for an ambitious all-day loop drive, which is especially doable during Portland's long summer days, drive to Tillamook, then work your way up the scenic U.S. 101 coastal highway to Astoria, returning to Portland via U.S. 30 along the Columbia River. This entire trip can be done in five to seven hours with limited stops, but to really make the most of this adventure, leave early in the morning and plan to return to Portland late in the evening.

MADE IN PORTLAND

Few cities have so ardently embraced maker culture as Portland, where there's an almost endless thirst for locally made clothing, shoes, and jewelry as well as smartly designed goods and household items in the style you might see on the cover of *Kinfolk* magazine. The trend extends to artisanal foods and beverages.

APPAREL AND ACCESSORIES

You'll find dozens of local, often cutting-edge, fashion designers and jewelry crafters around town, with many of them thriving in the same neighborhoods that also have indie lifestyle shops, such as Northwest 23rd Avenue in Nob Hill, Downtown's West End, the Pearl District, the Alberta Arts District, the parallel North Mississippi and North Williams corridors, Hawthorne, and the Central East Side. The city is also home to some of the world's leading sportswear companies, including Nike, Adidas, Columbia Sportswear, Under Armour, and Danner Boots.

DECOR AND LIFESTYLE GOODS

Many of Portland's top fashion boutiques also carry locally made—often eco-friendly—household goods and decorative items, like Bridge Nine Candles, Will Leather Goods, Hop City Soaps, Maija Rebecca cards and paper products, Scout journals and notebooks, and Terra Noir jars and mugs, to name a few. Held weekends throughout most of the year, the iconic **Portland Saturday Market** features more than 250 vendors and is a great one-stop source of shopping for local gifts and housewares.

EDIBLES AND DRINKABLES

A notable component of Portland's buzzy food scene are all the locally produced foods and beverages. Artisan chocolates are among the most prized Portland goodies—look for brands like Woodblock, Creo, Missionary, Buddha, and Alma. Other edibles include hazelnuts, honey, finishing salts, and jams. It's no secret that Portland and the surrounding area produce outstanding wine, craft beer, and spirits, but also be on the lookout for locally roasted coffee—Coava, Water Avenue, Proud Mary, and Trailhead are all standouts. Somewhat overlooked are the city's many exceptional teamakers, including Jasmine Pearl, Tea Chai Té, and Steven Smith. You can find these products at farmers markets and gourmet groceries, with World Foods Portland and Providore Fine Foods among the best bets.

VANCOUVER, WA

NORTH

NORTHWEST

NORTHEAST

SOUTHWEST

SOUTHEAST

Sightseeing ★★★★★ | Shopping ★★★★★ | Dining ★★★★☆ | Nightlife ★★★★☆

Typically, U.S. city centers turn into ghost towns after the office managers flick off the lights. But Downtown Portland isn't like most other city centers. It's a forward-thinking commercial and residential district with a clear sense of place—filled with green parks, plazas, and fountains. It feels like an urban planner's laboratory, crisscrossed by light-rail trains and streetcar tracks and compact enough to easily walk from the independent-minded West End, which borders the Pearl District, to the squeaky new Southwest Waterfront, complete with the futuristic Aerial Tram. Boutiques and chef-owned restaurants operate on the ground floors of glossy towers as well as historic buildings. Freelancers and entrepreneurs camp out in co-working spaces during the day, then stick around to mingle over happy-hour drinks on hotel rooftops and in subterranean cocktail dens. Sure, there's no denying the presence of chain restaurants and big-name stores, though they don't dominate the scene—you only need to cross the street from a fast-food joint to find a third-wave coffee roaster or a cluster of inventive food carts.—by Jon Shadel

Downtown

⊙ Sights

Aerial Tram

On a clear day, the short ride on the aerial tram is worth the ticket for a view that includes Downtown and the riverfront, Mt. Hood, and Mt. St. Helens. Operated by the Oregon Health & Science University (OHSU), the tram was designed to ferry commuters between the South Waterfront neighborhood and OHSU's main campus on Marquam Hill. Don't rush to get back on the tram; walk to the university's balcony area, where you can admire the cityscape below. Tram cabs typically depart every five minutes and get more crowded during the morning and evening commute hours. The recently developed neighborhood at the base, South Waterfront, offers a park and a few restaurants. ⊠ 3303 S.W. Bond Ave., South Waterfront ☎ 503/494–8283 ⊕ www.gobytram. com ⊡ $5.10.

Central Library

The elegant, etched-graphite central staircase and elaborate ceiling ornamentation make this no ordinary library. With a gallery space on the second floor and famous literary names engraved on the walls, the Georgian-style building is well worth a walk around. A free 20-minute tour of the impressive eco-roof garden is given a few times a month during the spring and summer seasons; call or go online for the required pre-registration. ⊠ *801 S.W. 10th Ave., Downtown* ☎ *503/988–5123* ⊕ *www. multcolib.org.*

Chapman and Lownsdale Squares

During the 1920s these parks were segregated by gender—a leafy reminder of how much society has progressed in the past century: Chapman, between Madison and Main Streets, was reserved for women, and Lownsdale, between Main and Salmon Streets, was for men. The elk statue on Main Street, which separates the parks, was given to the city by David Thompson, mayor from 1879 to 1882. It recalls the elk that grazed in the area in the 1850s. ⊠ *Between S.W. Salmon St. and S.W. Jefferson St. and S.W. 4th and 3rd Ave., Downtown.*

Director Park

Low on greenery but high on gathering space, this 2009 addition to the city's downtown park blocks was designed as a public piazza—it hides a 700-space parking garage below. A glass canopy–light display provides cover, and a fountain dedicated to teachers cools off summer visitors. Chess players enjoy the giant (it's 16 feet square) board with 25-inch-high pieces, available on a first-come, first-served basis. There's a branch of Elephants Delicatessen—great for salads, deli sandwiches, chocolates, and wine by the glass and bottle—with both indoor and outdoor seating adjacent

GETTING HERE

Early planners created 200-square-foot blocks in the city center—notably smaller than most other American cities. That pedestrian-friendly scale makes Downtown best explored on foot. Most MAX light-rail trains, buses, and streetcars converge here, efficiently connecting the urban core to outlying neighborhoods; bus and train lines meet along the Portland Transit Mall, spanning 5th and 6th Avenues, which makes transfers easy. Hop off westbound Blue and Red line MAX trains at the Washington Park Station to quickly reach popular attractions such as the Oregon Zoo.

to the piazza. ⊠ *815 S.W. Park Ave., Downtown* ⊕ *www.directorpark.org.*

Keller Fountain Park

A widely lauded example of public landscape architecture, this series of 18-foot-high stone waterfalls gushes across from the front entrance of the Keller Auditorium—a cool spot to dip your toes on a summer day. Each minute, 13,000 gallons of water fall and churn through the fountain's cascading platforms. ⊠ *SW 3rd Ave. and Clay St., Downtown* ☎ *503/274–6560* ⊕ *www.portlandoregon.gov.*

Oregon Historical Society Museum

Impressive eight-story-high trompe l'oeil murals of Lewis and Clark and the Oregon Trail invite history lovers into this Downtown museum, which goes beyond the dominant narratives of white colonists and

explorers to tell the story of the state through myriad perspectives, from prehistoric times through the racist era of "black-exclusion" laws to the challenges of the present day. The state-of-the-art permanent exhibit "Experience Oregon," which opened in 2019, comprises 7,000 square feet of interactive galleries displaying a pair of 9,000-year-old sagebrush sandals, an actual covered wagon, and hands-on games. ⊠ *1200 S.W. Park Ave., Downtown* ☎ *503/222–1741* ⊕ *www. ohs.org* ⊠ *$10.*

Pioneer Courthouse Square

Often billed as the living room, public heart, and commercial soul of Downtown, Pioneer Square is not entirely square, but rather an amphitheater-like brick piazza featuring five food carts. Special seasonal, charitable, and festival-oriented events often take place in this premier people-watching venue. Directly across the street is one of Downtown Portland's most familiar landmarks, the classically sedate **Pioneer Courthouse**; built in 1869, it's the oldest public building in the Pacific Northwest. A couple of blocks east of the square, you'll find **Pioneer Place Mall,** an upscale retail center that spans four city blocks. ⊠ *701 S.W. 6th Ave., Downtown* ⊕ *www.thesquarepdx.org.*

★ Portland Art Museum

The treasures at the Pacific Northwest's oldest arts facility span 35 centuries of Asian, European, and American art—it's an impressive collection for a midsize city. A high point is the Center for

Native American Art, with regional and contemporary art from more than 200 indigenous groups. The **Jubitz Center for Modern and Contemporary Art** contains six floors devoted entirely to modern art, including a small but superb photography gallery, with the changing selection chosen from more than 5,000 pieces in the museum's permanent collection. The film center presents the annual Portland International Film Festival in March. Also, take a moment to linger in the peaceful outdoor sculpture garden. Kids under 17 are admitted free. ⊠ *1219 S.W. Park Ave., Downtown* ☎ *503/226–2811, 503/221–1156 film schedule* ⊕ *www.portlandartmuseum. org* ⊠ *$20; free on the first Thursday of every month from 5–8 pm* ☉ *Closed Mon.*

Portland Building

Portlandia, the second-largest hammered-copper statue in the world, surpassed only by the Statue of Liberty, kneels on the second-story balcony of one of the earliest postmodern buildings in the United States. Built in 1982, and architect Michael Graves's first major design commission, this 15-story office building is buff color, with brown-and-blue trim and exterior decorative touches. Locals tend to either love or hate it, and its current need for a nearly $100 million renovation has plenty of critics calling—probably in vain—for its demolition. A huge

CURATOR'S GUIDE TO NATIVE AMERICAN ART

It's easy to lose track of time while exploring the Portland Art Museum's galleries dedicated to Native American art. The nationally renowned collection comprises more than 3,500 objects that includes work from Native masters, contemporary artists, and more than 200 groups from across the continent. The collection fills the Confederated Tribes of Grand Ronde Center for Native American Art, which spans the second and third floors of the Hoffman Wing. Keep your eyes peeled for these top picks from the center's curator Kathleen Ash-Milby, who came to the museum from the Smithsonian Institution.

Dzunuk'wa Feast Dish: One of the most sizeable pieces on view is a painted cedar dish in the form of a reclined figure—measuring more than 12 feet long and made by Charlie James, a celebrated carver and painter from the Kwakwaka'wakw First Nation of British Columbia.

Miniature Pomo Baskets: A few of the most mesmerizing items in the collection are also among the tiniest: a set of intricately-woven sedge and bulrush baskets created by Pomo artists around 1940. Nothing is larger than an inch.

Clay Figure by Virgil Ortiz: This pottery figure by the prolific potter and designer is a modern take on traditional Cochiti pottery, indicating a continuum between historic craft and the dynamic worlds of today's indigenous artists.

Model Tipi Cover: Dating to late 19th century, this Cheyenne tipi cover—adorned with glass beads, ink, dyed horsehair, and leather ties—showcases the cultural connections between art and architecture.

fiberglass mold of Portlandia's face is exhibited in the second-floor Public Art Gallery, which provides a good overview of Portland's 1% for Art Program, and the hundreds of works on display throughout the city. ⊠ *1120 S.W. 5th Ave., Downtown* ⊕ *www.portlandoregon.gov.*

★ Portland Farmers Market

On Saturdays year-round, local farmers, bakers, chefs, and entertainers converge at the South Park Blocks near the PSU campus for Oregon's largest open-air farmers' market—it's one of the most impressive in the country. It's a great place to sample the regional bounty and to witness the local-food obsession that's revolutionized Portland's culinary scene. There's plenty of food you can eat on the spot, plus nonperishable local items (wine, hazelnuts, chocolates, vinegars) you can take home with you. There's a smaller Wednesday market, May through November, on a different section of the Park Blocks (between S.W. Salmon and S.W. Main). On Mondays, June through September, the market is held at Pioneer Courthouse Square, and at other times the Portland Farmers Market is held in different locations around town, including Nob Hill/Northwest, Kenton/North Portland, King/Alberta, and Lents/Southeast, and some 40 other farmers' markets take place throughout metro Portland—see the website for a list. ⊠ *South Park Blocks at S.W. Park Ave. and Montgomery St., Downtown* ☎ *503/241-0032* ⊕ *www. portlandfarmersmarket.org* ☾ *Closed Sun.-Fri.*

Providence Park

Few Americans revere soccer as highly as Portlanders do, who have referred to Portland as "Soccer City, U.S.A." since the 1970s. To understand the level of enthusiasm, book tickets to see one of the two teams who claim Providence Park as their home turf: the Timbers, one of the most competitive teams in Major League Soccer, and the Thorns FC, which receives the highest average match attendance in the National Women's Soccer League. Grab seats in the Timbers Army section to take part in songs and chants, which get rowdy. Originally constructed in 1926, the stadium underwent an $85-million expansion that added 4,000 seats, new video boards, and a new store selling team paraphernalia. ⊠ *1844 S.W. Morrison St., Goose Hollow* ☎ *503/553-5400* ⊕ *www.timbers.com/providencepark.*

Tom McCall Waterfront Park

Named for a former governor revered for his statewide land-use planning initiatives, this park stretches north along the Willamette River for about a mile from near the historic Hawthorne Bridge to Steel Bridge. Broad and grassy, Waterfront Park affords a fine ground-level view of Downtown Portland's bridges and skyline. Once

an expressway, it's now the site for many annual celebrations, among them the Rose Festival, classical and blues concerts, Portland Pride, Cinco de Mayo, and the Oregon Brewers Festival. The arching jets of water at the **Salmon Street Fountain** change configuration every few hours, and are a favorite cooling-off spot during the dog days of summer. ■**TIP**➔ Both the Hawthorne Bridge and Steel Bridge offer dedicated pedestrian lanes, allowing joggers, cyclists, and strollers to make a full loop along both banks of the river, via Vera Katz Eastside Esplanade. ⊠ *S.W. Naito Pkwy. (Front Ave.), from Steel Bridge to south of Hawthorne Bridge, Downtown* ⊕ *www.portlandoregon. gov/parks.*

Travel Portland Visitor Center

You can pick up maps and literature about the city and the state here at the regional tourism board's official welcome center, located in a glass kiosk on the piazza at Director Park. ⊠ *877 S.W. Taylor St., Downtown* ☎ *503/275-8355, 877/678-5263* ⊕ *www.travelportland.com* ☾ *Closed Sun. Nov.-Apr.*

Yamhill National Historic District

Light-rail trains glide by many examples of 19th-century cast-iron architecture on the MAX line between the Skidmore and Yamhill stations, where the streets are closed to cars. Take a moment at the Yamhill station to glance around at these old buildings, which have intricate rooflines and facades. Nearby, on Southwest Naito Parkway at Taylor Street, is **Mill Ends Park,** which sits in the middle of a traffic island. This patch of whimsy, at 24 inches in diameter, has been recognized by *Guinness World Records* as the world's smallest official city park. ✉ *Between SW Naito Pkwy., SW 3rd Ave., SW Morrison, and SW Taylor Sts., Downtown.*

 Shopping

★ Canoe

Form meets function at this design boutique with a niche selection of clean-lined, modern goods and gifts for every room in the home. You'll find curvy thick-glass bowls, modern lamps with sheer paper shades, polished-stone trays, Bigelow natural-bristle toothbrushes, and Chemex coffee kettles, with some goods produced locally and exclusively for Canoe, and others imported from Asia and northern Europe. ✉ *1233 S.W. 10th Ave., Downtown* ☎ *503/889–8545* ⊕ *www.canoe.design* ⊙ *Closed Mon.*

Columbia Sportswear

A local legend and global force in recreational outdoor wear, Columbia Sportswear is especially strong in all-weather jackets, pants, and durable shoes. The national brand's Downtown flagship store, just two blocks from Pioneer Courthouse Square, stocks the latest styles. You'll find another outpost at the airport. ✉ *911 S.W. Broadway, Downtown* ☎ *503/226–6800* ⊕ *www. columbia.com.*

Finnegan's Toys & Gifts

Downtown Portland's largest toy store, Finnegan's stocks artistic, creative, educational, and other types of toys and games. ✉ *820 S.W. Washington St., Downtown* ☎ *503/221–0306* ⊕ *www.finnegan-stoys.com.*

Nike Portland

It's safe to assume that Nike's flagship Portland store, just a short drive from the company's mammoth HQ campus in Beaverton, has the latest and greatest in swoosh-adorned products. The high-tech setting has athlete profiles, photos, and interactive displays. ✉ *638 S.W. 5th Ave., Downtown* ☎ *503/221–6453* ⊕ *www.nike.com.*

Portland Outdoor Store

If you want real-deal western gear—saddles, Stetsons, boots, and shirts—head to this old-school, no-nonsense store which stub-bornly resists all that is trendy, both in clothes and decor. The red neon sign, depicting a cowboy riding a bucking horse, is a Downtown icon. ✉ *304 S.W. 3rd Ave., Downtown* ☎ *503/222–1051* ⊕ *www.portlandout-doorstore.us* ⊙ *Closed Sun.*

Portland Pendleton Shop

This store stocks clothing by the famous local apparel maker, whose woolen mills were established in 1863 and continue to produce sturdy, brightly patterned blankets and rugs as well as men's and women's shirts, sweaters, outer-wear, and gear that's as popular with octogenarians as with twenty-somethings. ✉ *825 S.W. Yamhill St.,*

Downtown ☎ 503/242–0037 ⊕ www.
pendleton-usa.com.

Rich's Cigar Store

One of the longest-operating
retailers in the city, Rich's has a lot
to brag about. It not only stocks the
most cigars in the state but also one
of the widest selections of magazines and periodicals on the West
Coast, including obscure fashion
and culture glossies from around
the world. ⊠ 820 S.W. Alder St.,
Downtown ☎ 503/228–1700 ⊕ www.
richscigarstore.com.

★ Stand Up Comedy

As much a boutique as conceptual
art space, Stand Up Comedy's
proprietor has a contagious sense
of humor. Founded by former
performing arts curator Diana
Kim, the influential shop showcases her penchant for the absurd
and surreal as well as her eye for
cutting-edge styles in high fashion,
with hard-to-find international
designers represented alongside
local women's labels. ⊠ 511 S.W.
Broadway, Downtown ☎ 503/233–3382
⊕ www.standupcomedytoo.com.

underU4men

Stocking an exhaustive selection
of trendy men's underwear, this
boutique has a strong following
with Portland's gay community,
but any guy with a discerning eye
for quality boxer briefs and ribbed
trunks will appreciate underU4men
and its helpful sales staff. In
addition to more than 50 underwear brands, from good old Levi's
boxers to sexy Unico and Andrew
Christian briefs, the shop also

carries thousands of swimsuits and
a range of apothecary products.
⊠ 800 S.W. Washington St., Downtown
☎ 503/274–2555 ⊕ www.underu4men.
com.

☕ Coffee and Quick Bites

★ Behind the Museum Cafe

$ | Japanese. Decorated with
antiques and crafts (all for sale),
this Japanese teahouse feels like
the sort of café you'd find adjacent to a Tokyo museum's gift
store. But true to its name, this
shop resides on a street of condos
behind the Portland Art Museum,
where it serves fine tea, sake,
and a light menu of sandwiches,
onigiri (Japanese rice ball), and
tea-based treats. **Known for:** finely
milled matcha; ceremonial-style
tea service; pit-stop for museum
goers. *Average main: $8* ⊠ 1229 S.W.
10th Ave., Downtown ☎ 503/477–6625
☾ No dinner.

Case Study Coffee Roasters

$ | Café. A first-rate indepen-
dent café on a heavily trafficked
Downtown corner by MAX and
streetcar stops, Case Study serves
small-batch, house-roasted coffee
in a variety of formats, from Chemex
to Aeropress to crowds of regulars.
There is an additional Downtown
location on S.W. 4th Avenue as well
as coffeehouses in Hollywood and
the Alberta Arts District. **Known
for:** lattes made with scratch-made
syrups; a pasty case stocked with
goods from various local bakers;
slow-drip cold brew. *Average main:*
$5 ⊠ 802 S.W. 10th Ave., Downtown

☎ *503/477–8221* ⊕ *www.casestudy-coffee.com.*

★ Good Coffee

$ | Café. The Woodlark Hotel yielded its plant-filled lobby to the latest outpost from Portland roaster Good Coffee. The marble bar complements the sprawling seating area—a living room for an army of young freelancers, who set up shop at the communal table, on the blue banquet seats lining the street-facing windows, and the plush couches and armchairs. **Known for:** one of Portland's best cappuccinos; intriguing seasonal drink menu; tea lattes and matcha. *Average main: $5* ✉ *Woodlark Hotel, 813 S.W. Alder St., Downtown* ☎ *503/548–2559* ⊕ *www.goodwith.us* ⊙ *No dinner.*

Upper Left Roasters

$ | Café. In the historic Meier & Frank building, a glazed terra-cotta tower adjacent to Pioneer Courthouse Square, Upper Left Roasters has put a jolt of fresh energy into the Downtown coffee shop scene with this lobby espresso bar. The Scandinavian-inspired space, defined by dark woods and anchored by a high-top communal table, is perfect for a quick shopping or sightseeing break. **Known for:** nitro cacao-nib cold brew on tap; a menu of savory toasts; matcha sourced from Tea Bar. *Average main: $5* ✉ *555 S.W. Morrison St., Suite 100, Downtown* ☎ *503/477–8469* ⊕ *www.upperleftroasters.com* ⊙ *Closed Sat. and Sun. No dinner.*

🍴 Dining

★ Bullard

$$$$ | Steakhouse. In a city with the density of restaurants that Portland has, it takes a lot to stoke the level of buzz surrounding the opening of Bullard, a festive next-generation steakhouse in the lobby of The Woodlark Hotel. Drawing on his roots in Texas, Top Chef alum Doug Adams brings a Southwest-meets-Oregon flair ("Tex-Oregana," according to *The Oregonian*'s food critic) to signature dishes such as beef carpaccio and San Antonio chicken that lives up to the hype. **Known for:** mains large enough for two; house-smoked meats; pickleback shots. *Average main: $35* ✉ *Woodlark Hotel, 813 S.W. Alder St., Downtown* ☎ *503/222–1670* ⊕ *www.bullardpdx.com.*

★ Departure Restaurant + Lounge

$$$ | Asian. This extravagant rooftop restaurant and lounge on the top floor of The Nines hotel seems fresh out of L.A.—a look and feel that is, indeed, a departure from Portland's usual no-fuss vibe. The retro-chic interior has an extravagant, space-age, airport-lounge feel, and the outdoor patio—furnished with low, white couches and bright-orange tables and chairs—offers panoramic views of the Downtown skyline. **Known for:** chef's tasting service with wine pairings; dedicated vegan menu; fantastic skyline views. *Average main: $25* ✉ *Nines Hotel, 525 S.W. Morrison St., Downtown*

☎ 503/802–5370 ⊕ www.departure-portland.com ⊗ No lunch.

Duck House Chinese Restaurant

$ | Chinese. The rather bland blocks surrounding Portland State University's campus don't often rank high for dining, but this Szechuan-centric Chinese restaurant and bar is a clear exception. Its pub-like atmosphere draws suits from nearby offices for lunch, and the wide-ranging menu inspires families to make the trek into the city from the suburbs for a dinnertime feast when the kitchen sometime struggles to meet the demand. **Known for:** housemade dumplings; generous platters of Peking duck; Oregon craft beer on tap. *Average main: $14* ⊠ *1968 S.W. 5th Ave., Downtown* ☎ *971/801–8888* ⊕ *www.duckhousepdx.com* ⊗ *Closed Tues.*

Higgins

$$$ | Pacific Northwest. One of Portland's original farm-to-table restaurants, this classic eatery, opened in 1994 by renowned name-sake chef Greg Higgins, has built its menu—and its reputation—on its dedication to local, seasonal, organic ingredients. Higgins' dishes display the diverse bounty of the Pacific Northwest, incorporating ingredients like heirloom tomatoes, forest mushrooms, mountain huckleberries, Pacific oysters, Oregon Dungeness crab, and locally raised pork. **Known for:** house-made charcuterie plate; tender duck confit; casual bistro menu in adjacent bar. *Average main: $30* ⊠ *1239 S.W. Broadway, Downtown* ☎ *503/222–9070*

⊕ www.higginsportland.com ⊗ No lunch weekends.

★ Imperial

$$$ | Pacific Northwest. Tall concrete pillars, exposed brick and ductwork, soft overhead lighting, and rustic wood tables and floors create a warehouse vibe at one of Portland's most defining restaurants, located inside the Hotel Lucia. Open for breakfast, lunch, and dinner, and serving up exemplary contemporary Pacific Northwest fare, menu highlights include Dungeness crab omelet, duck meatballs, grilled king salmon with corn puree and chanterelles, and meaty fare from the wood-fired rotisserie grill. **Known for:** Flat Top happy-hour burger; stellar cocktail program; wood-fired rotisserie-grill fare. *Average main: $25* ⊠ *Hotel Lucia, 410 S.W. Broadway, Downtown* ☎ *503/228–7221* ⊕ *www.imperialpdx.com.*

Mother's Bistro & Bar

$$ | American. Chef and cookbook author Lisa Schroeder dedicates her home-style, made-with-love approach to food to the comforting foods prepared by mothers everywhere. Clearly the theme resonates, as evidenced by the long waits on weekends, and even some weekday mornings for breakfast, which is arguably the best time of the day to sample Schroeder's hearty cooking; try the wild salmon hash with leeks or the French toast with a crunchy cornflake crust. **Known for:** down-home American comfort fare; fantastic breakfasts; drinks in the swanky Velvet Lounge bar. *Average main: $17* ⊠ *121 S.W. 3rd Ave., Downtown* ☎ *503/464–1122* ⊕ *www. mothersbistro.com.*

Murata

$$ | Japanese. Slip off your shoes and step inside one of the tatami rooms or pull up a chair at the sushi bar at this unassuming but outstanding Downtown Japanese restaurant. So ordinary looking it barely stands out among the office towers near Keller Auditorium, the restaurant draws a crowd of locals and Japanese businesspeople who order from the wide-ranging but well-executed menu. **Known for:** tempura; grilled salmon cheeks; sashimi. *Average main: $21* ⊠ *200 S.W. Market St., Downtown* ☎ *503/227–0080* ⊗ *Closed Sun. and no lunch Sat.*

Portland City Grill

$$$$ | American. On the 30th floor of the U.S. Bank Tower, the Portland City Grill has bragging rights for best dinner view in town, which makes up for the rather unremarkable steakhouse fare. **Known for:** Portland's highest-up happy hour; extensive regional wine list; "Bridge view" buffet brunch on Sunday. *Average main: $55* ⊠ *111 S.W. 5th Ave., Downtown* ☎ *503/450–0030* ⊕ *www.portlandcitygrill.com* ⊗ *No lunch Saturday.*

Shigezo Izakaya

$ | Japanese. This first U.S. outpost of a popular Tokyo izakaya franchise is on the leafy Park Blocks, steps from several theaters and museums, and offers a reasonably priced, extensive menu, especially during happy hour, which runs a lot longer than in most restaurants in town. Choose a seat in the lively bar area, with both tables and counter seating, or one of the darker booths in the main dining room. **Known for:** sharing-friendly menu; okonomi-yaki pork and squid pancakes; robata skewers. *Average main: $15* ⊠ *910 S.W. Salmon St., Downtown* ☎ *503/688–5202* ⊕ *www.shigezo-pdx. com.*

🍸 Bars and Nightlife

★ Abigail Hall

Inspired by the legacy of Oregon suffragist Abigail Scott Duniway, the first woman registered to vote in Multnomah County, this elegant hotel lounge looks like a time capsule for a reason. A historian helped the design team recreate the early 1900s floral aesthetic of the historic Ladies Reception Hall, which originally inhabited this room. Behind the bar, the bartenders seem less tied to the history of the space, mixing up more than a dozen creative cocktails with quippy names. ⊠ *Woodlark Hotel, 813 S.W. Alder St., Downtown* ☎ *503/548–2559* ⊕ *www.abigailhallpdx.com.*

Driftwood Room

Once your eyes adjust to the romantically dim lighting, you'll find a curved bar, leather banquette seating, and polished-wood ceilings and walls in this Old Hollywood–themed bar in the Hotel deLuxe. The trendy cocktails are garnished with herbs culled from the hotel's garden. ✉ *Hotel deLuxe, 729 S.W. 15th Ave., Goose Hollow* ☎ *503/219–2094* ⊕ *www.hoteldeluxeportland. com.*

★ Headwaters at the Heathman

At the elegant Heathman Hotel, you can enjoy Russian tea service in the eucalyptus-paneled Tea Court or beer, wine, and cocktails in the marble Headwaters lounge, a venerable Old World space that received a revamp in 2016 when local celeb chef Vitaly Paley took over. This is one of the city's most popular see-and-be-seen venues, especially before or after shows at nearby theaters and concert halls. ✉ *Heathman Hotel, 1001 S.W. Broadway, Downtown* ☎ *503/790–7752* ⊕ *www.headwaterspdx.com.*

Huber's

The city's oldest restaurant (est. 1879) is notable for its old-fashioned feel and iconic Spanish coffee cocktail, which is set aflame at your table. The old bar in the back has great character. Huber's is on the ground floor of the historic Oregon Pioneer Building, which became the snazzy Hi-Lo Hotel in 2017. ✉ *Hi-Lo Hotel, 411 S.W. 3rd Ave., Downtown* ☎ *503/228–5686* ⊕ *www.hubers.com.*

Luc Lac Vietnamese Kitchen

With a reputation as an after-work eating and drinking hangout among local Portland chefs and restaurant workers, this always-hopping Vietnamese joint offers well-executed cocktails, such as the Single Knight: Four Roses Single Barrel bourbon, pho syrup, Angostura orange bitters, and a Lapsang souchong tea ice cube. The kitchen turns out delicious eats until midnight on weekdays and 4 am on weekends. ✉ *835 S.W. 2nd Ave., Downtown* ☎ *503/222–0047* ⊕ *www. luclackitchen.com.*

Raven & Rose

Located in the ornate Victorian two-level Ladd Carriage House amid Downtown's office towers, this British Isles-inspired spot serves English-style pub fare and a worldly list of beers, wines, and cocktails in the Rookery Bar upstairs. Downstairs, you'll find a main dining room and a small lounge area. There's live music select evenings. ✉ *1331 S.W. Broadway, Downtown* ☎ *503/222–7673* ⊕ *www.ravenandrosepdx.com* ☾ *Closed Mon.*

Southpark Seafood

With its extensive wine list and proximity to Downtown theaters and museums, this wine and cocktail bar is a perfect spot for a post-concert drink, with a notable list of Northwest bottles. Don't miss the sustainably fished seafood and dozen-plus varieties of oysters. ✉ *901 S.W. Salmon St., Downtown* ☎ *503/326–1300* ⊕ *www.southparkseafood.com.*

🎭 Performing Arts

★ Arlene Schnitzer Concert Hall

The 2,776-seat Arlene Schnitzer Concert Hall, built in 1928 in an Italian rococo revival style, hosts rock concerts, choral groups, lectures, and concerts by the Oregon Symphony and others. "The

Schnitz," as locals call it, is one of the venues that make up the Portland'5 Centers for the Arts umbrella organization. ⊠ *1037 S.W. Broadway, Downtown* ☎ *503/248-4335* ⊕ *www.portland5.com.*

Artists Repertory Theatre

With a reputation for commissioning and staging new work by Pulitzer Prize-winning playwrights, this celebrated theater company performs seven to nine productions a year including regional premieres and classics. Starting with the 2019–20 season, the Artists Repertory is taking the show on the road—staging productions at other venues around the city, while they build new theaters on the site of its Downtown headquarters. Check the website for its "ART on Tour" showtimes and locations. ⊠ *Downtown* ☎ *503/241-1278* ⊕ *www.artistsrep.org.*

Chamber Music Northwest

Some of the most sought-after soloists, chamber musicians, and recording artists from the Portland area and abroad perform here during the five-week summer concert series; performances take place at a few different venues, primarily Reed College's Kaul Auditorium and the Lincoln Performance Hall at Portland State University. ⊠ *Box Office, 2300 SW 1st Ave, Suite 103, Downtown* ☎ *503/294-6400* ⊕ *www.cmnw.org.*

Keller Auditorium

With 3,000 seats and outstanding acoustics, Keller Auditorium hosts performances by the Portland Opera and Oregon Ballet Theatre, as well as country and rock concerts and touring Broadway shows. The Keller is one of several venues that form the Portland'5 Centers for the Arts. ⊠ *222 S.W. Clay St., Downtown* ☎ *503/248-4335* ⊕ *www.portland5.com.*

Northwest Dance Project

Founded in 2004, this first-rate contemporary-dance company performs several shows—typically including a world premier or two—each season at different venues around town, including the Newmark Theatre and PSU's Lincoln Performance Hall. ⊠ *Downtown* ☎ *503/828-8285* ⊕ *www.nwdanceproject.org.*

Northwest Film Center Whitsell Auditorium

Located adjacent to and operated by the Portland Art Museum, the Northwest Film Center's Whitsell Auditorium screens art films, documentaries, and independent features, and presents the three-week Portland International Film Festival every February. ⊠ *1219 S.W. Park Ave., Downtown* ☎ *503/221-1156* ⊕ *www.nwfilm.org.*

Oregon Ballet Theatre

This respected company produces several classical and contemporary works a year, including a much-loved holiday *Nutcracker.* Most performances are at Keller Auditorium and the Portland Center

for the Arts' Newmark Theatre.
✉ Box Office and Studios, 0720 S.W. Bancroft St., Downtown ☎ 503/222–5538, 888/922–5538 ⊕ www.obt.org.

Oregon Children's Theatre
This kid-centric company puts on four to five shows a year for school groups and families at Downtown's Newmark and Winningstad theaters. ✉ 1111 S.W. Broadway, Downtown ☎ 503/228–9571 ⊕ www.octc.org.

★ Oregon Symphony
Established in 1896, the symphony is Portland's largest classical group—and one of the largest orchestras in the country. Its season officially starts in September and ends in May, with concerts held at Arlene Schnitzer Concert Hall, but throughout the summer the orchestra and its smaller ensembles can be seen at Waterfront Park and Washington Park for special outdoor summer performances. It also presents about 40 classical, pop, children's, and family concerts each year. ✉ Ticket Office, 909 S.W. Washington St., Downtown ☎ 503/228–1353 ⊕ www.orsymphony.org.

Portland Baroque Orchestra
The city's baroque group performs music composed before 1840 on period instruments in a season that runs October to April. Performances are held at Reed College's Kaul Auditorium, First Baptist Church, and Trinity Episcopal Cathedral. ✉ Box Office, 610 S.W. Broadway, Suite 605, Downtown ☎ 503/222–6000 ⊕ www.pbo.org.

★ Portland'5 Centers for the Arts
The city's top performing arts complex hosts opera, ballet, rock shows, symphony performances, lectures, and Broadway musicals in its five venues: the Arlene Schnitzer Concert Hall, the Keller Auditorium, and the three-in-one Antoinette Hatfield Hall, which comprises the Brunish, Newmark, and Winningstad theatres. The majority of the region's top performing companies call these venues home, including the Portland Opera, the Oregon Symphony, the Oregon Ballet Theatre, and the Portland Youth Philharmonic. ✉ Box Office, 1111 S.W. Broadway, Downtown ☎ 503/248–4335 ⊕ www.portland5.com.

Portland Opera
This well-respected opera company performs five or six productions a year, most of them Downtown at Keller Auditorium or the Newmark Theatre, but also occasionally across the river at the Hampton Opera Center. ✉ Downtown ☎ 503/241–1802, ⊕ www.portland-opera.org.

Waterfront Blues Festival
One of the nation's premier blues gatherings, the four-day Waterfront Blues Festival, a benefit for the Oregon Food Bank, has been drawing big crowds and big names in blues over the July 4 weekend since 1987. Past performers have included Keb' Mo', Susan Tedeschi, Johnny Winter, and Sharon Jones & the Dap-Kings. ✉ Tom McCall

Waterfront Park, Downtown ⊕ www.
waterfrontbluesfest.com.

White Bird Dance
Since its founding in 1997, White
Bird Dance has been dedicated to
bringing exciting local, regional,
national, and international dance
performances to Portland stages
including the Arlene Schnitzer
Concert Hall and the Newmark
Theatre. ⊠ Downtown ☎ 503/245–
1600 ⊕ www.whitebird.org.

West End

Sights

★ West End
Sandwiched between the Pioneer
Square area and the swanky Pearl
District, this triangular patch of
vintage buildings—interspersed
with a handful of contemporary
ones—has evolved since the early
2000s into one of the city's most
eclectic hubs of fashion, nightlife,
and dining. Boutique hotels like the
Ace and Sentinel rank among the
city's trendiest addresses. Along
Harvey Milk Street, formerly the
heart of Portland's LGBTQ scene,
there's still a popular gay bar, but
now you'll also find noteworthy
restaurants and lounges like Clyde
Common, Bamboo Sushi, and
Multnomah Whiskey Library. Among
the many independent shops, check
out Cacao chocolate shop, Frances
May clothier, and Union Way—an
enclosed pedestrian mall with a
handful of tiny storefronts. ⊠ S.W.
13th to S.W. 9th Aves., between W.
Burnside St. and S.W. Yamhill St.,
West End.

Shopping

Boys Fort
If the name of this colorful West End
emporium brings back memories
of hanging out with friends in a rad
basement rec room, you'll likely
love this offbeat store curated by
designers R. Rolfe and Jake France.
They've stocked this high-ceilinged
corner shop with a mix of artful
items, including earthy-hued terra-
cotta planters, model sailboats,
and mounted wooden faux deer
heads, plus old posters and games.
⊠ 1001 S.W. Morrison St., West End
☎ 503/241–2855 ⊕ www.boysfort.com.

Cacao
Chocolate fiends and sweet-tooths
get their fix at this inviting storefront
and café in the West End. Browse
the huge selection of ultrafine,
single-origin, artisanal chocolates
from around the world, or order
a cup of luscious house-made
drinking chocolate. ⊠ 414 S.W. 13th
Ave., West End ☎ 503/241–0656
⊕ www.cacaodrinkchocolate.com.

★ Frances May
Commanding a prime corner shop
in the fashion-forward West End,
this grandmother-and-grand-
daughter-owned clothing retailer is
one of the Pacific Northwest's most
defining trendsetters—a favorite
of stylish locals who come for that
cool, understated look (casual to
dressy) that Portlanders are known
for. You'll find made-here labels

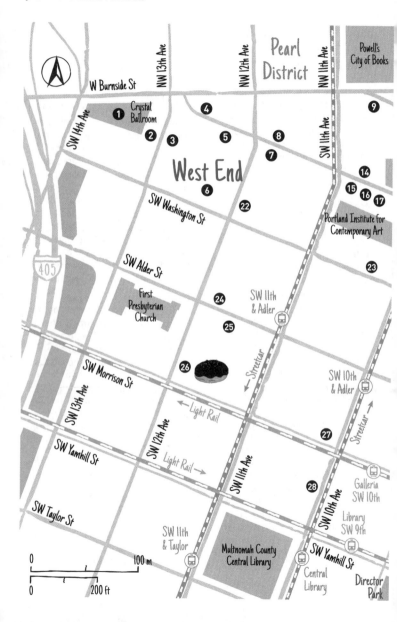

NW 10th Ave

NW 9th Ave

W Burnside St

SW Oak St

SW 10th Ave

SW 9th Ave

SW Harvey Milk St

O'Bryant Square

SW Washington St

SW Alder St

SW Park Ave

Downtown

SW Morrison St

SW 9th Ave

★ Teachers Fountain

SIGHTS
West End 6

SHOPPING
Boys Fort 27
Cacao 3
Frances May............. 23
Maak Lab 10
Maloy's Jewelry
Workshop 28
North of West........... 13
Tender Loving
Empire 20
Union Way.................. 9
Wildfang................... 19

COFFEE & QUICK BITES
Blue Star Donuts 26
Courier Coffee.......... 11
Ruby Jewel
Ice Cream 22
Stumptown Coffee
Roasters 16

DINING
Bamboo Sushi 7
Boxer Ramen 14
Clyde Common.......... 17
Jake's Famous
Crawfish 5
Kenny & Zuke's
Delicatessen............. 15
Maurice..................... 12
Nong's Khao
Man Gai...................... 2
Tasty n Alder 24

BARS & NIGHTLIFE
McMenamins
Crystal Ballroom 1
Multnomah
Whiskey Library 25
Pépé le Moko............. 21
Ringlers Annex
Cellar Bar..................... 4
Scandals 8

PERFORMING ARTS
Living Room
Theaters 18

like gender-neutral, organic line Olderbrother, as well as European faves like Acne and APC. Frances May also stocks jewelry, art books, and the city's own OLO Fragrances. ⊠ *1003 S.W. Washington St., West End* ☎ *503/227-3402* ⊕ *www.francesmay. com.*

Maak Lab

Scent designers at this combo studio and storefront capture the aromas of the Pacific Northwest, from fir trees and cedar to lavender and blossoming roses. Shop for signature fragrances, soaps, candles, and other apothecary goods, or try your hand at making your own scent in one of the weekly hands-on workshops. ⊠ *916 W. Burnside St., West End* ☎ *503/893-9933* ⊕ *www.maaklab.com.*

Maloy's Jewelry Workshop

Walking into this store feels like walking into an antique shop that specializes in fine jewelry, including some pieces from the 18th century. Rare and vintage designs, many of them purchased from luxury estates, fill the sparkling glass cases. ⊠ *711 S.W. 10th Ave., West End* ☎ *503/223-4720* ⊕ *www.maloys. com* ☾ *Closed Sun.*

North of West

Embodying the growing conscious-ness about ethical fashion, this eclectic boutique opened in 2014 as a collaboration between several Portland designers, who shared a vision for opening a mission-driven store that elevated locavore goods and small-scale manufacturing. Today, you'll find the eponymous

North of West line mingling with like-minded women's and kids' apparel, apothecary, and houseware brands. ⊠ *203 S.W. 9th Ave., West End* ☎ *503/208-3080* ⊕ *www.shopnor-thofwest.com.*

Tender Loving Empire

The retail shop of the eponymous Portland record label founded by Jared and Brianne Mees carries not only music but also cool hand-printed cards, posters, and T-shirts, along with an artistic selection of handcrafted lifestyle goods, from pastel miniature vases and squiggle-shaped earrings to ceramic fox trinkets and illustrated prints. You'll find additional loca-tions on Hawthorne, in Nob Hill, at Bridgeport Village, and in the airport. ⊠ *412 S.W. 10th Ave., West End* ☎ *503/548-2925* ⊕ *www.tender-lovingempire.com.*

Union Way

A modern take on an old-fashioned European shopping arcade, this indoor alley spans one block from Harvey Milk to Burnside streets (right across the street from Powell's City of Books) and contains about a half-dozen diverting boutiques, plus Wailua Shave Ice and a branch of the trendy Japanese-inspired restaurant Boxer Ramen. Most of these shops specialize in apparel and accesso-ries, including Tanner Goods, Bridge & Burn, and Danner sports and outerwear. ⊠ *1022 W. Burnside St., West End* ☎ *503/ 235-5743.*

Wildfang

Founded by two former Nike employees, this queer-owned, women-centric retailer makes its values immediately clear, with its "Wild Feminist" T-shirt among its best-sellers. Wildfang's house collection of punkish, tomboy-inspired apparel shares this gallery-like shop with other minimally stylish brands that challenge gender conventions in the fashion world. ⊠ 404 S.W. 10th Ave., West End ☎ 503/964–6746 ⊕ www.wildfang. com.

Coffee and Quick Bites

Blue Star Donuts

$ | Bakery. If you have time for just one Portland doughnut shop, choose this light-filled spot on the street level of a glassy tower in the West End. Blue Star opens at 7 am and remains open until that day's fresh-baked stock sells out of popular flavors like blueberry-bourbon-basil, bacon-maple, and Valrhona chocolate crunch with a Boston-cream-style filling. **Known for:** brioche-based doughnuts; wildly inventive flavors; serving Stumptown Coffee. *Average main: $4* ⊠ 1155 S.W. Morrison St., West End ☎ 503/265–8410 ⊕ www.bluestardonuts.com.

Courier Coffee

$ | Café. In between pulling dialed-in shots of espresso, baristas at this scrappy West End café spin LPs from a vast collection of vinyl, ranging from underground hip hop to Taylor Swift. Rotating art gives the demitasse-size shop a DIY gallery vibe. **Known for:** single-origin pour-overs; house-baked treats; Japanese-style shaved ice in the summer. *Average main: $5* ⊠ 923 S.W. Oak St., West End ☎ 503/545–6444 ⊕ www.couriercoffeeroasters. com ⊗ No dinner.

Ruby Jewel Ice Cream

$ | Café. Portland's *other* critically acclaimed ice-cream shop (Salt & Straw tends to get far more attention), Ruby Jewel started in 2004 with ice-cream sandwiches in unusual flavors, such as lemon cookie with honey-lavender ice cream and cinnamon-chocolate cookie stuffed with espresso ice cream. Ruby Jewel's five cafés, including this central one in Downtown's West End, also dole out cones and dishes of ice cream with flavors like caramel with salted dark chocolate and chèvre with Pinot-grape swirl. **Known for:** ice cream sandwiches locals line up for; root beer floats; relationships with regional farms and producers. *Average main: $5* ⊠ 428 S.W. 12th Ave., West End ☎ 971/271–8895 ⊕ www.rubyjewel.com.

Stumptown Coffee Roasters

$ | Café. A pioneer in Portland's artisanal coffee experience, Stumptown Coffee Roasters has expanded into a nationally revered brand. There are five local cafés, where hip baristas, well-versed in all things coffee, whip up delicious espresso drinks. **Known for:** quintessential Portland roasts; sectionals and couches to lounge on in the Ace's lobby; pick-me-up before exploring the nearby Powell's City of Books. *Average main: $4* ⊠ *Ace Hotel, 1026 S.W. Harvey Milk St., West End* ☎ *855/711–3385* ⊕ *www.stumptown-coffee.com* ☾ *No dinner.*

🍴 Dining

Bamboo Sushi
$$ | Sushi. Claiming to be the world's first certified sustainable sushi restaurant, this Portland-based chainlet partners with non-profits such as the Marine Stewardship Council and Monterey Bay Aquarium to ensure it sources its seafood from eco-conscious fishing operations. Bamboo has five locations throughout the metro area, including this stylish branch in Downtown's West End, where the counter seating fills for the weekday happy hour, served until 6 pm. **Known for:** creative, non-traditional signature rolls; choose-your-own sake flights; happy-hour nigiri set. *Average main: $18* ⊠ *404 S.W. 12th Ave., West End* ☎ *503/444–7455* ⊕ *www.bamboosushi.com.*

Boxer Ramen
$ | Ramen. This often crowded and convivial ramen shop, at the entrance of the Union Alley shopping arcade across from the Ace Hotel, is tiny in size and menu, but popular for its quick-service soups, including spicy red miso with pork belly and egg, and shiitake mushroom shoyu. Seating is at a few small wooden tables and a short bar, so prepare for a wait at lunchtime or on weekend evenings. *Average main: $13* ⊠ *1025 S.W.*

Portland may not have a dedicated contemporary art museum, but many of its streets increasingly feel like one. In the past decade, artists from around the world have descended on the city and painted large-scale murals on vacant walls—notably in the West End area, where you'll find a concentration of striking street art. To spot two of the most colorful works, curated by the Forest For The Trees NW art project, pause at the intersection of Southwest 12th Avenue and Harvey Milk Street.

Harvey Milk St., West End, West End ☎ *503/894–8260* ⊕ *www.boxerramen. com.*

Clyde Common
$$$ | Pacific Northwest. While chefs have come and gone, and Portland's dining scene evolved considerably since Clyde Common opened with much fanfare in 2007, two things remain consistent: the open kitchen turns out European-inspired plates driven by seasonal Oregon-sourced ingredients and revered cocktail master Jeffrey Morgenthaler still makes one of the finest Negronis in Portland. **Known for:** barrel-aged cocktails; seasonal farm-to-table menu; outstanding happy hour. *Average main: $27* ⊠ *Ace Hotel, 1014 S.W. Harvey Milk St., West End* ☎ *503/228–3333* ⊕ *www. clydecommon.com* ☾ *No lunch weekdays.*

Jake's Famous Crawfish

$$$ | Seafood. Diners have been enjoying fresh Pacific Northwest seafood in Jake's warren of wood-paneled dining rooms for more than a century. The back bar came around Cape Horn during the 1880s, and the chandeliers hanging from the high ceilings date from 1881. **Known for:** almost endless sheet of daily seafood specials; Dungeness crab and Bay shrimp cakes; Oregon Triple Berry Martini. *Average main: $28 ⊠ 401 S.W. 12th Ave., West End* ☎ 503/226-1419 ⊕ www.mccormicka-ndschmicks.com.

Kenny & Zuke's Delicatessen

$ | Deli. The reputation of this Jewish deli beside the Ace Hotel is based largely on its much-revered pastrami, which is cured for seven days, then smoked for 10 hours and steamed for 3. The open and airy Downtown space serves omelets, Benedicts, biscuits, and breakfast sandwiches all day, along with a wide selection of soups, salads, and meaty sandwiches. **Known for:** best Reuben in town; house-made bagels; breakfast all day. *Average main: $14 ⊠ 1038 S.W. Harvey Milk St., West End* ☎ 503/222-3354 ⊕ www.kennyandzukes.com.

★ Maurice

$$ | Café. Described by baker-owner Kristen Murray as a "modern pastry luncheonette," this dainty West End café has just a handful of wooden booth and counter seats and a minimalist-inspired white-on-white aesthetic. The menu features exquisite French–Scandinavian pastries, cakes, and sandwiches, as well as a full gamut of drinks, including wine, beer, cocktails, teas, and coffee. **Known for:** ever-changing, hand-written menu; assorted Swedish fika (snack) pastries; revelatory black-pepper cheesecake. *Average main: $20 ⊠ 921 S.W. Oak St., West End* ☎ 503/224-9921 ⊕ www.mauricepdx.com ⊘ Closed Mon. No dinner.

★ Nong's Khao Man Gai

$ | Thai. What started as a Downtown food cart serving deceptively simple poached chicken and rice—*khao man gai,* a popular Thai street-food dish that originated in China's Hainan province—has evolved into a brick-and-mortar restaurant with a cult following. Stop in to taste why Bangkok-native Nong Poonsukwattana has earned praise everywhere from the *New York Times* to *Bon Appétit.* **Known for:** variations of only one dish—khao man gai; tiny eat-in area; fast service for take-out. *Average main: $11 ⊠ 417 S.W. 13th Ave., West End* ☎ 503/208-2402 ⊕ www.khaomangai.com.

Tasty n Alder

$$$ | Eclectic. Brunch draws even weekday crowds at this always-happening Downtown venture of celebrated Portland chef John Gorham, what you could label as a "modern steakhouse," though the globe-trotting, tapas-focused menu evades easy categorization. For dinner, Tasty n Alder turns up the class, with a selection of steaks from family-run ranches, along with well-crafted original cocktails. **Known for:** brunch till 2 pm every day; "grown ass" milkshakes (with alcohol, of course); Korean-style fried chicken. *Average main: $24* ⊠ *580 S.W. 12th Ave., West End* ☎ *503/621–9251* ⊕ *www.tastynalder.com.*

 Bars and Nightlife

McMenamins Crystal Ballroom

With a 7,500-square-foot spring-loaded dance floor built on ball bearings to ramp up the energy, this historic former dance hall draws local, regional, and national acts every night but Monday. Past performers include Sleater-Kinney, Jefferson Airplane, Emmylou Harris, Tame Impala, and Angel Olsen. ⊠ *1332 W. Burnside St., West End* ☎ *503/225–0047* ⊕ *www.crystal-ballroompdx.com.*

★ Multnomah Whiskey Library

Smartly dressed bartenders roll drink carts around the seductively clubby room—with beam ceilings, wood paneling, leather chairs, a wood-burning fireplace, and crystal chandeliers—pouring cocktails table-side. The emphasis, of course, is whiskey and bourbon—Multnomah has such an extensive collection in its "library" that staff need rolling ladders to access the bottles perched on the tall shelves lining the exposed-brick walls. ⊠ *1124 S.W. Alder St., West End* ☎ *503/954–1381* ⊕ *www.mwlpdx.com.*

★ Pépé le Moko

A neon "cocktails" sign glows at the street-level entrance to this Mediterranean-influenced cocktail bar. Pass through a pantry-size

kitchen and descend a flight of stairs to a somewhat claustrophobic tunnel beneath the original Ace Hotel, where you enter the boozy domain of Portland's bartending poet Jeffrey Morgenthaler. Nibble on a charcuterie plate while sipping sweet-ish concoctions like espresso martinis and Amaretto sours into the wee hours of the night. ⊠ *407 S.W. 10th Ave., West End* ☎ *503/546–8537* ⊕ *www.pepelemokopdx.com.*

Ringlers Annex Cellar Bar

Sip on beer, port, or single-malt scotch in the cavernous basement of Ringlers Annex, a pie-shaped corner pub in the atmospheric Crystal Hotel, right where Harvey Milk and Burnside streets meet. It's part of the famously offbeat McMenamins brewpub empire. ⊠ *1223 S.W. Harvey Milk St., West End* ☎ *503/384–2700* ⊕ *www.mcme-namins.com/ringlersannex.*

Scandals

This low-key bar is the lone remaining LGBTQ hangout in the West End, which used to be the city's gay nightlife district (most of the gay bars are now spread around the city, with a concentration in Old Town). There's a pool table, and light food service noon to closing. The plate-glass windows offer a view of Harvey Milk Street, and there's also popular sidewalk seating. ⊠ *1125 S.W. Harvey Milk St., West End* ☎ *503/227–5887* ⊕ *www.scandalspdx. com.*

 **Performing Arts**

Living Room Theaters

The boutique cinema, which has a lobby restaurant with a full bar, shows 3-D blockbuster, foreign, and independent films in, true to its name, living-room-like theaters furnished with spacious seats and movable couches and tables. You can dine and drink from your seat. ⊠ *341 S.W. 10th Ave., West End* ⊕ *pdx. livingroomtheaters.com.*

Washington Park and West Hills

 Sights

Council Crest Park

The highest point in Portland, at 1,073 feet, this 43-acre bluff-top patch of greenery is a superb spot to take in sunsets and sunrises. Along with nearly 180-degree views of the Portland metro area, a clear day also affords views of the surrounding peaks—Mt. Hood, Mt. St. Helens, Mt. Adams, Mt. Jefferson, and Mt. Rainier. A bronze fountain depicting a mother and child has been erected in the park twice; first in the 1950s and second in the 1990s. The peaceful piece was stolen in the 1980s, uncovered in a narcotics bust 10 years later, and then returned to the park. Trails connect Council Crest with Marquam Nature Park and Washington Park. ■ **TIP→** It's quite busy on weekends so visit on a weekday, if possible. ⊠ *1120 SW Council Crest Dr., West Hills* ⊕ *www. portlandoregon.gov/parks.*

Hoyt Arboretum

Some 12 miles of trails, which connect with others in Washington Park and Forest Park, wind through the 189-acre arboretum, which was established in 1928 and contains more than 2,000 species of plants and one of the nation's largest collections of coniferous trees; pick up trail maps at the visitor center. Guided 90-minute tours ($3 suggested donation) are offered most Saturdays and Sundays at 11 am and 1 pm from April through October. Also here are the Winter Garden and a memorial to veterans of the Vietnam War. The visitor center is a half mile from the Washington Park MAX station. ⊠ *4000 S.W. Fairview Blvd., Washington Park* ☎ *503/865–8733* ⊕ *www.hoytarboretum.org* ☜ *Free.*

★ International Rose Test Garden

This glorious park within Washington Park comprises three terraced gardens, set on 4½ acres,

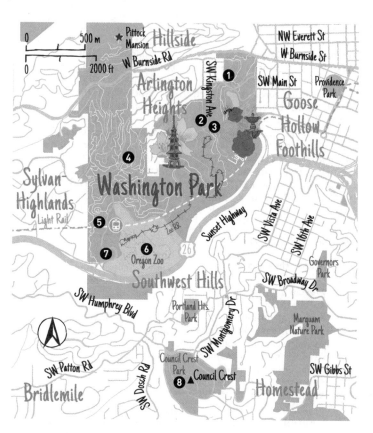

where more than 10,000 bushes and some 550 varieties of roses grow. The flowers, many of them new varieties, are at their peak in June, July, September, and October. From the gardens you can take in views of the Downtown skyline and, on clear days, the slopes of Mt. Hood, 50 miles to the east. Summer concerts take place in the garden's amphitheater. It's a pretty but hilly 30- to 40-minute walk from Downtown, or you can get here via MAX light rail (either to Washington Park or Kings Hill/S.W. Salmon Street stations); then transfer to Bus No. 63 or Washington Park shuttle (May–October only). ⊠ 400 S.W. Kingston Ave., Washington Park ☎ 503/227-7033 ⊕ www.portland-oregon.gov/parks.

Oregon Holocaust Memorial

This memorial to those who perished during the Holocaust bears the names of surviving families who live in Oregon and southwest Washington. A bronzed baby shoe, a doll, broken spectacles, and other strewn possessions await notice on the cobbled courtyard. Soil and ash from six Nazi concentration camps is interred beneath the black granite wall. The memorial is operated by the Oregon Jewish Museum and Center for Holocaust Education in Old Town, which hosts rotating history and art exhibits, films, concerts, and lectures. ⊠ S.W. Washington Way and S.W. Wright Ave., Washington Park ☎ 503/226-3600 ⊕ www.ojmche.org.

Oregon Zoo

This animal park in the West Hills, famous for its Asian elephants, is undergoing a two-decade-long series of major improvements and expansions to make the zoo more sustainable and provide more stimulating spaces, education, and conservation opportunities, as well as improved guest amenities and event spaces. New in recent years are the Condors of the Columbia habitat, which includes a deep pool for condor bathing, a 30-foot aviary, and an elevated viewing area to see the condors in flight; and the Elephant Lands area, which features feeding stations, mud wallows, varied terrain, and deep pools to keep the elephants active, as well as one of the world's largest indoor elephant facilities. A state-of-the-art Zoo Education Center opened in 2017. Other major draws include the Africa Savanna with rhinos, hippos, zebras, and giraffes; Steller Cove, an aquatic exhibit home to Steller sea lions and a family of sea otters; and a troop of chimpanzees. More than a dozen summer concerts, featuring nationally known pop stars, take place at the zoo from mid-June through August. Take the MAX light rail to the Washington Park station. ⊠ 4001 S.W. Canyon Rd., Washington Park ☎ 503/226-1561 ⊕ www.oregonzoo.org ⊠ $17.95.

Portland Children's Museum

Colorful sights and sounds entertain kids of all ages where hands-on play is the order of the day. Visit nationally touring exhibits; catch a story time, a sing-along, or a puppet show in the theater; create sculptures in the clay studio; splash hands in the waterworks display; or make a creation from junk in the Maker Studio. The museum shares the same parking lot as the Oregon Zoo and can also be reached via the MAX light rail Washington Park stop. ⊠ *4015 S.W. Canyon Rd., Washington Park* ☎ *503/223–6500* ⊕ *www.portlandcm.org* 🎫 *$11.*

★ Portland Japanese Garden

One of the most authentic Japanese gardens outside Japan, this serene landscape unfolds over 12½ acres of Washington Park, just a short stroll up the hill from the International Rose Test Garden. Designed by a Japanese landscape master, there are five separate garden styles: Strolling Pond Garden, Tea Garden, Natural Garden, Sand and Stone Garden, and Flat Garden. The Tea House was built in Japan and reconstructed here. An ambitious expansion designed by renowned Japanese architect Kengo Kuma added a tea garden café, library, art gallery, and a new gift shop in 2017. The east side of the Pavilion has a majestic view of Portland and Mt. Hood. Take MAX light rail to Washington Park station, and transfer to Bus No. 63 or the Washington Park Shuttle (May–October only). ■TIP→ Knowledgeable volunteers guide daily public tours, which are free with admission; call ahead for times. ⊠ *611 S.W. Kingston Ave., Washington Park* ☎ *503/223–1321* ⊕ *www.japanese-garden.com* 🎫 *$16.95.*

World Forestry Center Discovery Museum

This handsomely designed, contemporary museum across from the Oregon Zoo contains interactive and multimedia exhibits about forest sustainability. A white-water raft ride, smoke-jumper training simulator, and Timberjack tree harvester all provide different perspectives on Pacific Northwest forests. On the second floor the forests of the world are explored in various travel settings. A canopy lift ride hoists visitors to the 50-foot ceiling to look at a Douglas fir. ⊠ *4033 S.W. Canyon Rd., Washington Park* ☎ *503/228–1367* ⊕ *www.worldforestry.org* 🎫 *$8* ⊗ *Closed Tues.–Wed. early Sept.–late May.*

Pearl District and Old Town/ Chinatown

VANCOUVER, WA

NORTH

NORTHWEST

NORTHEAST

SOUTHWEST

SOUTHEAST

Sightseeing ★★★★☆ | Shopping ★★★★★ | Dining ★★★☆☆ | Nightlife ★★★★☆

Bordering Old Town to the west and Downtown and the West End to the north, the Pearl District comprises a formerly rough-and-tumble warren of warehouses and railroad yards that has been steadily morphing into a mixed-use neighborhood of stylish condos, restaurants, and retailers since the late 1990s. Much of the Pearl is new construction, but dozens of the district's handsome, historic industrial buildings have been converted into trendy, loft-style housing and commercial concerns, too. You'll find some of the city's most buzzed-about galleries, design shops, and clothiers in this neighborhood, plus quite a few hot spots for dining and drinking, many of them on the upscale side. Independently owned businesses dominate the landscape, but the Pearl has quite a few chains as well, especially on the three or four blocks nearest to Burnside Street. A great time to visit is during the monthly First Thursday parties, held in the evening at art galleries and along a few blocks of Northwest 13th Avenue. Also, be sure to pick up a copy of the neighborhood magazine, The Pearl, or check it out online at wwww.ExploreThePearl.com for the latest activities and events.—*by Andrew Collins*

. . . .

The original city center of Portland, Old Town/Chinatown fringes Downtown and the Pearl District, and while it's a bit seedy in places, it exudes character and is home to a number of cool shops and eateries, including the hip food hall Pine Street Market. This 20-square-block historic district—bounded by Oak Street to the south, Hoyt Street to the north, and the Park Blocks to the west—includes buildings of varying ages and architectural designs. Before it was renovated, this was skid row. Older buildings continue to be remodeled, mostly into businesses or transitional housing (there are fewer than 60 market-rate residential units in

the entire neighborhood). Portland doesn't have a gay district per se—the scene permeates just about every neighborhood of this extremely LGBTQ-welcoming city—but you'll find the highest concentration of Portland's gay nightspots in Old Town (and a couple of others close by in the West End).

Pearl District

 Sights

Blue Sky Gallery
Since 1975, this nonprofit organization located in the historic DeSoto Building has been staging critically acclaimed rotating shows that feature emerging and established

talents from parts far and near. Admission to this gallery is free, and the 20 to 25 shows presented throughout the year are often accompanied by opening receptions and artists talks. Visitors are also welcome to stop in and browse the more than 1,000 photography-related titles in the gallery library. The independent artists co-op Nine Gallery is in the same building and shares Blue Sky's hours. ⊠ *122 NW 8th Ave., Pearl District* ☎ *503/225–0210* ⊕ *www.blueskygallery.org* ▢ *Free* ☉ *Closed Mon.*

Ecotrust Building

Officially named, but rarely referred to as, the Natural Capital Center, this striking building has a handful of organic and environment-friendly businesses and other retail outlets, including Hot Lips Pizza, Laughing Planet Café, and a wonderful little Latinx-owned coffeehouse, Perlita. Built in 1895 and purchased by Ecotrust in 1998, the former warehouse has been adapted to serve as a landmark in "green" building practices. Guided tours are available by appointment and showcase the original "remnant wall" on the west side of the parking lot as well as the "eco-roof," a grassy rooftop, with its great view of the Pearl District. ⊠ *721 N.W. 9th Ave., Pearl District* ☎ *503/227–6225* ⊕ *www.ecotrust.org* ▢ *Free.*

The Fields Park

Situated at the northern tip of the Pearl and offering one of the largest public lawns in the city center, this 3.2-acre park affords

GETTING HERE

Adjoining Downtown and with several parking garages (there are good ones at Naito and Davis and at Marshall and Station Way), the Pearl and Old/Town Chinatown are easy to reach. The MAX red and blue lines have stops along 1st Avenue, and the green and yellow lines stop along 5th and 6th Avenues. And the Portland streetcar line passes through the Pearl District on its way from Nob Hill to Downtown.

sweeping views of the Fremont Bridge, Willamette River, and the neighborhood's many soaring glass towers. It's a great place for a picnic (there are several cafés nearby), it's hugely popular with dog walkers (there's even an enclosed run), and it has a well-designed playground with cargo nets for kids to gambol around on. Several events, including the Portland Craft Beer Festival and Cider Summit, take place here throughout the year. ⊠ *1099 N.W. Overton St., Pearl District* ⊕ *www. explorethepearl.com.*

Jamison Square Park

This gently terraced park surrounded by tony lofts, shops, and restaurants contains a soothing fountain that mimics nature. Rising water gushes over a stack of basalt blocks, gradually fills the open plaza, and then subsides. Colorful 30-foot tiki totems by pop artist Kenny Scharf stand along the park's west edge. There are tables and chairs in the park and wading in the fountain is encouraged. The

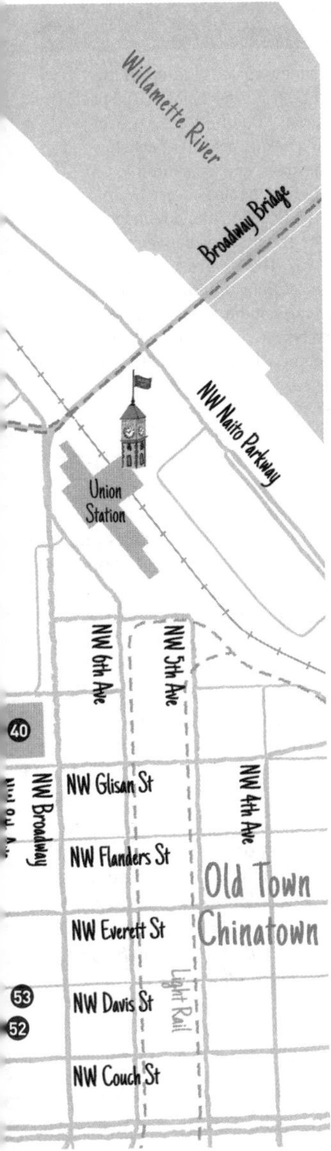

Willamette River
Broadway Bridge
NW Naito Parkway
Union Station
NW 6th Ave
NW 5th Ave
NW 4th Ave
40
NW Glisan St
NW Broadway
NW Flanders St
Old Town
NW Everett St
Chinatown
Light Rail
53
52
NW Davis St
NW Couch St

SIGHTS

Blue Sky Gallery 52
Ecotrust Building 15
The Fields Park 1
Jamison Square Park 14
Lovejoy Columns...... 34
Oregon Jewish Museum and Center for Holocaust Education.................. 53
Pacific Northwest College of Art (PNCA) 40
Tanner Springs Park 5

SHOPPING

First Thursday.......... 11
Halo Shoes 43
HAY............................ 10
J. Pepin Art Gallery 42
Keen Garage............. 22
Lizard Lounge 16
MadeHere PDX......... 47
Nau............................ 32
Oblation Papers 25
PDX Contemporary Art.... 38
Powell's City of Books 46
Thelonious Wines 39
World Foods Portland.................... 49

COFFEE & QUICK BITES

Greenleaf Juicing Co................ 13
Little Chickpea......... 12
Nuvrei 37
Pop Bagel 35
Sisters Coffee Co. 6
Tea Bar 3

DINING

Andina....................... 23
Arden 36
Can Font 4
Carlita's 2
Deschutes Brewery Portland Public House........................ 44
Eleni's Philoxenia 51
Fuller's Coffee Shop 50
Irving Street Kitchen 17
Lovejoy Bakers........... 9
Mediterranean Exploration Company................... 27
Montesacro Pinseria Romana 18
Oven and Shaker...... 31
Prasad 48
The Star 19
Tanner Creek Tavern....................... 41
Tilt 28
Verde Cocina 20
Von Ebert Brewing 29

BARS & NIGHTLIFE

Botanist Bar PDX 8
Cerulean Wine Bar 7
Cider Bite 24
Pink Rabbit 30
River Pig Saloon 21
Teardrop Cocktail Lounge 33
10 Barrel Brewing Co............... 26

PERFORMING ARTS

Portland Center Stage 45

streetcar stops right at the park. ⊠ *N.W. 10th Ave. and Lovejoy St., Pearl District* ⊕ *www.explorethepearl. com* ⊠ *Free.*

Lovejoy Columns

This pair of cement columns are all that's left of the Lovejoy Ramp, a viaduct that existed from 1927 to 1999 to elevate the Broadway Bridge over the once-busy freight tracks that existed in this neighborhood. Between 1948 and 1952, artist and Greek immigrant Tom E. Stefopoulos covered the original 12 columns with Greek mythology-inspired murals and phrases. The existing columns were brought out of storage in 2005, and in 2006, the original artwork was restored and reconstructed using archival photography. You can view these early works of street art in a small courtyard at Northwest Flanders Street and 10th Avenue. ⊠ *316 NW 10th Ave., Pearl District* ⊕ *www. pdxstreetart.org.*

★ Oregon Jewish Museum and Center for Holocaust Education

This institution, which interprets the stories and lives of the state's vibrant Jewish community, also functions as an educational and inspirational resource that focuses on promoting tolerance and combating discrimination and persecution. The museum was established in 1999 and is the force behind Washington Park's poignant Oregon Holocaust Memorial, but it wasn't until 2017 that it moved into this beautiful new permanent home inside the 1916 DeSoto Building, on

> **ART IN THE WILD**
>
> A strikingly curious vestige of the Pearl District's gritty industrial past, the Lovejoy Columns are a pair of soaring bridge piers that artist, calligrapher, and Greek immigrant Tom E. Stefopoulos covered with fanciful, Greek mythology-inspired murals and phrases between 1948 and 1952. There were originally a dozen columns, but most were lost when the viaduct they supported, which bisected the neighborhood, was demolished in 1999. You can view these early works of street art in a small courtyard at Northwest Flanders Street and 10th Avenue.

the leafy Park Blocks. The gallery on the upper floor contains permanent collections, including artifacts and artwork, and oral histories of the state's earliest Jewish residents as well as the profoundly moving historical exhibit on both the Holocaust and the valiant struggles of Jewish, Asian American, African American, Hispanic, LGBTQ, and other minority communities in the face of often strenuous intolerance in Oregon. ■**TIP**→ The ground floor features Lefty's, an excellent little lunch spot that has delicious sandwiches, salads, soups, rugelach, and other treats. ⊠ *724 N.W. Davis St., Old Town/Chinatown* ☎ *503/226–3600* ⊕ *www.ojmche.org* ⊠ *$8* ⊗ *Closed Mon.*

Pacific Northwest College of Art (PNCA)

Begun in 1909 as part of the Portland Museum of Art, the city's oldest college of art resides inside a dramatically transformed—by renowned Oregon architect Brad Cloepfil—1919 post office building overlooking the North Park Blocks. Apart from adding a heady dose of youthful creative energy to the neighborhood, PNCA presents free exhibitions in its public gallery spaces, which include the Center for Contemporary Art & Culture. The school also stages readings, lectures, and other events, often in its airy mezzanine space that's suspended by a series of steel cables. In 2018, PNCA opened the Glass Building just across the river at 2139 North Kerby Avenue. Set in beautifully adapted former warehouse, it also contains a public gallery space that focuses on works by the college's sculpture students, whose studios are in this building. ⊠ 511 N.W. Broadway, Pearl District ☎ 503/226-4391 ⊕ www.pnca.edu ⊗ Galleries closed weekends.

Tanner Springs Park

Tanner Creek, which once flowed through the area, lends its name to this unusual urban wetland park that's surrounded by soaring modern condo towers. Today the creek flows underground, and this quiet, man-made oasis and spring with alder groves was built in the middle of the Pearl District as a reminder of what the area was once like. The Artwall was created using hundreds of upright railroad tracks and hand-painted fused glass. ⊠ NW 10th Ave. and NW Marshall St., Pearl District ⊕ www.explorethepearl.com/places/tanner-springs-park ⊠ Free.

Shopping

★ First Thursday

This gallery walk the first Thursday of every month gives art appreciators a chance to check out new exhibits while enjoying music, wine, and light appetizers. Typically the galleries, which are largely located in the Pearl District, are open in the evening from 6 to 9, but hours vary. Beyond the galleries, you'll find a lively scene of street musicians, local art vendors, and food and craft beer stalls along N.W. 13th Avenue between roughly Hoyt and Kearney Streets, which is pedestrian only during First Thursday. ⊠ Pearl District ☎ 503/227-8519 ⊕ www.explorethepearl.com.

Halo Shoes

This dapper little boutique has earned a loyal following for its well-curated shoes for women and men. The selection is eclectic, from fire-engine red pumps to sturdy leather boots to hand-sewn dress sneakers from brands like Red Wing, Pantanetti, Jil Sander, and the Last Conspiracy. Beyond shoes, Halo also stocks designer denim, leather coats, and fanciful Antipast dress socks from Japan. ⊠ 938 N.W. Everett St., Pearl District ☎ 503/331-0366 ⊕ www.haloshoes.com.

HAY

The first U.S. brick-and-mortar location of the Danish homewares maker known for its clean lines and fun pops of color, HAY carries an especially nice selection of kitchen and bath items, from tiny stuff (colorful toothbrushes, penguin sponges, geometric trivets) to bigger pieces (pendant lamps, lounge chairs, work desks). You'll also find cleverly designed gadgets and accents pieces for just about every room in the home as well as patios and lawns. ✉ *815 N.W. 13th Ave., Pearl District* ☎ *503/420–3155* ⊕ *www.us.hay.com.*

J. Pepin Art Gallery

This highly respected contemporary gallery in the Pearl stands out for its unusual mission: the space represents renowned painters, photographers, and other creative spirits who use their experiences coping with mental illness to inspire their work and raise awareness. ✉ *319 N.W. 9th Ave., Pearl District* ☎ *503/274–9614* ⊕ *www.jpepinartgallery.com.*

★ Keen Garage

Known for its wildly popular and often playfully colorful hiking sandals, boots, and water shoes, this spacious showroom occupies a splendidly restored 1907 steamship factory that also houses this eco-concious company's headquarters. In addition to just about any kind of footwear you could need to tackle Pacific Northwest's great outdoors, you'll also find backpacks and messenger bags along with socks, pants, shirts, and other rugged outerwear. There's also a phone booth in the store from which you can call politicians in Washington to express support for a variety of environmental issues, from land and water conservation to clean air. ✉ *505 N.W. 13th Ave., Pearl District* ☎ *971/200–4040* ⊕ *www.keenfootwear.com.*

Lizard Lounge

Shop until your caffeine levels drop at this expansive men's and women's fashion source in the Pearl, where staff will pour you a complimentary cup of Stumptown coffee as you browse that particularly Portland mix of hip and hipster chic. Lizard Lounge carries everything from major mid-range brands like Levi's and Ray Bans to higher-end clubbing labels, like G-Star, Nudie Jeans, and Naked & Famous. There's also a good selection of gifts and household items. ✉ *1323 N.W. Irving St., Pearl District* ☎ *503/416–7476* ⊕ *www.lizardloungepdx.com.*

★ Made Here PDX

This spacious showroom across from Powell's carries an impressive and eclectic assortment of locally made culinary goods, housewares, fashion, jewelry, arts and crafts—even handcrafted skis and snowboards. The quality of everything here is consistently high—it's a perfect way to get a sense of Portland's vibrant "maker" culture, all under one roof. There's a second location on North Mississippi Avenue. ✉ *40 N.W. 10th Ave., Pearl District* ☎ *503/224–0122* ⊕ *www.madehereonline.com.*

Nau

Specializing in men's and women's sustainable clothing, from rugged hoodies and urbane down jackets to dressier threads made with cotton, Tencel, and other breathable fabrics, Portland-based Nau ships all over the world, but you can try on products and ask questions at this sleek flagship retail store in the Pearl District. ⊠ *304 N.W. 11th Ave., Pearl District* ☎ *503/224-9697* ⊕ *www.nau.com.*

Oblation Papers

Employing antique presses and old-world processes, this dapper shop in the Pearl District houses a paper mill, letterpress shop, and retail store where you can find one-of-a-kind cards, stationery, albums, and journals. The quality, handcrafted cards featuring vintage posters or images of local wildlife make wonderful keepsakes and gifts. ⊠ *516 N.W. 12th Ave., Pearl District* ☎ *503/223-1093* ⊕ *www.oblationpapers.com.*

★ PDX Contemporary Art

One of the Pearl District's longest-running and most respected art spaces, this large gallery features rotating exhibitions in a range of materials from an impressive roster of both local and national artists. The striking space, inside one of the neighborhood's oldest buildings, was designed by famous Portland architect Brad Cloepfil (famous for the Seattle Art Museum, Museum of Arts and Design in New York City, and many others). ⊠ *925 N.W. Flanders St., Pearl District* ☎ *503/222-0063* ⊕ *www.pdxcontemporaryart.com.*

★ Powell's City of Books

The largest retail store of used and new books in the world covers an entire city block and rises three stories on the edge of the Pearl District. A local legend, and rightfully so, Powell's also carries rare and collectible books and contains a popular coffeehouse, World Cup. There are also branches in Portland International Airport as well as a large outpost in the heart of the Hawthorne District, with its own coffeehouse, the Fresh Pot. ⊠ *1005 W. Burnside St., Pearl District* ☎ *503/228-4651* ⊕ *www.powells.com.*

Thelonious Wines

This bi-level bottle shop and wine bar differs from others of its kind in that it focuses exclusively on unusual, hard-to-find wines, from small productions of Pinot Noir from outstanding but lesser-known Oregon vineyards to interesting wines from unexpected places (bubbly from Tasmania, dry whites from Slovenia). Several single pours and flights are available, and you can pair your tasting with wine and charcuterie in the cozy upstairs loft with tables fashioned out of wine crates. ⊠ *516 N.W. 9th Ave., Pearl District* ☎ *503/444-7447* ⊕ *www.theloniouswines.com* ⊘ *Closed Mon.–Tues.*

A BOOK LOVER'S GUIDE TO POWELL'S

Visiting this Portland landmark, the largest independent bookstore in the world, with more than 1.5 million new and used books along with a good selection of locally made gifts and goodies, can easily take up several hours. Here are a few tips on how to make the most of your time.

Get Your Bearings
The store is so big that maps are available at the info kiosks and rooms are color-coded according to book type. Start at the main entrance (at Burnside and 10th), a light-filled room with prominent displays of staff picks, fun gifts and merchandise, top sellers, favorite used titles, and cash registers. A second entrance at the opposite corner (Couch and 11th) has some of the same features as well as an area where you can sell your own books for cash or, at a much better rate, store credit. There are staffed info desks on each floor where you can also look up titles on guest computers.

Don't Miss...
On the top floor, the Rare Book Room is a must, even if you're not planning to splurge for an 1829 volume of the *Waverly Novels* or an autobiography signed by Anwar Sadat; there are rare prints and mint-condition first editions in just about every genre. Be sure to look for the pillar bearing signatures of prominent sci-fi authors who have passed through the store that's protected by a jagged length of Plexiglas. Also check online for upcoming author readings, which take place three to five times a week and draw some of the world's top literary names.

Coffee Break
If you need a refreshment or a pleasant space to work, visit the store's branch of World Cup Coffee & Tea on the ground floor—you'll find scones, cookies, and muffins.

Take a Tour
The best way to see all of the store's key points of interest and learn about its storied history is by taking a free 45-minute guided tour offered every Sunday morning at 10 am on a first-come, first-served basis.

World Foods Portland
This family-run gourmet grocery market in the Pearl stocks a wide range of both international and local cheeses, chocolates, craft beers, wines, and other delicious foods, and it especially stands out for its Middle Eastern and Mediterranean packaged and prepared foods, including falafel, lamb shawarma, and fresh-baked baklava. ■**TIP**➔ A stop here is a must if you're planning a picnic, and there's pleasant indoor and sidewalk seating on-site. ⊠ *830 N.W. Everett St., Pearl District* ☎ *503/802-0755* ⊕ *www. worldfoodsportland.com.*

 Coffee and Quick Bites

Greenleaf Juicing Company
$ | Café. The healthy sipping and snacking options at this grab-and-go café in the Pearl go well beyond cold-pressed juices and

smoothies packed with antioxidant-rich greens, fruits, and nuts. They also offer healthy steamed soups, granola cups, and acai bowls, which are perfect in the morning when you've grown tired of expensive and heavy hotel breakfasts. **Known for:** the Sunrise acai bowl (with strawberries, coconut, and banana); ginger-orange soup; seasonal warm oatmeal and quinoa bowls during the colder months. *Average main: $7 ⊠ 810 N.W. 12th Ave., Pearl District ☎ 971/271–8988 ⊕ www.green-leafjuice.com.*

Little Chickpea

$ | Bakery. If the premise of this hip vegan bakery and ice cream shop in a contemporary space in the Pearl sounds quixotic—chickpea flour is the base ingredient of everything from the ice cream to the fig-fennel scones and olive loaf breads—it works because the food is genuinely tasty. And that's a big boon for folks who crave sweets and ice cream but can't do dairy, gluten, soy, or nuts. **Known for:** vegan- and gluten-free cookies and pastries; dairy-free ice cream in novel flavors like cherry-chai and mint-matcha; high-quality coffee drinks. *Average main: $5 ⊠ 1241 N.W. Johnson St., Pearl District ⊕ www.littlechickpea.com.*

★ Nuvrei

$ | Bakery. You'll find some of the tastiest sweets—including heavenly pistachio-rose croissants and blueberry-blackberry scones—in town at this cozy patisserie and café a few blocks south of Jamison Square. Be sure to check out the ever-changing selection of fluffy macarons. **Known for:** house-made macarons; savory quiches and croissants; double-chocolate flourless cookies. *Average main: $9 ⊠ 404 N.W. 10th Ave., Pearl District ☎ 503/972–1701 ⊕ www.nuvrei.com ⊗ No dinner.*

Pop Bagel

$ | Bakery. This cute little storefront near Jamison Square Park, with another location Downtown, bakes and sells dozens of satisfyingly chewy pretzel-style bagels each day. The flavors are conventional (salt, poppy seed, etc.), but some interesting cream cheese toppings are available, including pineapple and brown-butter sage. **Known for:** lox sandwiches; the baked egg breakfast bagel; distinctive house-made cream cheese spreads. *Average main: $9 ⊠ 433 N.W. 10th Ave., Pearl District ☎ 971/302–6110 ⊕ www.popbagel.co ⊗ No dinner.*

Sisters Coffee Co.

$ | Café. This airy bi-level cafe in the northern blocks of the Pearl is one of the most inviting spots in the neighborhood to sip nitro cold brew or single-origin pour-overs. Get comfy in one of the plush leather chairs, and consider ordering one of the delicious breakfast items (available until 1 pm). **Known for:** nitro cold brew on tap; breakfast sandwiches and tacos; plenty of laptop-conducive tables and counters. *Average main: $8 ⊠ 1235 N.W. Marshall St., Pearl District ☎ 971/279–2957 ⊕ www.sisterscoffee.com ⊗ No dinner.*

Tea Bar

$ | Café. This minimalist space with white walls and blond-wood tables and chairs on the ground floor of one of the Pearl's tallest residential towers has giant windows looking out over Tanner Springs Park, which is also a lovely spot to sip one of the cafe's signature milk teas and tea lattes or savor a dish of lavender-matcha vegan ice cream. **Known for:** coconut-milk soft-serve ice cream; boba milk teas in taro, vanilla rose, and other notable flavors; ginger-lemon tea toddies with local raw honey. *Average main: $7* ✉ *1055 N.W. Northrup St., Pearl District* ☎ *503/227-0464* ⊕ *www.iloveyouso-matcha.com.*

⏍ Dining

★ Andina

$$$ | Peruvian. This popular upscale Pearl District restaurant offers an inventive menu—a combination of traditional Peruvian and contemporary "Novoandina" cuisines—served in a large but nook-filled space that features live music most evenings. The extensive seafood offerings include several ceviche, grilled octopus, and a Peruvian-style paella that abounds with shellfish. **Known for:** Peruvian-style pisco sours; stylish yet casual lounge with great happy hour; ceviche with mixed fish and shellfish. *Average main: $28* ✉ *1314 N.W. Glisan St., Pearl District* ☎ *503/228-9535* ⊕ *www.andinares-taurant.com.*

★ Arden

$$$ | Pacific Northwest. From the custom wine cellar that forms the back wall of the dining room to the rows of bottles in the front window, the emphasis on viticulture is clear the minute you walk into this intimate bistro known for its seasonally sourced Pacific Northwest cuisine. The menu—available à la carte or as a four-course prix-fixe—changes daily according to availability but might feature local king salmon or bavette steak. **Known for:** cured meats and caviar on the lounge menu; exceptional selection of hard-to-find wines; an excellent prix-menu with wine pairings. *Average main: $30* ✉ *417 N.W. 10th Ave., Pearl District* ☎ *503/206-6097* ⊕ *www.ardenpdx.com* ☾ *Closed Mon. No lunch.*

Can Font

$$$ | Catalan. With tall windows and one interior wall covered with a giant photo of Gaudí's modernist Barcelona masterpiece, Casa Milà, elegant and relatively dressy—by Portland standards—Can Font serves artfully plated Spanish food, with an emphasis on Catalonia fare, such as bone marrow with grilled Catalan bread and duck breast and leg confit with smoked mushrooms and brûléed apples. You'll also discover a few dishes from other parts of Spain, such as gazpacho and several varieties of paella. **Known for:** tapas-sized open-face sandwiches and other light snacks on the bar menu; an impressive list of sherries and ports; zarzuela de mariscos (a rich shellfish stew

with a saffron and roasted-almond seafood broth). *Average main: $29* ✉ *1015 N.W. Northrup St., Pearl District* ☎ *503/224–3911* ⊕ *www.canfontportland.com* ⊗ *Closed Mon. No lunch.*

Carlita's

$ | Southwestern. Although you may be lured to this modern take on a Mexican cantina by the extensive list of creative cocktails and premium tequilas, mezcals, and whiskies, Carlita's also serves up remarkably good Northwest-meets-Mexico fare. Pacific ahi ceviche, several types of house-made salsa (the kicky ghost-pepper crema is notable), and tacos filled with smoked pork belly, blackened salmon, and wild mushrooms are presented in generous portions. **Known for:** generous afternoon and late-night happy hours; impressive mezcal and tequila selection; good-sized tacos with interesting fillings. *Average main: $9* ✉ *1101 N.W. Northrup St., Pearl District* ☎ *971/352–6991* ⊕ *www.carlitaspdx.com.*

★ Deschutes Brewery Portland Public House

$$ | American. The Portland branch of the Bend-based Deschutes Brewery typically has more than 25 beers on tap, including nationally acclaimed mainstays Mirror Pond Pale Ale, Inversion IPA, and Black Butte Porter, plus seasonal and experimental brews. On the food side, the kitchen has really upped its game in recent years, making this a worthy destination for elevated pub fare, such as Manila clams steamed in cider, porter-braised and smoked

pork shoulder with grits, and plenty of sandwiches and salads. **Known for:** limited-release and seasonal beers; the IPA pretzel with cheese sauce and porter mustard; marionberry cobbler. *Average main: $18* ✉ *210 N.W. 11th Ave., Pearl District* ☎ *503/296–4906* ⊕ *www.deschutes-brewery.com.*

Eleni's Philoxenia

$$ | Greek. A self-taught cook who grew up on the island of Crete, chef-owner Eleni Touhouliotis serves up flavorful Greek fare in this unassumingly romantic neighborhood bistro where lamb, rabbit, and shellfish figure prominently on the menu. Share a variety of the more than 40 tapas-size dishes, from traditional dips to refreshing salads to hearty pastas, and note the well-chosen selection of wines, including a number of Greek favorites. **Known for:** the midweek $30 per person Eleni's choice tasting menu; kouneli stifatho (an earthy casserole of tender braised rabbit and baby onions); saganaki cheese flambéed with cognac. *Average main: $20* ✉ *112 N.W. 9th Ave., Pearl District* ☎ *503/227–2158* ⊕ *www.elenisrestaurant.com* ⊗ *Closed Mon. No lunch.*

Fuller's Coffee Shop

$ | Diner. This Edward Hopper-esque corner diner with an endearing red neon sign and seating around a series of wood-grain counters has been doling out reliably good greasy-spoon fare since 1947, back before this formerly working-class neighborhood morphed into the slick Pearl District. The no-nonsense fare—buttermilk pancakes, corned beef hash, country-fried steak, chiliburgers, fried seafood—is filling and cheap. **Known for:** deep-fried Oregon razor clams; pig in a blanket (sausage rolled in a German pancake with syrup and powdered sugar); chicken-fried steak. *Average main: $8 ⌖ 136 N.W. 9th Ave., Pearl District ☎ 503/222-5608 ⊕ www.fullerscoffee-shop.com ⊗ Closed Mon. No dinner.*

★ Irving Street Kitchen

$$$ | Modern American. You might come to this hip Pearl District restaurant set inside a gorgeously transformed warehouse building just because you heard about the rich butterscotch pudding with roasted-banana caramel and peanut butter bonbons (it's available to go, sold in its own adorable canning jar); but chances are, once you see the exposed-brick-and-wood-beam walls, Edison bulb chandeliers, inviting central bar, and patio seats on a converted loading dock, you'll want to stay. And you'll be glad you did, as the well-executed Southern-influenced American dinner and brunch fare—including pan-fried soft-shell crab, organic fried chicken, and country ham with biscuits—is superb. **Known for:** wine by the glass on tap; terrific weekend brunch; decadent desserts. *Average main: $27 ⌖ 701 N.W. 13th Ave., Pearl District ☎ 503/343-9440 ⊕ www. irvingstreetkitchen.com ⊗ No lunch weekdays.*

Lovejoy Bakers

$ | American. A satisfying lunch or breakfast stop when you're strolling around the Pearl's shops and galleries, or a great spot to grab a takeout meal to enjoy at nearby Jamison Square or Tanner Springs parks, this glass-walled bakery also has sidewalk tables and Adirondack chairs out front along the wooden boardwalk that runs up and down 10th Avenue. Known for its bounteous salads and sandwiches, from roasted beets, grapefruit, and chevre over frisee greens to lamb meatloaf with crispy onions and harissa aioli, Lovejoy also offers a mouthwatering array of sweet treats. **Known for:** a good beer and wine selection, along with mimosas; seasonal made-from-scratch soups; personal blackberry, salted-caramel chocolate, and other tarts. *Average main: $10 ⌖ 939 N.W. 10th Ave., Pearl District ☎ 503/208-3113 ⊕ www. lovejoybakers.com ⊗ No dinner.*

★ Mediterranean Exploration Company

$$ | Mediterranean. Developed by cookbook author and celeb-chef John Gorham, this vegetarian-friendly tribute to Mediterranean cuisine occupies a handsome former warehouse on historic 13th Avenue in the Pearl. MEC (for short) is an energy-filled, open space with a mix of communal and individual tables (the food is served family-style)—it's surprisingly affordable considering the extraordinary quality and generous portions, particularly if you opt for the $50 tasting menu. **Known for:** chicken and lamb kebabs; Middle East–inspired cocktails; cardamom ice cream served with a pour-over of robust Turkish coffee. *Average* *main: $22* ⊠ *333 N.W. 13th Ave., Pearl District* ☎ *503/222-0906* ⊕ *www. mediterraneanexplorationcompany. com* ☉ *No lunch.*

Montesacro Pinseria Romana

$$ | Italian. The Italian-born owner of this lively spot decorated with rustic antiques based the concept on the modest working-class taverns—called *fraschette*—of the countryside outside Rome. In addition to serving appetizingly light blistered-crust *pinsas* (similar to pizzas), the Montesacro offers a vast selection of cheeses and charcuterie, vegetables marinated in olive oil and herbs, and a terrific list of interesting wines. **Known for:** the Maranella pinsa with broccolini, spicy pork sausage, and burrata; vanilla and wild fennel panna cotta with olive oil; fantastic charcuterie and cheese selection. *Average main: $20* ⊠ *1230 N.W. Hoyt St., Pearl District* ☎ *503/208-2992* ⊕ *www. montesacropdx.com* ☉ *Closed Mon.*

Oven and Shaker

$$ | Pizza. A joint venture between James Beard Award–nominated chef Cathy Whims and renowned cocktail mixologist Ryan Magarian, this aptly named late-night spot specializes in creatively topped wood-fired pizzas and deftly crafted cocktails that rely heavily on local spirits and fresh juices. The salads and appetizers are also terrific, especially the radicchio version of a classic Caesar salad. **Known for:** great happy early evening and late-night pizza deals; Tuscan brownie sundae with vanilla gelato, chocolate sauce; the Maple Pig

pizza with apple butter, pork belly, smoked ham, maple mascarpone, and ricotta. *Average main: $19* ⊠ *1134 N.W. Everett St., Pearl District* ☎ *503/241-1600* ⊕ *www.ovenand-shaker.com.*

Prasad

$ | Vegetarian. Adjacent to the Yoga Pearl studio and drawing a decidedly health-minded clientele, this popular vegan restaurant and juice bar offers a great selection of hearty bowls, salads, tempeh scrambles, and breakfast items. In warm weather there's sidewalk seating, and the large central glass garage door is open to the sunshine. **Known for:** a fully gluten-free and organic menu; fresh-squeezed juice and smoothies; chia waffles topped with fresh fruit, almonds, coconut, and maple syrup. *Average main: $9* ⊠ *925 N.W. Davis St., Pearl District* ☎ *503/224-3993* ⊕ *www.prasadpdx. com.*

The Star

$ | Pizza. A newcomer to the Pearl with deep roots in the San Francisco Bay Area, this casually stylish pizzeria—known for both thin-crust and (arguably more impressive) cornmeal-based deep-dish pies—occupies a sunny corner building on historic 13th Avenue with tall windows and a fireplace. Among the deep-dish pizzas, the All-Star with four kinds of meat is sure to satisfy, while among the thin-crust pies, you can't go wrong ordering the garlicky white pie with tomatoes, zucchini, and feta. **Known for:** cornmeal-based, deep-dish pizzas; the burrata caprese salad; noteworthy cocktail and wine selection. *Average main: $22 ⊠ 1309 N.W. Hoyt St., Pearl District ☎ 503/300–7827 ⊕ www.thestarportland.com.*

Tanner Creek Tavern

$$ | American. While both dining and drinking happen here, it's the airy, window-lined bar off the lobby of Pearl's surprisingly snazzy Hampton Inn that draws the biggest crowds, thanks to its lively buzz and—in warm weather—seating that spills out onto the sidewalk. Tuck into plates of familiar fare with creative twists, or for a more intimate and elegant repast, opt for a table in the intimate dining room overlooking an exhibition kitchen. **Known for:** a fantastic happy hour with big portions of creative pub fare; flatbread pizzas with inventive seasonal toppings; deviled duck wings with balsamic-mustard glaze. *Average main: $20 ⊠ Hampton Inn & Suites Portland-Pearl District, 875 N.W. Everett St., Pearl District ☎ 971/865–2888 ⊕ www.tannercreektavern.com.*

TILT

$ | American. A slightly snazzier but still informal outpost of a classic blue-collar burger joint in Portland's industrial Swan Island neighborhood (there's a third location just across the river from downtown on East Burnside), Tilt is a worthy stop for massive burgers, sandwiches, biscuits and gravy with fried chicken, house-made jalapeno tots, and hand-dipped pie shakes. On the right side of this cavernous order-at-the-counter space, there's a full bar as well as a coffee counter

serving espresso drinks. **Known for:** the Island Trucker (a beef patty topped with honey-cured ham, beer-battered onion rings, grilled pineapple, teriyaki sauce, and Swiss cheese); plenty of patio seating; extensive craft-beer selection. *Average main: $11 ⊠ 1355 N.W. Everett St., Pearl District ☎ 503/894–9528 ⊕ www.tiltitup.com ▭ No credit cards.*

Verde Cocina

$$ | Mexican. Noted especially for its Mexican-inspired weekend brunch dishes—chilaquiles and huevos rancheros—piled high with fresh Oregon veggies and served in the restaurant but also at the PSU Farmers Market, this friendly space in the Pearl also scores high marks for hearty bowls and platters at lunch and dinner. Salmon fajitas, tofu or grilled chicken chimichurri bowls, and quinoa-filled chile rellenos are among the top dishes, which tend to be light and healthy, although you can add the decadent thick and smoky candied pork belly bacon to many dishes. **Known for:** heaps of fire-roasted vegetables that accompany many dishes; gluten-free and vegan choices; creative craft cocktails. *Average main: $17 ⊠ 524 N.W. 14th Ave., Pearl District ☎ 503/894–9321 ⊕ www.verdecocinamarket.com.*

Von Ebert Brewing

$ | American. Unquestionably, the tremendously varied and interesting beers—barrel-aged ales, small-batch seasonal sours, gluten-frees, German- and Belgian-styles—are the key draw of this cavernous brewpub, but the kitchen also turns out legit pub fare that makes this a great choice even for the hops-averse. Many of the best dishes have an Eastern European slant, such as the smoked trout salad and the bratwurst sandwich, but the pizzas are great as well. **Known for:** charcuterie and cheese platter; innovative seasonal beers; burgers and other hefty sandwiches. *Average main: $12* ⊠ *131 N.W. 13th Ave., Pearl District* ☎ *503/820–7721* ⊕ *www.vonebertbrewing.com.*

 Bars and Nightlife

★ Botanist Bar PDX

This classy, food-forward basement lounge opened in 2019 to rave reviews for its use of high-quality artisan spirits and fresh-juice, shrubs, and spirits. The bar snacks here are substantive and delicious—whitefish ceviche, tuna poke nachos, Korean BBQ chicken. And a popular boozy brunch is offered on Sundays. ⊠ *1300 N.W. Lovejoy St., Pearl District* ☎ *971/533–8064* ⊕ *www.botanist-barpdx.com.*

Cerulean Wine Bar

Based in the Columbia Gorge town of Hood River and known for elegant Pinot Noir, Pinot Gris, Tempranillo Rosé, and other fine estate wines, this family-owned winery and wine bar shares a handsome, timber-ceilinged warehouse space with a contemporary art gallery. Stop in to sample wines, perhaps order a glass or two, and snack on delicious appetizers. ⊠ *1439 N.W. Marshall St., Pearl District* ☎ *503/308–9137*

⊕ *www.ceruleanwine.com* ☉ *Closed Mon. in winter.*

Cider Bite

It's impressive just how extensive a selection of artisan ciders, many of them produced in the Northwest, are available on tap in this narrow storefront space with chunky varnished-wood tables. The best approach: choose a flight of six 5-ounce pours, and if you're unsure of your cider tastes, consult the detailed tasting notes on the menu. Shareable appetizers and sandwiches are served, too. ⊠ *1230 N.W. Hoyt St., Pearl District* ☎ *503/765–5655* ⊕ *www.ciderbite.com.*

★ Pink Rabbit

This elegant space with ambient pink lighting and suspended bubble lamps, named for a song by indie band The National, serves playfully named but seriously crafted cocktails like the sherry-and-gin-centric Sucker's Luck and the mezcal-driven Quiet Company. The Asian-influenced bar snacks are distinctively delicious—try taro tots with Thai ranch and chili sauce or the oxtail burger. The darkly seductive space makes an inviting milieu before or after a show at nearby Portland Center Stage. ⊠ *232 N.W. 12th Ave., Pearl District* ⊕ *www.pinkrabbitpdx.com.*

River Pig Saloon

This often-packed homage to the hardscrabble mill and timber workers of Portland's Victorian era is a great place to hobnob with locals or catch a game on the large-screen TVs. Try a pickleback (whiskey served neat with a shot of house-made pickle juice) or one of the excellent lamb or bison burgers, and on nice days relax on the wood-plank deck out front. ⊠ *529 N.W. 13th Ave., Pearl District* ☎ *971/266-8897* ⊕ *www.riverpigsaloon.com.*

Teardrop Cocktail Lounge
One of the original craft-cocktail bars in the Pearl, Teardrop continues to draw a loyal following for its well-crafted drinks, several of which clock in at just $7 each at happy hour. The bar snacks are tasty, too. ⊠ *1015 N.W. Everett St., Pearl District* ☎ *503/445-8109* ⊕ *www.teardroplounge.com.*

10 Barrel Brewing Co.
Order a flight to experience the full range of beer styles offered by this acclaimed, Bend-based brewer that's especially known for its hop bombs, like the blood orange–inflected Blood Runs Cold. The pub grub includes pretty good pizzas, but 10 Barrel's most beloved attribute is its expansive roofdeck with sweeping views of the Pearl District. ⊠ *1411 N.W. Flanders St., Pearl District* ☎ *503/224-1700* ⊕ *www.10barrel.com.*

🎫 Performing Arts

★ Portland Center Stage
Housed in a handsomely restored 1891 armory, Portland Center Stage puts on around 10 contemporary and classic works on two stages in the LEED-certified green building between September and June. These are first-rate produc-tions with exceptional on-stage and behind-the-scenes talents. ⊠ *Gerding Theater at the Armory, 128 N.W. 11th Ave., Pearl District* ☎ *503/445-3700* ⊕ *www.pcs.org.*

Old Town/Chinatown

👁 Sights

Japanese-American Historical Plaza
In this particularly striking section of Tom McCall Waterfront Park that's dotted with cherry trees that bloom brilliantly in early spring, take a moment to study the evocative figures cast into the bronze columns at the plaza's entrance. They show Japanese and Japanese-Americans before, during, and after World War II—living daily life, fighting in battle for the United States, and marching off to internment camps. Simple blocks of granite carved with haiku poems describing the war experience powerfully evoke this dark episode in American history. ■TIP→ Consider visiting the plaza in conjunction with the nearby—and related—Oregon Nikkei Legacy Center museum. ⊠ *N.W. Naito Pkwy. and Couch St., in Tom McCall Waterfront Park, Old Town/Chinatown* ⊕ *www.oregonnikkei.org/plaza.htm* 🎟 *Free.*

★ Lan Su Chinese Garden
In a twist on the Joni Mitchell song, the city of Portland and private donors took down a parking lot and unpaved paradise when they created this wonderland near the Pearl District and Old Town/Chinatown.

It's the largest Suzhou-style garden outside China, with a large lake, bridged and covered walkways, koi- and water lily–filled ponds, rocks, bamboo, statues, waterfalls, and courtyards. A team of 60 artisans and designers from China literally left no stone unturned—500 tons of stone were brought here from Suzhou—in their efforts to give the windows, roof tiles, gateways (including a "moongate"), and other architectural aspects of the garden some specific meaning or purpose. Also on the premises are a gift shop and an enchanting two-story teahouse, operated by local Tao of Tea company, overlooking the lake and garden. ⊠ *239 N.W. Everett St., Old Town/Chinatown* ☎ *503/228-8131* ⊕ *www.lansugarden.org* 🖾 *$12.95.*

Oregon Maritime Museum

Local model makers created most of this museum's models of ships that once plied the Columbia River. Contained within the stern-wheeler steamship *Portland*, this small museum provides an excellent overview of Oregon's maritime history with artifacts and memorabilia. The Children's Corner has nautical items that can be touched and operated. The *Portland* is the last steam-powered stern-wheel tugboat operating in the United States, and volunteer-guided tours include the pilot house and engine room. ■TIP→ Occasional four-hour cruises on the ship are also offered, about once a month, in summer; the cost is $88. ⊠ *Foot of S.W. Pine St., in Waterfront Park, Old Town/Chinatown*

☎ *503/224-7724* ⊕ *www.oregon-maritimemuseum.org* 🖾 *$7* 🕙 *Closed Sun.–Tues. and Thurs.*

Oregon Nikkei Legacy Center Museum

This Japanese American historical museum, just a short walk from the related historical plaza in Waterfront Park, pays homage to the dynamic Nikkei (Japanese emigrant) community that has thrived in Portland for generations. The museum occupies the stately 19th-century Merchant Hotel building, and the excellent rotating exhibits use art, photography, personal histories, and artifacts to touch on all aspects of the Japanese American experience in Portland and the Northwest, including the dark period during World War II of forced relocation to concentration camps situated throughout the U.S. West. ■TIP→ You can also view an excellent interactive permanent history exhibit on the Nikkei Center's website. ⊠ *121 N.W. 2nd Ave., Old Town/Chinatown* ☎ *503/224-1458* ⊕ *www.oregonnikkei.org* 🖾 *$5* 🕙 *Closed Mon.*

★ Pine Street Market

In a city where restaurants rank among the top sightseeing attractions, this bustling food hall in a handsome late-Victorian Old Town building offers visitors a one-stop opportunity to try food from some of Portland's most celebrated chefs. In one massive room, you'll find nine small restaurants with counter service and plenty of common seating. Highlights include one of the first U.S. branches of Tokyo's famed **Marukin Ramen,** juicy Southern-style burgers and throwback cocktails at **Bless Your Heart** (from John Gorham of Tasty n Sons fame), Spanish-inspired tapas and rotisserie chicken at **Pollo Bravo,** and a soft-serve ice-cream stand called **Wiz Bang Bar** operated by Salt & Straw. Bring your appetite, and brace yourself for long lines on weekends. ⊠ *126 S.W. 2nd Ave., Old Town/Chinatown* ⊕ *www.pines-treetpdx.com* ✉ *Free.*

Portland Chinatown Museum

Begun as a temporary exhibit on the city's Chinatown—more than 10 percent of Portland's population identified as Chinese American in the 1900s, making it the second largest such community in the country—at the Oregon Historical Society Museum, this museum opened a 2,500-square-foot permanent space in late 2018 in the heart of Chinatown. Exhibits here document the community's continuously important contribution to the city, including the vibrant Chinese American–owned businesses that have prospered here since Portland's founding, as well as art, music, food, and important aspects of the community. The museum also presents rotating art and history exhibits as well as occasional concerts, lectures, and oral-history presentations. ⊠ *127 N.W. 3rd Ave., Old Town/Chinatown* ☎ *503/224–0008* ⊕ *www.portlandchinatownmuseum. org* ✉ *$8* ⊘ *Closed Mon.–Wed.*

★ Portland Saturday Market

On weekends from March to Christmas Eve, the west side of the Burnside Bridge and the Skidmore Fountain area hosts North America's largest ongoing open-air handicraft market, with some 400 vendors. If you're looking for jewelry, yard art, housewares, and decorative goods made from every material under the sun, check out the amazing collection of works by talented artisans on display here. The market also opens for holiday shopping during the week preceding Christmas Day, a period known as the Festival of the Last Minute. Entertainers and food booths add to the festive feel. ■**TIP**➔ Be careful not to mistake this market for the food-centric PSU Portland Farmers Market, which also takes place on Saturday, on the other side of Downtown. ⊠ *2 S.W. Naito Pkwy. at foot of S.W. Ankeny, in Waterfront Park, Old Town/Chinatown* ☎ *503/222–6072* ⊕ *www.portlandsat-urdaymarket.com* ✉ *Free* ⊘ *Closed Jan., Feb., and weekdays.*

Skidmore Fountain

This unusually graceful fountain, built in 1888, is the centerpiece of **Ankeny Square,** a plaza around which the Portland Saturday Market takes place. Two nymphs uphold the brimming basin on top; citizens once quenched their thirst from the spouting lions' heads below, and horses drank from the granite troughs at the base of the fountain. ⊠ *SW Ankeny St. and 1st Ave., Old Town/Chinatown* 🎫 *Free.*

Union Station
You can always find your way to Union Station by heading toward the huge neon "go by train" sign atop the 150-foot-tall Romanesque Revival clock tower that looms high above the building. Originally opened in 1896, the station's vast lobby area, with high ceilings and marble floors, is worth a brief visit if you hold any nostalgia for the heyday of rail travel in the United States. Amtrak trains stop here, and the old-school restaurant adjoining the station, Wilfs, is an elegant spot for a bite to eat or watching live jazz in the evening. ⊠ *800 NW 6th Ave., Old Town/Chinatown* ⊕ *www.amtrak. com/stations/pdx* 🎫 *Free.*

White Stag Sign
Perched atop the historic White Stag Building, this flashing neon-and-incandescent-bulb sign is one of Portland's iconic images. Installed in 1940, the sign was originally used to advertise White Stag Sportswear, but in 2010, the City of Portland acquired the sign and changed the lettering to "Portland Oregon." The sign, also known as the Portland Oregon Sign, is a popular spot to take photos, especially during the holidays when the stag's nose glows

red à la Rudolph. ⊠ *70 N.W. Couch St., Old Town/Chinatown.*

 Shopping

Compound Gallery
One of a few spots in Old Town that specialize in urban streetwear fashion, this expansive boutique carries Herschel backpacks, Japanese Kidrobot vinyl art toys, and clothing, footwear, and hats from trendy brands like Stüssy, UNDFTD, and Bape. The shop also collaborates on new products with local designers and artists. ⊠ *107 N.W. 5th Ave., Old Town/Chinatown* ☎ *503/796-2733* ⊕ *www.compound-gallery.com.*

Floating World Comics
Although the diverse selection of comics is the key draw at this spacious Old Town shop, you'll also find witty and humorous books (from *Twin Peaks* viewing guides to *How to Talk to Your Cat About Gun Safety*), young adult graphic novels, vinyl records, and decidedly irreverent artwork. The staff knows the material well and works hard to

stock a provocative and offbeat selection of works, many of them self-published or produced by small indie presses. ⊠ *400 N.W. Couch St., Old Town/Chinatown* ☎ *503/241–0227* ⊕ *www.floatingworldcomics.com.*

Hello from Portland

Head to this bright and fun storefront with a whimsical postcard-style sign when you're seeking that perfect PDX-themed gift for friends back home. You'll find colorful window stickers with playful sayings, bags of Stumptown Coffee and Jacobsen Salty Caramels, evergreen-print mugs, and plenty of other sometimes clever, sometimes goofy keepsakes and goodies. ⊠ *514 N.W. Couch St., Old Town/Chinatown* ☎ *971/279-2787* ⊕ *www.hello-fromportland.net.*

INDEX

Avid hunters of vintage sneakers flock to this Old Town consignment shop that carries highly sought-after new and used shoes—Air Jordan, Nike Dunk, Yeezy Boost, Vans, Asics—plus a few select hoodies and beanies. ⊠ *114 N.W. 3rd Ave., Old Town/Chinatown* ☎ *503/208-3599* ⊕ *www.indexpdx.com.*

★ Kiriko

Shibori-style hand-dyed and intricately sewn textiles—both contemporary and vintage—form the basis for most of the products in this gorgeous Old Town shop that practically bursts at the seams with kimonos, boros, dresses, neckties, socks, dopp kits, wallets, and other items for the home and wardrobe. It's easy to lose yourself in this colorful space, where you'll also discover plates, bowls, tea sets, and pottery works. ⊠ *325 Couch St., Old Town/Chinatown* ☎ *503/222-0335* ⊕ *www.kirikomade.com.*

Orox Leather

The name of this fourth-generation shop that specializes in finely crafted leather belts, wallets, handbags, and other accessories is a play on the owners' home states ORegon and OXaca. Be sure to have a look in the bin of seconds, experiments, and other one-of-a-kind items at drastically reduced prices. ⊠ *450 N.W. Couch St., Old Town/Chinatown* ☎ *503/954-2593* ⊕ *www.oroxleather.com* ☉ *Closed Sun.*

★ Pendleton Home Store

At this flagship lifestyle store—the headquarters are in the same building—of the world-famous textile and furniture purveyor, you can browse the company's new products before they're available online or in Pendleton's other shops around the country. The company's classic camp blankets—many of them with patterns inspired by

Native American weavings and U.S. national parks—are a huge draw, but you'll also find pillows, pet beds, hats, backpacks, totes, sweaters, and other apparel. ⊠ *210 N.W. Broadway, Old Town/Chinatown* ☎ *503/535-5444* ⊕ *www.pendleton-usa.com* ☉ *Closed Sun.*

★ Serra Dispensary

A beautifully designed cannabis shop in which carefully curated marijuana is displayed in blue ceramic dishes inside blond-wood cases, Serra stands out for its knowledgeable staff and decidedly artisanal aesthetic. They'll lend you a bronze magnifying glass if you want a closer inspection of the products, which also include cannabis-infused local chocolates, gummies, and other edibles. There's a similar branch in Southeast on Belmont Street. ⊠ *220 S.W. 1st Ave., Old Town/Chinatown* ☎ *971/279-5613* ⊕ *www.shopserra.com.*

🍵 Coffee and Quick Bites

Voodoo Doughnut

$ | Bakery. The long lines outside this Old Town 24/7 doughnut shop, marked by its distinctive pink-neon sign, attest to the fact that this irreverent bakery is almost as famous a Portland landmark as Powell's Books. The aforementioned sign depicts one of the shop's biggest sellers, a raspberry-jelly-topped chocolate voodoo-doll doughnut, but all of the creations here, some of them witty, some ribald, bring smiles to the faces of customers— even those who have waited 30

minutes in the rain. **Known for:** offbeat doughnut flavors; the bacon maple bar doughnut; long lines. *Average main: $4* ⊠ *22 S.W. 3rd Ave., Old Town/Chinatown* ☎ *503/241-4704* ⊕ *www.voodoodoughnut.com.*

🍴 Dining

Dan & Louis Oyster Bar Restaurant

$$ | Seafood. This Old Town landmark, located near the river and Voodoo Doughnuts, has oysters baked Rockefeller-style, stewed, and on the half shell, but the venerable 1907 restaurant offers plenty of other tasty local seafood, including steamed clams, Dungeness crab stew, and beer-battered cold-smoked-salmon. The collection of steins, plates, and marine art fill beams, nooks, crannies, and nearly every inch of wall space. **Known for:** oyster stew; mix-and-match fried or sauteed combination dishes; endearingly old-fashioned ambience. *Average main: $21* ⊠ *208 SW Ankeny St., Old Town/Chinatown* ☎ *503/227-5906* ⊕ *www.danandlouis. com.*

Kalé

$ | Japanese. A cozy counter-service option for a quick but satisfying meal near the riverfront, this fast-casual Japanese curry parlor makes up in food quality what it lacks in ambience. The kitchen serves slow-cooked-from-scratch vegetable, beef, and chicken rice curries, which can be enhanced with a number of extra toppings: pickles, spinach, hard-boiled eggs, and more. **Known for:** vegan and gluten-free options; Katsu chicken cutlets that can be added to any dish; chilled and canned Japanese coffee. *Average main: $10 ⊠ 50 S.W. Pine St., Old Town/Chinatown ☎ 503/206-4114 ⊕ www.kalepdx.com ⊗ Closed Sun.*

Kasbah Moroccan Cafe

$ | Moroccan. Although it's open only from 11 am until 5 pm most days (until 8 on Fridays and Saturdays), this colorful but unpretentious corner cafe is a welcome destination when you're craving a flavorful breakfast (served all day) or rich tagine, perhaps after a night of revelry in the many nearby bars. The Moroccan mint teas and spiced coffees are the perfect accompaniment to this exquisitely seasoned food, which also includes couscous plates, beet and carrot salads, and Merguez lamb and harissa sandwiches. **Known for:** refreshing Moroccan mint tea; kefta meatballs and eggs for breakfast; seafood tagine with chermoula and lemon. *Average main: $9 ⊠ 201 N.W. Davis St., Old Town/Chinatown ☎ 971/544-0875 ⊗ Closed Sun. No dinner Mon.–Thurs.*

★ Lechon

$$$ | South American. The menu of wood-fired, carne-intensive dishes at this bustling spot reads like a greatest hits of South American recipes, from Peruvian fried chicken bites with fermented hot honey to brisket empanadas with ancho aioli to Argentinian-style 28-day dry-aged rib eye steaks with cilantro butter. An added appeal is the location inside a handsome historic building just across the street from Tom McCall Waterfront Park, making it one of the closest dining options to the city's riverfront. **Known for:** plenty of seafood and vegetarian options; an emphasis on locally sourced and organic ingredients; great late-night tapas menu. *Average main: $25 ⊠ 113 S.W. Naito Pkwy., Old Town/Chinatown ☎ 503/219-9000 ⊕ www.lechonpdx. com ⊗ No lunch weekends.*

Lovely Rita

$$ | Modern Mexican. A long room facing Burnside Street contains this buzzy yet surprisingly relaxed space in the ultra-hip Hoxton hotel filled with Oriental rugs and plush, colorfully upholstered sofas and chairs—the sort of space that's perfect for whiling away a lazy afternoon. The daily (until 3 pm) brunch and nightly dinner fare mixes Northwest ingredients with international bistro fare, liked Dungeness crab sandwiches, albacore crudo, and summer squash gnocchi. **Known for:** stylish and comfy seating; all-day brunch fare; heavenly pastries during brunch. *Average main: $21 ⊠ Hoxton Hotel, 15 N.W. 4th Ave., Old Town/Chinatown ☎ 503/770-0500 ⊕ the-hoxton.com.*

Mi Mero Mole

$ | Mexican. Graffiti and murals decorate one concrete wall of this colorful Old Town eatery that serves some of the most flavorful Mexico City–style street food in town. Regulars come for the tacos, burritos, quesadillas, and bowls filled with pork adobo, albondigas (meatballs) with a tomato-chipotle sauce, shrimp Veracruzana, roasted green chiles with a crema sauce, and about 10 other options, but there's also tasty ceviche and tamales with a daily-changing selection of flavors. **Known for:** chilaquiles and breakfast burritos in the morning; extensive list of fine tequilas and mezcals, plus several handcrafted margaritas; the mole sampler with four types (pork mole verde, chicken, lamb, and butternut squash). *Average main: $13* ⊠ *32 N.W. 5th Ave., Old Town/Chinatown* ☎ *971/266-8575* ⊕ *www.mmmtaco-spdx.com.*

🍸 Bars and Nightlife

Ascendant Beer Company
Visit this warmly inviting brewpub in the quieter northern end of Old Town to quaff British-style lagers and ales—including a much-heralded red stout—and enjoy live music on certain nights. Original timber beams and red-brick walls create a pubby ambience, and there's sidewalk seating as well. ⊠ *412 N.W. 5th Ave., Old Town/Chinatown* ☎ *503/564-2739* ⊕ *www.ascendantbeer.com.*

Basement Bar
Although officially part of the trendy Hoxton Hotel in Old Town, this speakeasy is located beneath the lobby and reached by an unmarked black door around the corner from the building's main entrance. Once inside this warmly lighted subterranean lair, you can curl up with

a friend on a leather sofa, order a spendy but splendid cocktail, and munch on pork belly buns and crab rangoon dip. ⊠ *2 N.W. 5th Ave., Old Town/Chinatown* ☎ *503/770-0400* ⊕ *www.thehoxton.com* ⊘ *Closed Sun.–Tues.*

C.C. Slaughters Nightclub & Lounge
The most popular gay and lesbian dance club in the city, "C.C.'s" also has a quieter cocktail bar in front called the Rainbow Room. ⊠ *219 N.W. Davis St., Old Town/Chinatown* ☎ *503/248-9135* ⊕ *www.ccslaughter-spdx.com.*

Darcelle XV Showplace
The namesake performer and owner of this legendary drag cabaret, Darcelle (whose real name is Walter Cole), turned 89 in 2019, and he continues to pack the house with his hilariously ribald and outrageous shows. At this bona fide slice of West Coast LGBTQ history, shows include a roster of some of the city's funniest and sassiest talents. The walls inside are lined with photos of glam performers who have performed on this stage. ⊠ *208 N.W. 3rd Ave., Old Town/Chinatown* ☎ *503/222-5338* ⊕ *www.darcellexv.com* ⊘ *Closed Sun.–Tues.*

★ Ground Kontrol Classic Arcade
Revisit your teen years at this massive, old-school Old Town arcade filled with more than 100 classic arcade games and about 50 pinball machines, including vintage Atari, Super Nintendo, and Killer Queen. There are two full bars and a kitchen serving reliably

good nachos, sandwiches, and ice cream sundaes—and now that you are no longer a teen, you can have as much as you like. Over 21 after 5 pm. ⊠ *115 N.W. 5th Ave., Old Town/Chinatown* ☎ *503/796-9364* ⊕ *www.groundkontrol.com.*

Kells Irish Restaurant & Pub

There's terrific music here nightly, including traditional Celtic tunes on Sundays, at this old-school pub, plus decent Irish food and imported ales. ⊠ *112 S.W. 2nd Ave., Old Town/Chinatown* ☎ *503/227-4057* ⊕ *www.kellsportland.com.*

Roseland Theater

This spacious theater holds 1,410 people (standing-room only except for the 21+ balcony seating area), primarily stages rock, alternative, and blues shows, plus occasional comedians. Legends like Miles Davis and Prince have performed here, and more recent acts have included Hot Chip, Ingrid Michaelson, and Cat Power. ⊠ *10 N.W. 6th Ave., Old Town/Chinatown* ☎ *855/227-8499* ⊕ *www.roselandpdx.com.*

★ Stag

Drawing a diverse crowd of hipsters, tourists, and old-school clubbers, this Old Town hot spot cheekily bills itself a "gay gentlemen's lounge." Mounted antlers, leather chairs, and exposed-brick walls lend a rustic air, and male strippers dance on a small stage toward the back of the main room; a side bar contains a pool table. ⊠ *317 N.W. Broadway, Old Town/Chinatown* ☎ *971/407-3132* ⊕ *www.stagpdx.com.*

Valentine's

One of the more intimate venues in town to catch live rock, alternative, funk, and other edgy performances, bi-level Valentine's is set along a pedestrian-only stretch of Ankeny Street, just down the block from iconic Voodoo Doughnuts. For a break from the inside action, enjoy your drink at one of the picnic tables out front. ⊠ *232 S.W. Ankeny St., Old Town/Chinatown* ☎ *503/248-1600* ⊕ *www.valentinespdx.com.*

Nob Hill and Vicinity

A young generation of restaurateurs, distillers, bartenders, and designers have sparked a renaissance in Nob Hill, a mixed-use district of Victorian homes converted into boutiques and turn-of-the-century apartments housing street-level cafés. Once the epicenter of the city's fashion and culinary scenes, the neighborhood stagnated in the early 2000s, losing much of its edge as upstart chefs and shopkeepers set their sights on the quickly gentrifying east side of the Willamette River. Recently, though, much of that entrepreneurial energy has shifted back to the Northwest quadrant, especially in Slabtown—a swathe of formerly industrial blocks stretching north from N.W. Lovejoy Street—where a warren of converted warehouses and shiny condos buzz with late-night dining and cocktail lounges. Helmed by the sprawling and truly wild Forest Park to the west and the Pearl District to the east, compact Nob Hill feels like an action-packed village where old-school and new-wave Portlanders meet up for pints at the same bars—so go ahead, pull up a chair.—by Jon Shadel

◉ Sights

Aria Gin

Four years of testing and hundreds of recipe revisions resulted in an award-winning British-inspired dry gin, the sole focus of this distillery and tasting room, just a block away from Bull Run Distilling. Enjoy the batch-distilled spirit neat or in a flight of cocktails, and bring home a bottle along with their selection of artisan mixers and bar tools. ⊠ 2304 N.W. Savier St., Slabtown ⊕ www.ariagin.com ☉ Closed Mon. and Tues.

Bull Run Distilling

A pioneer of Portland's burgeoning craft spirits scene, head distiller Lee Medoff opened this Slabtown distillery in a 7,000-square-foot warehouse in 2010, with a dream of creating an iconic single-malt Oregon whiskey. Today, Bull Run operates two of the largest commercial stills in the state, turning out acclaimed whiskeys, vodkas, and aquavit. ⊠ 2259 N.W. Quimby St., Slabtown ☏ 503/224–3483 ⊕ www.bullrundistillery.com ☉ Closed Mon. and Tues.

Couch Park

When the sun comes out, pack picnic provisions and follow the locals to this urban park, where you can spread out a blanket and lounge on several sloping, grassy hills beneath dozens of shady trees. Admire the Temple Beth Israel, a domed Byzantine-style neighborhood icon that's just across the street. The park's newly built, ADA-accessible playground and designated off-leash area make this a popular spot for families and dog owners alike. ⊠ *N.W. 19th Ave. and Glisan St., Nob Hill* ☎ *503/823–7529* ⊕ *www.portlandoregon.gov/parks.*

★ Forest Park

One of the nation's largest urban wildernesses (5,157 acres), this city-owned, car-free park has more than 50 species of birds and mammals and more than 80 miles of trails through forests of Douglas fir, hemlock, and cedar. Running the length of the park is the 30-mile Wildwood Trail, which extends into adjoining Washington Park (and is a handy point for accessing Forest Park), starting at the Vietnam Veterans Memorial in Hoyt Arboretum. You can access a number of spur trails from the Wildwood Trail, including the 11-mile Leif Erikson Drive, which picks up from the end of N.W. Thurman Street and is a popular route for jogging and mountain biking. ■ TIP→ You can find information and maps at the Forest Park Conservancy office, at 210 N.W. 17th Avenue, and website. ⊠ *Leif Erikson Dr. entrance, end of N.W. Thurman St., 833 SW 11th Ave, Suite 800, Forest Park* ☎ *503/223–5449* ⊕ *www.forestparkconservancy.org.*

GETTING HERE

Despite its name, Nob Hill is, in fact, quite flat and its dense grid of tree-lined streets makes it eminently walkable and bikeable. From the Pearl District, it's an easy stroll to reach N.W. 21st and 23rd Avenues on foot. Or hop on the North South Line streetcar in both the Pearl and Downtown. You can also reach the neighborhood via the 15, 24, and 77 buses, which have multiple convenient stops.

★ Freeland Spirits

Founded by an agricultural educator, this craft spirits producer sets itself apart from its neighbors with expert-led tours that take you behind the scenes of the only women-run distillery in Oregon. Freeland takes the tasting room concept to new heights, too, with an ever-changing food menu and a full cocktail program centered on the house gin and bourbon. With philodendrons lining streetside windows, the bar is a relaxing place to sip the latest spirit release. ■ TIP→ To guarantee you catch one of the daily afternoon tours, make sure you reserve a spot on Freeland's website, bookable up to two months in advance. ⊠ *2671 N.W. Vaughn St., Slabtown* ☎ *971/279–5692* ⊕ *www. freelandspirits.com* ☉ *Closed Mon. and Tues.*

★ Pittock Mansion

Henry Pittock, the founder and publisher of the *Oregonian* newspaper, built this 22-room, castlelike mansion, which combines French

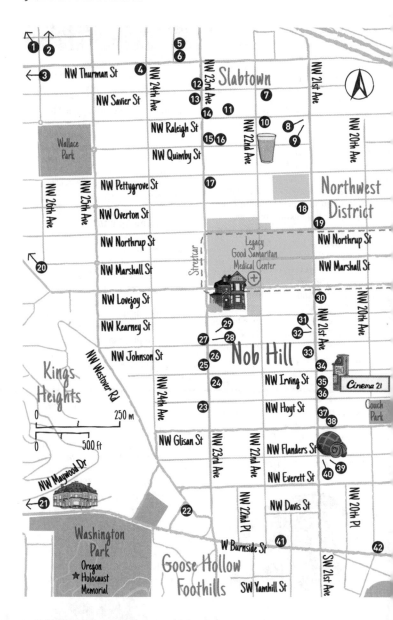

SIGHTS

SHOPPING

COFFEE & QUICK BITES

DINING

BARS & NIGHTLIFE

PERFORMING ARTS

Renaissance and Victorian styles. The opulent manor, built in 1914, is filled with art and antiques. The 46-acre grounds, northwest of Washington Park and 1,000 feet above the city, offer superb views of the skyline, rivers, and the Cascade Range, including Mt. Hood and Mt. St. Helens. The mansion is a half-mile uphill trek from the nearest bus stop. The mansion is also a highly popular destination among hikers using Forest Park's well-utilized Wildwood Trail. ⊠ *3229 N.W. Pittock Dr., Forest Park* ☎ *503/823–3623* ⊕ *www.pittockmansion.org* 🏷 *$12* 🕙 *Closed Jan.*

Portland Audubon Society

The 150-acre sanctuary has a few miles of trails, including one known for ample woodpecker sightings, as well as access to the miles of trails in the adjoining Forest Park. There's also a hospital for injured and orphaned birds here, as well as a gift shop stocked with books and feeders. The society supplies free maps and sponsors a flock of bird-related activities, including guided bird-watching events. ⊠ *5151 N.W. Cornell Rd., Forest Park* ☎ *503/292–6855* ⊕ *www.audubonportland.org.*

Slabtown

A formerly industrial slice of Northwest, this mini neighborhood epitomizes New Portland, with a walking-scale grid of stylish apartment buildings and repurposed warehouses filled with some of the city's most hyped restaurants. Come hungry, as the food scene is the star of Slabtown. Tasty highlights include cocktail lounges like Solo Club and Bar West, inventive tapas at Spanish eatery Ataula, craft beer at the bi-level Breakside Brewery, and handmade pasta at Grassa. While Slabtown loosely refers to the blocks stretching north from Lovejoy Street to the Willamette River, most of the action is sandwiched between Northrup and Thurman Streets. ⊠ *Blocks stretching north of Lovejoy St., Slabtown.*

Shopping

★ Betsy & Iya

Bright Santa Fe-esque colors and sleek geometric forms define the handmade earrings, bracelets, rings, cuffs, necklaces, and other stylish accessories at this beloved jewelry studio. On weekdays during production hours (between 10 am and 5 pm), complimentary artisan-led tours show you the magic happening in the production space, where you might glimpse anything from stone setting to metal soldering. ⊠ *1777 N.W. 24th Ave., Slabtown* ☎ *503/227–5482* ⊕ *www. betsyandiya.com.*

Daedalus Books

Upon stepping into this compact bookseller, which largely focuses on obscure and second-hand tomes, you may get the sense that you've stumbled into a scholar's expansive library. Browsing the shelves reveals the quirks and curiosities of the independent shopkeeper, whose selections lean heavily on the humanities and social sciences—ranging from art and literature to philosophy and politics. ⊠ *2074 N.W. Flanders St., Nob Hill* ☎ *503/274-7742* ☾ *Closed Sun.*

Gem Set Love

Portland's premier estate and vintage jewelry shop, known formerly as Gilt, occupies a dapper Craftsman bungalow along a fashionable stretch of Nob Hill's N.W. 23rd. Inside you'll find an ever-changing inventory of radiant gold and silver rings, bracelets, earrings, and necklaces, many inlaid with dazzling gems. The antique wedding and engagement rings are especially popular. ⊠ *720 N.W. 23rd Ave., Nob Hill* ☎ *503/226-0629* ⊕ *www.gem-set-love.com* ☾ *Closed Sun.–Mon.*

MindRite Dispensary

Budtenders are to recreational cannabis dispensaries what baristas are to coffee shops—the best ones get to know the preferences of their clientele and tune their suggestions accordingly. Beyond MindRite's stellar selection of high-quality flower and artisan edibles, what sets this low-key outpost apart from other nearby dispensaries is that it's

With cranes towering overhead and new restaurants opening at a fever pace, Slabtown may look like a neighborhood built from scratch, but this chunk of Nob Hill has a prolific history as host to a 1905 world's fair. A pivotal moment in Portland's growth, the Lewis and Clark Centennial Exposition drew 1.5 million visitors, who marveled at such innovations as motorized blimps and moving picture shows. The regal exhibition halls no longer stand, but some hotels built for the expo have since been converted into apartments.

helmed by some of Portland's most award-winning budtenders. (Yes, there are awards for budtenders.) In other words, this is the spot to go if you want help discovering the type of high you enjoy. ⊠ *1780 N.W. Marshall St., Nob Hill* ☎ *503/477-4430* ⊕ *www.mindritepdx.com.*

New Renaissance Bookshop

Between Overton and Pettygrove, this expansive bookstore is dedicated to New Age and metaphysical books as well as crystals, meditation cushions, wind chimes, and more. It's also a place to get astrology, palmistry, tarot, and other readings. ⊠ *1338 N.W. 23rd Ave., Slabtown* ☎ *503/224-4929* ⊕ *www. newrenbooks.com.*

Russo Lee Gallery

A longtime staple of the Portland arts scene, the Russo Lee Gallery displays contemporary Northwest work of all styles, including landscapes and abstract expressionism. ✉ *805 N.W. 21st Ave., Nob Hill* ☎ *503/226-2754* ⊕ *www.laurarusso. com* ☽ *Closed Sun.–Mon.*

Twist

This sprawling space in Nob Hill is well stocked with contemporary American ceramics, glass, furniture, sculpture, and handcrafted jewelry often with a whimsical touch. ✉ *30 N.W. 23rd Pl., Nob Hill* ☎ *503/224-0334* ⊕ *www.twistonline.com.*

★ Vía Raíz

"Made in Mexico" is the manifesto at Vía Raíz. The Spanish name of this tiny, 220-square-foot boutique translates to "via roots," which sums up the shopkeeper's approach to elevating contemporary Mexican designers and artisans. Expect a rotating display of modern crafts, art, accessories, home goods, and coffee table books. ✉ *2774 N.W. Thurman St., Slabtown* ☎ *503/303-3450* ⊕ *www.viaraiz.com* ☽ *Closed Mon.–Tues.*

Will Leather Goods

This upscale leather brand nick-named its Nob Hill outpost the "Family House," which makes sense since it both occupies a converted old home and sells practical leather goods that have remained stylish for generations. Shop for handcrafted Western and Americana handbags, wallets, purses, journals, and other travel accessories. ✉ *816 N.W. 23rd Ave., Nob Hill* ☎ *503/290-7479* ⊕ *www. willleathergoods.com.*

Portland's evergreen setting, with temperate rain forests within city limits and a snowcapped volcano shimmering on the horizon, gives photographers eye candy in all directions. For the most striking view of Downtown, head to the overlook on the grounds of Pittock Mansion. While the historic home charges admission, the landscaped estate is a public park, so you're free to explore until 9 pm. On a clear evening, you might get lucky enough to snap the skyline twinkling with Mt. Hood looming in the distance.

 Share your photo with us!
@FodorsTravel #FodorsOnTheGo

The Yo! Store

This playful storefront in the Film Exchange building—a retail and design complex—showcases the personal tastes of its owner, a fashion stylist and well-traveled British expat. Colorful textiles, vintage women's apparel, local apothecary brands, and European kidswear labels mingle in this self-dubbed "lifestyle shop," where serendipity seems to be the organizing principle. ⊠ *935 N.W. 19th Ave., Nob Hill* ☎ *503/841–5879* ⊕ *www.yoportland.com* ☉ *Closed Mon.*

 Coffee and Quick Bites

Coffeehouse Northwest

$ | Café. With hardwood floors, Jacobethan brick walls, and rotating work from local artists, Coffeehouse Northwest is the quintessential Portland café—and one of the city's pioneering specialty shops, the first to serve single-origin beans. Expect first-rate drinks made with shots of espresso from Dovetail Coffee Roasters. **Known for:** rock-star baristas; vegan and gluten-free treats from the artisan Shoofly Bakery; sidewalk seating along a gritty strip of West Burnside Street. *Average main: $4* ⊠ *1951 W. Burnside St., Nob Hill* ☎ *503/248–2133* ⊕ *www. sterlingcoffeeroasters.com* ☉ *No dinner.*

Commissary Cafe

$ | Café. The concept for this cinema-inspired café comes from the history of the building it occupies—a former distribution hub for America's major film studios. Art Deco lighting and design touches subtly reference the Golden Age of Hollywood, while the proprietor named her simple menu of sandwiches and salads in honor of stars from the silver screen. **Known for:** a popular spot for hanging

with friends; light weekend brunch without any lines; fine espresso drinks prepared with locally roasted beans. *Average main: $7* ⊠ *915 N.W. 19th Ave., Suite A, Nob Hill* ☎ *503/593–5992* ⊕ *www.commissary-cafe.com* ☉ *No dinner.*

Moberi

$ | Café. This spin-your-own-smoothie bar rose to national prominence in 2014 after the founder appeared on the TV show *Shark Tank* to pitch his stationary bicycle blender. Today fitness-conscious guests at the flagship café let electric blenders do most of the hard work—pureeing produce mostly sourced from nearby growers in the Willamette Valley. **Known for:** acai bowls generously topped with fresh fruit; vegan-centric breakfast hot spot; made-to-order tea drinks. *Average main: $14* ⊠ *1755 N.W. 23rd Ave., Slabtown* ☎ *503/890–9333* ⊕ *www.moberi.com.*

★ Smith Teamaker

$ | Café. At the center of Portland's locally steeped tea scene is Smith Teamaker's birthplace—a rustic tasting room opened in 2009 by the late entrepreneur Steven Smith, who the *New York Times* said "helped transform the nation's tea-drinking habits." Duck inside to learn about the tea's origin stories, sample different varieties at the tea bar, and leave with a few gift boxes. **Known for:** tea flights; tea lattes; chocolate and tea pairings. *Average main: $5* ⊠ *1626 N.W. Thurman St., Slabtown* ☎ *503/719–8752* ⊕ *www. smithtea.com.*

★ Sterling Coffee Roasters

$ | **Café.** Flights of batch-roasted espresso arrive in scotch glasses at this elegant, houseplant-filled café—a darling of Portland's specialty coffee community that doubles as a living room for the neighborhood. In contrast to the light, fruit-forward notes of many third-wave roasters, Sterling's house beans taste unapologetically chocolatey and seem roasted with milky drinks in mind. **Known for:** lively neighborhood café; pastry case filled with treats from Northeast Portland's Bakeshop; free refill on "for-here" mugs of drip coffee. *Average main: $4* ⊠ *518 N.W. 21st Ave., Nob Hill* ☎ *503/248–2133* ⊕ *www.sterling.coffee* ⊗ *No dinner.*

World Cup Coffee and Tea

$ | **Café.** Step into an old-school slice of Portland's circa-1999 coffee-shop scene. This pioneering roaster continues to serve organic coffee and espresso at its flagship Nob Hill location as well as at the coffee bar within Powell's City of Books on Burnside. **Known for:** chai lattes; butterscotch oatmeal cookies; assorted fair-trade teas. *Average main: $4* ⊠ *1740 N.W. Glisan St., Nob Hill* ☎ *503/228–4152* ⊕ *www. worldcupcoffee.com* ⊗ *No dinner.*

🍴 Dining

★ Ataula

$$$ | **Tapas.** The son of a cook from Spain's Aragon region, renowned chef-owner Jose Chesa brings his passion for Spanish cuisine to this small restaurant on a side street just off N.W. 23rd Avenue. The food is served tapas-style, with everything meant to be shared, including the heaping paella platters. **Known for:** picturesque sidewalk seating; the dessert of toasted bread with olive oil, chocolate, and salt; outstanding wine list. *Average main: $29* ⊠ *1818 N.W. 23rd Pl., Slabtown* ☎ *503/894–8904* ⊕ *www.ataulapdx. com* ⊗ *Closed Mon. No lunch.*

Besaws

$$ | **American.** Brunch is the signature meal at the longest-operating restaurant in Northwest Portland, which opened in 1903 as a beer parlor serving famished loggers and dockworkers. While the restaurant relocated from its original home in 2016 to the ground floor of shiny-new Slabtown condo, Besaws's hefty helpings of American standards could still please the appetites of lumberjacks. **Known for:** hour-plus waits for weekend brunch; dedicated "day-drinking" cocktail menu; a group-friendly spot for special occasions. *Average main: $20* ⊠ *1545 N.W. 21st Ave., Slabtown* ☎ *503/228– 2619* ⊕ *www.besaws.com.*

★ Bhuna

$ | **Indian.** This counter-service café—with a retro décor inspired by 1960s Air India posters—is Portland's first to focus solely on the flavors of the Kashmir region of India, which the chef proudly dubs "Indian soul food." Cooks artfully smother the various rice bowls with such savory toppings as coconut Chettinad chicken and then garnish each with yogurt-based raita and pickles. **Known for:** healthy portions of artfully spiced mains; collaborations with craft breweries; gluten-free and vegetarian dishes. *Average main: $15 ⌧ 704 N.W. 21st Ave., Nob Hill* ☎ *971/865-2176* ⊕ *www. bhunarestaurant.com* ⊘ *Closed Mon.*

Caffé Mingo
$$$ | Italian. The weekly regulars may have aged along with this 1990s-era Italian joint, but the cooks aren't resting on their laurels. Pass by before happy hour, and you may see lasagna dough hanging in the dining room—such touches elevate the scratch-made comfort fare that continues to draw crowds. **Known for:** connections to regional farms; a classic menu that changes weekly; handmade pasta. *Average main: $23 ⌧ 807 N.W. 21st Ave., Nob Hill* ☎ *503/226-4646* ⊕ *www.caffemingonw.com* ⊘ *Closed Mon., no lunch.*

Fish Sauce
$ | Vietnamese. A greatest-hits selection of Vietnamese dishes—culled from the owner's family recipe book—plus the bartenders' knack for craft cocktails make this a favorite neighborhood haunt. On sunny afternoons, the patio fills up like clockwork for the standout happy hour, with deals on more than a dozen of the restaurant's most-loved small plates and entrees. **Known for:** dinner crowds of hip Nob Hill locals; flights of Japanese whiskey; gluten-free and vegetarian dishes. *Average main: $15 ⌧ 407 N.W. 17th Ave., Nob Hill* ☎ *971/386-2196* ⊕ *www.fishsaucepdx. com* ⊘ *Closed Sun.*

Grassa
$ | Italian. "Grassa" means fatty in Italian, which tells you a lot about the simple-but-decadent menu at this fast-casual trattoria, a carb-heavy staple of Portland's food scene. Lines creep out the door for the bowls of scratch-made pasta, which range from the elegant flavors of squid-ink tonnarelli to crowd-pleasing classics like pork-belly macaroni. **Known for:** quick spot for crowd-pleasing dinner; spinning vinyl rock-and-roll LPs; Oregon wine on tap. *Average main: $15 ⌧ 1506 N.W. 23rd Ave., Slabtown* ☎ *971/386-2196* ⊕ *www.grassapdx. com.*

★ HunnyMilk
$$$ | American. There's a universal appeal to the whimsical brunch served at HunnyMilk, a weekend pop-up turned brick-and-mortar stalwart where tables are set with crayons and coloring paper. It's one of those rare spots where food critics scribble alongside families with young kids, who endure the often-long waits for inventive takes on American breakfast staples that push such humble plates as French toast and waffles to playful new heights. **Known for:** pre-fixe brunch with savory and sweet options; mimosas prepared with fresh-squeezed juices; kid-friendly menu options. *Average main: $23 ⌧ 1981 W. Burnside St., Nob Hill* ☎ *503/719-7349* ⊕ *www.hunnymilk.com* ⊘ *Closed Mon.-Tues. No dinner.*

Ken's Artisan Bakery

$ | Café. Golden crusts are the trademark of Ken's rustic breads, croissants, tarts, and puff pastries, perfect for breakfast and lunch. Sandwiches, barbecue pulled pork, and croque monsieur are served on thick slabs of freshly baked bread, and local berries fill the flaky pastries. **Known for:** French-inspired luncheonette; buttery croissants; Monday night pizza pop-up till 9:30 pm. *Average main: $12* ✉ *338 N.W. 21st Ave., Nob Hill* ☎ *503/248-2202* ⊕ *www.kensartisan. com* ✺ *No dinner Tues.–Sun.*

Kornblatt's Deli

$ | Deli. This New York-style kosher deli and bagel bakery evokes a 1950s diner. The thick sandwiches are made with fresh bread and lean, fresh-cooked meats, and the tender home-smoked salmon and pickled herring are simply mouthwatering. **Known for:** breakfast hashes, served all-day; "eggle" bagel sandwiches; Reuben on rye. *Average main: $12* ✉ *628 N.W. 23rd Ave., Nob Hill* ☎ *503/242-0055* ⊕ *www.kornblattsdelipdx.com.*

Le Happy

$ | French. This tiny creperie just outside the hubbub of the Pearl District can serve as a romantic dinner-date spot or just a cozy place to enjoy a cocktail and a late-night snack. You can get sweet crepes with fruit, cheese, chocolate, and cream or savory ones with meats and cheeses; in addition, the dinner menu is rounded out with salads and steaks. **Known for:** $15-a-bottle wine specials on Wednesdays; the Monte Cristo brunch-breakfast crepe with strawberry preserves; the bacon-and-cheddar crepe with a side of Pabst Blue Ribbon. *Average main: $10* ✉ *1011 N.W. 16th Ave., Slabtown* ☎ *503/226-1258* ⊕ *www. lehappy.com* ✺ *No lunch weekdays, no dinner Sun.*

★ Paley's Place

$$$$ | French. Open since 1995 in an old Victorian house, this nationally acclaimed bistro helped put Portland's farm-forward restaurant scene on the map. Helmed by James Beard Award-winning chef-owner Vitaly Paley, who also operates Downtown's Imperial restaurant, Paley's serves Pacific Northwest meets French cuisine prepared with organic ingredients. **Known for:** iconic restaurant in a converted Victorian; glass case filled with an extensive cheese selection; porch and patio seating. *Average main: $34* ✉ *1204 N.W. 21st Ave., Slabtown* ☎ *503/243-2403* ⊕ *www. paleysplace.net* ✺ *No lunch.*

Papa Haydn

$$$ | American. There's one reason people frequent this buzzy 23rd Avenue bistro: its luscious desserts, like the banana coconut cream pie, the berry cobblers, and the *boccone dolce* (Swiss meringues layered with whipped cream and seasonal fruit and drizzled with semi-sweet chocolate). **Known for:** big slices of cake; affogato with house-made ice cream; flights of dessert wines. *Average main: $25* ✉ *701 N.W. 23rd*

Ave., Nob Hill ☎ 503/228–7317,
⊕ www.papahaydn.com.

RingSide Steakhouse

$$$$ | Steakhouse. This retro-
cool Portland institution has been
famous for its beef since it opened
in 1944, though seafood lovers will
find plenty of choices as well. Dine
in cozy booths on rib eye, prime rib,
and New York strip, which come
in regular- or king-size cuts, as
well as Dungeness crab, broiled
lobster tails, deep fried prawns,
and plank-roasted steelhead trout.
Known for: one of the few white-
tablecloth dining rooms in town;
late-night happy hour; sweet Walla
Walla onion rings. Average main:
$70 ⊠ 2165 W. Burnside St., Nob Hill
☎ 503/223–1513 ⊕ www.ringside-
steakhouse.com ⊗ No lunch.

St. Honoré Boulangerie

$ | Café. Named for the patron saint
of bakers, this French bakery on
a quiet corner in Slabtown serves
light meals and pastries. Start the
day off with a plain or chocolate
croissant, or café au lait, but return
for lunch (or dinner) and the delicious quiche, sandwiches, salads,
savory puff pastries, and tarts.
Known for: resident Francophile
master baker; pleasant sidewalk
seating; a rainbow of macarons.
Average main: $9 ⊠ 2335 N.W.
Thurman St., Slabtown ☎ 503/445–
4342 ⊕ www.sainthonorebakery.com.

St. Jack

$$$$ | French. This always-crowded
Slabtown restaurant takes its inspiration from the bouchons, or rustic
cafés, of Lyon, the culinary capital of
France. The menu changes weekly,
with recurring favorites including
such sharable plates as pan-seared
scallops, drenched in a cognac,
leek, and Gruyère sauce, with a
bread-crumb crunch. Known for:
superbly crafted house cocktails;
mussels served with baguette;
aged cheese menu. Average main:
$30 ⊠ 1610 N.W. 23rd Ave., Slabtown
☎ 503/360–1281 ⊕ www.stjackpdx.
com ⊗ No lunch.

23Hoyt

$$ | Eclectic. While this upscale
tavern serves fine dinner plates,
it's happy hour and brunch that
draws scene-y Nob Hill revelers to
23Hoyt. With a cool, clean ambience
and the owner's private collection
of contemporary art on the walls,
this corner establishment makes an
excellent place to partake in early-
evening or weekend noshing. Known
for: cocktails made with house-
infused spirits; recurring drag
brunch; a wide selection of small
plates. Average main: $22 ⊠ 529 N.W.
23rd Ave., Nob Hill ☎ 503/445–7400
⊕ www.23hoyt.com ⊗ No lunch.

🍸 Bars and Nightlife

Bantam Tavern

Named for the miniature variety
of fowl, this shot glass-sized pub
is refreshing for what it's not. In a
city nearly obsessed with themed
cocktail lounges, this 2018 addition
to the 21st Avenue bar circuit has
no discernible concept but plenty
of character. In other words, it's a
snug neighborhood hangout with
a brief tap list of Pacific Northwest

A TALE OF TWO STREETS

Spend any time in this corner of Northwest Portland and you'll hear locals refer to nearly everything in relation to 21st and 23rd—shorthand for the neighborhood's two marquee avenues. Paralleling each other for more than a dozen blocks, these commercial thoroughfares share the same Victorian-era charm, but each maintains a distinct vibe and deserves at least a few hours of exploring on its own.

N.W. 23rd Avenue

The city's original boutique street came on the scene in the 1990s as the fashionable spot for a shopping spree. Today, retail remains the main draw, with designer boutiques inhabiting converted regal homes and the ground floors of walk-up apartments. Yes, national brands are here, but you'll also find plenty of locally-owned shops

worthy of a treasure hunt—especially on the street's northern end. Out-of-town visitors clog the sidewalks on summer weekends, when 23rd is at its busiest; show up on a weekday to avoid the crowds.

N.W. 21st Avenue

If 23rd is where tourists flock during the day, this is where Nob Hill residents play at night. Here you can hang out in low-key bars with karaoke, dine in casual restaurants, or visit a beloved arthouse cinema. Aside from a few stellar cafés, there's not much happening during business hours, so come in the early evening when the street lights up with diners, and revelers spill out of the many dive bars littering the main drag (seven sweet blocks sandwiched between Lovejoy and Everett streets).

and German beers, classic and draft cocktails, and a concise selection of shareable entrees for late-night snacking. ✉ 922 N.W. 21st Ave., Nob Hill ☎ 503/274–9032 ⊕ www.bantam-tavern.com.

★ Bar West

A minimal aesthetic defines this on-trend hangout in Slabtown. Potted plants hang above the pale mint-colored bar and candles illuminate tables lining the street-facing windows. Expert bartenders shake up classic cocktails and fizzy highballs prepared with locally inspired ingredients like Douglas fir brandy, and a curated list of Pacific Northwest and Old World wines. In line with many of Portland's food

establishments, the food menu is farm-driven and changes seasonally. ✉ 1221 N.W. 21st Ave., Slabtown ☎ 503/208–2852 ⊕ www.westportland.com.

Breakside Brewery

A large-scale mural of a rather serious-looking man marks the exterior of this craft brewery, where the atmosphere inside is far more convivial. Famous for its prolific range of beers and a face-sized soft pretzel, the industrial-styled brewpub spans two floors, with a sunny dining hall, a covered patio, and a mezzanine bar. Don't miss the rotating taps that showcase the brewmaster's experimental spirit. Breakside also has a second brewpub on Dekum Street in Inner Northeast Portland and a tasting room in the suburban community of Milwaukie. ✉ *1570 N.W. 22nd Ave., Slabtown* ☎ *503/444-7597* ⊕ *www.breakside.com.*

The Fireside

Warmed by an open fire pit and a roaring fireplace, and decorated with lots of wood and leather, this cozy campfire-chic spot on Nob Hill's retail strip serves one of the best happy hours in Northwest, wallet-friendly appetizers made from Oregon-sourced ingredients, and well-crafted cocktails. ✉ *801 N.W. 23rd Ave., Nob Hill* ☎ *503/477-9505* ⊕ *www.pdxfireside.com.*

Muu-Muu's

A lively crowd packs the cool booths at this self-described "big-world diner," an old-school hangout on bar-lined 21st Avenue. Stop in before a movie at Cinema 21 next door for well-poured cocktails, globally inspired small plates, and daily happy hour. ✉ *612 N.W. 21st Ave., Nob Hill* ☎ *503/223-8169* ⊕ *www.muumuus.net.*

★ Pope House Bourbon Lounge

Of the half-dozen hopping bars clustered around the intersection of 21st Avenue and Glisan Street, this whiskey lover's haven is the clear standout. Set in a Victorian home, with a covered porch and pocket-size patio, Pope House prides itself on its collection of more than 40 different Kentucky bourbon brands that pair well with the selection of Southern-accented small plates.

✉ *2075 N.W. Glisan St., Nob Hill* ☎ *503/222-1056* ⊕ *www.popehouselounge.com.*

Taste on 23rd

Order a flight of "crisp" whites or "soft" reds (they're all grouped by sensory descriptors), and maybe a plate of prosciutto-wrapped dates or artichoke-Brie dip from the food menu at this Nob Hill wine bar and bottle shop, located in a pretty, olive-green Victorian house. There's a solid beer and sake selection, too. ✉ *2285 N.W. Johnson St., Nob Hill* ☎ *503/477-7238* ⊕ *www.tasteon23rd.com.*

Twenty First Ave Kitchen & Bar

Ready to show off your inner pop diva? Karaoke every night of the week is the main draw at Twenty First Ave. Open until 2:30 am, this dive has dimly lighted booth seating and an expansive garden patio and outdoor bar. ✉ *721 N.W. 21st Ave., Nob Hill* ☎ *503/222-4121* ⊕ *www.twentyfirstave.com.*

★ Solo Club

A Mediterranean air flows through this jewelry box of a bar, which specializes in highball cocktails and *amari*, Italian after-dinner digestifs. The bi-level Solo Club, with salt-block adored pillars and turquoise tiles, has a piazza-like patio that appeals to the parents of toy poodles, corgis, and other adorable dogs. ✉ *2110 N.W. Raleigh St., Slabtown* ☎ *971/254-9806* ⊕ *www.thesoloclub.com.*

Performing Arts

BodyVox

Led by Emmy Award-winning choreographers, BodyVox performs energetic contemporary dance–theater works at its state-of-the-art space in a converted carriage house. ✉ *1201 N.W. 17th Ave., Nob Hill* ☎ *503/229–0627* ⊕ *www.bodyvox. com.*

★ Cinema 21

An arthouse three-screen movie theater in Nob Hill, Cinema 21 shows independent and foreign films. It regularly hosts special showings, touring cinematic events, and the annual Portland Queer Film Festival in September. ✉ *616 N.W. 21st Ave., Nob Hill* ☎ *503/223–4515* ⊕ *www.cinema21.com.*

Mission Theater

First opened in 1987, the Mission Theater was the first McMenamins brew theater. It shows recent Hollywood hits, art films, and cult classics—as well as hosts live musical performances. ✉ *1624 N.W. Glisan St., Nob Hill* ☎ *503/223–4527* ⊕ *www.mcmenamins.com/ mission-theater.*

Third Rail Repertory Theatre

This talented rep company performs five often edgy, sometimes dark, and typically funny plays, at the CoHo Theatre in Nob Hill. ✉ *CoHo Theatre, 2257 N.W. Raleigh St., Nob Hill* ☎ *503/235–1101* ⊕ *www.third-railrep.org.*

Inner North and Northeast

VANCOUVER, WA

NORTH

NORTHWEST

NORTHEAST

SOUTHWEST

SOUTHEAST

Sightseeing ★☆☆☆☆ | Shopping ★★★★☆ | Dining ★★★★☆ | Nightlife ★★★★★

C ontaining the Moda Center basketball and concert arena, the Oregon Convention Center, and an eclectic mix of both new and old industrial, commercial, and residential areas, the portions of North and Northeast Portland closest to the Willamette River and Downtown abound with noteworthy restaurants and also reflect the city's changing aesthetic over its history. In these blocks bound by the river to the west, Burnside Street to the south, 33rd Avenue to the east, and Fremont Street to the north, you'll find rows of beautifully restored late-19th- and early-20th-century homes in the peaceful, leafy neighborhoods of Laurelhurst, Kerns, Irvington, and Eliot. Interstates 5 and 84 are a couple of ugly if necessary swaths of concrete that cut parts of the area off from one another, and a good chunk of Inner Northeast is dominated by a roughly 75-block rectangle of prosaic urban renewal surrounding the convention center and Lloyd Center Mall. There are advantages to using the area as a base: there are several hotels around the convention center that are generally cheaper than those Downtown, and all four of the city's MAX lines as well as a streetcar line serve the area.—*by Andrew Collins*

Although lacking in museums and sightseeing opportunities, Inner North and Northeast have several noteworthy pockets of dining, nightlife, and retail. Just across the Burnside Bridge from Downtown, the once industrial Burnside Bridgehead contains a cluster of new condo towers with ground-floor shops and restaurants and arguably the most interesting pod of contemporary architecture in the city. Farther east in Kerns, especially around the intersection of Burnside and 28th, you'll discover a slew of first-rate dining spots (see the Inner Southeast chapter for coverage of the southern half of this area). Still more first-rate restaurants as well as a notable crop of cutting-edge breweries await in Eliot and, to a lesser extent, pretty Irvington, which are both north of the Lloyd District.

◉ Sights

East Burnside and 28th Avenue
A roughly T-shaped dining and retail district that's less defined but no less popular and impressive than some of the East Side's other culinary and shopping hot spots (like the Alberta Arts District and Southeast Division Street), this diverse neighborhood comprises a slew of mostly food-related ventures along East Burnside Street from about 22nd to 28th Avenues.

Then, where Burnside meets 28th Avenue, you'll find several blocks of first-rate eateries as well as a handful of boutiques in either direction, heading north up to about Glisan Street and south—into an area covered in the Inner Southeast chapter once you cross Burnside Street—down to about Stark Street. The historic Laurelhurst Theater anchors the intersection of 28th and Burnside, and top foodie haunts in these parts include Heart Coffee Roasters, Güero, Screen Door, Tusk, Navarre, Alma Chocolate, PaaDee and Langbaan, Laurelhurst Market, Crema Coffee + Bakery, Fifty Licks, Ken's Artisan Pizza, and several others (see the Inner Southeast chapter for listings of any businesses in this area with S.E. addresses). ■TIP→ The neighborhood isn't close to any light-rail stops, but you can get here easily from Downtown via Bus 20, and street parking is free and pretty easy to find. ⊠ *E. Burnside St. from 22nd to 28th Aves., and 28th Ave. from N.E. Glisan to S.E. Stark Sts., East Burnside/28th Ave.*

Portland Institute for Contemporary Art (PICA)

Founded in 1995 with a mission to foster the development of the city's contemporary artists and provide venues for them to perform and exhibit their work, PICA existed as an itinerant organization until landing in this permanent home—an 18,000-square-foot former warehouse—in 2017. The organization developed the Time-Based Art (TBA) Festival, which takes place over 10

GETTING HERE

These closer-in sections of North and Northeast are connected to Downtown, Old Town, and the Pearl District by several short bridges that can be easily traversed on foot or by car, bus, streetcar, and MAX trains. Closer to the river, and also around the Lloyd District, you'll find some metered parking and quite a few pay lots and garages, and as you get a bit farther out, free street parking is plentiful. But you really don't need a car to explore this part of the city.

days in mid-September and has become an internationally respected celebration of music, visual art, film, workshops, and other performances. Most TBA events take place here at PICA's campus. Beyond TBA, PICA welcomes the public for a variety of events as well as Wednesday through Friday afternoons. ⊠ *15 N.E. Hancock St., Lloyd District/Convention Center* ☎ *503/242–1419* ⊕ *www.pica.org* ⊠ *Free* ۞ *Closed Sat.–Tues.*

Portland Trail Blazers

The NBA's Portland Trail Blazers play their 82-game season—with half the games at home—in the Moda Center, which can hold up to 20,000 spectators. The MAX train pulls up just a couple blocks from the arena's front door. ⊠ *Moda Center, 1 N. Center Ct., Rose Quarter, Lloyd District/Convention Center* ☎ *503/797–9600* ⊕ *www.nba.com/blazers.*

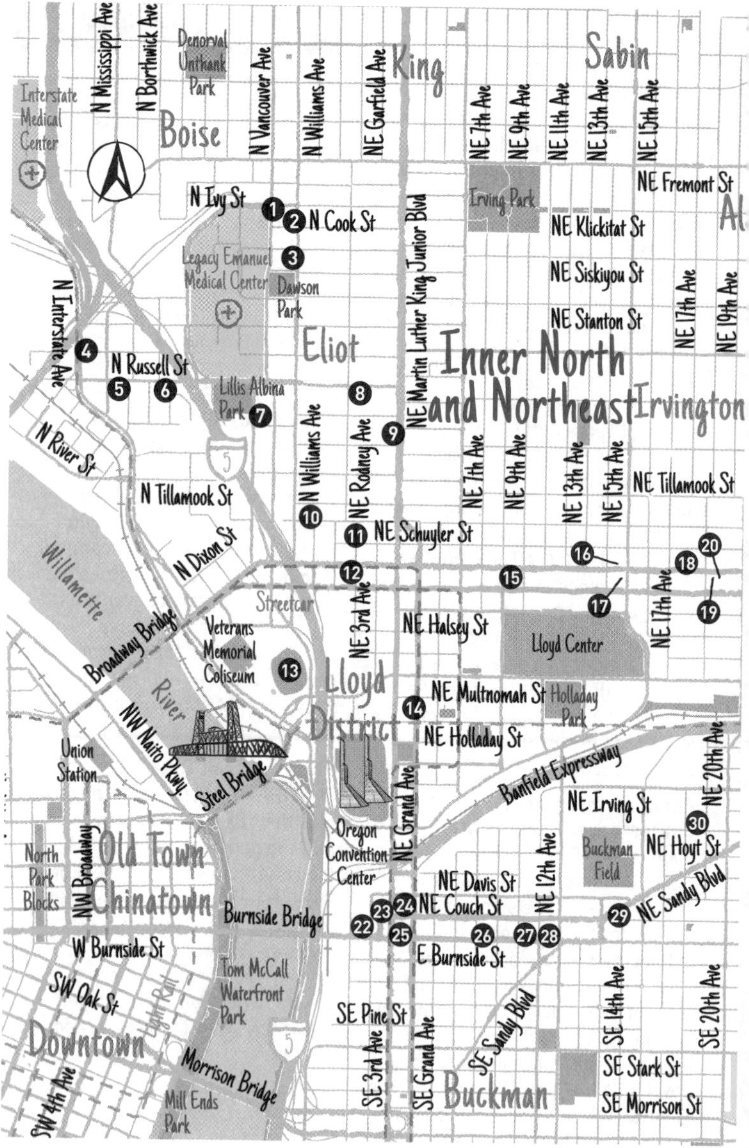
N Mississippi Ave
N Borthwick Ave
Denorval Unthank Park
N Vancouver Ave
N Williams Ave
NE Garfield Ave
King
Sabin
Interstate Medical Center
Boise
NE 7th Ave
NE 9th Ave
NE 11th Ave
NE 13th Ave
NE 15th Ave
NE Fremont St
Irving Park
N Ivy St
N Cook St
NE Klickitat St
Legacy Emanuel Medical Center
Dawson Park
NE Siskiyou St
NE Stanton St
NE Martin Luther King Junior Blvd
NE 17th Ave
NE 19th Ave
N Interstate Ave
Eliot
Inner North and Northeast
Irvington
N Russell St
Lillis Albina Park
N River St
N Williams Ave
NE Rodney Ave
NE 7th Ave
NE 9th Ave
NE 13th Ave
NE 15th Ave
N Tillamook St
NE Tillamook St
NE Schuyler St
N Dixon St
Willamette
Streetcar
NE 3rd Ave
NE 17th Ave
Broadway Bridge
Veterans Memorial Coliseum
NE Halsey St
Lloyd Center
River
Lloyd District
NE Multnomah St
Holladay Park
NW Naito Pkwy.
NE Holladay St
Union Station
Steel Bridge
Banfield Expressway
NE 20th Ave
NE Grand Ave
NE Irving St
Oregon Convention Center
NE 12th Ave
Buckman Field
NE Hoyt St
North Park Blocks
NW Broadway
Old Town Chinatown
NE Davis St
NE Couch St
NE Sandy Blvd
Burnside Bridge
W Burnside St
E Burnside St
Tom McCall Waterfront Park
SW Oak St
Light Rail
SE Pine St
SE Sandy Blvd
SE 14th Ave
SE 20th Ave
Downtown
SE 3rd Ave
SE Grand Ave
SE Stark St
Morrison Bridge
SW 4th Ave
Mill Ends Park
Buckman
SE Morrison St

NE Mason St
NE Dunckley St
NE Alameda St
NE Ridgewood Dr
NE 33rd Ave
Wilshire Park

ameda

0   500 m
0   1000 ft

NE 21st Ave
NE 24th Ave
NE 27th Ave
NE 29th Ave
NE 31st Ave

NE Knott St
NE Brazee St
NE Thompson St
Grant Park
Grant Park

NE Hancock St
NE Broadway
NE Schuyler St
21

NE Weidler St
Sullivan's
Gulch
NE 28th Ave
Light Rail
84

NE Pacific St
31
NE Oregon St
32
33
Oregon Park
NE Hoyt St

34
37
39 40
38 41
42
NE Glisan St
35 36
Kerns
44
45
NE Davis St

52
50
51 53
43
46
47 48 49
E Burnside St

SE 28th Ave
SE Ash St
Laurelhurst Park

SE Oak St

Lone Fir
Cemetery
SE Stark St
Sunnyside

SIGHTS

East Burnside
and 28th Avenue 51

Portland Institute for
Contemporary Art
(PICA) 10

Portland
Trail Blazers.............13

Wild Roots Spirits 25

SHOPPING

Alma Chocolate........45

Beam & Anchor..........4

Cosube 23

Creo Chocolate 12

Jasmine
Pearl Tea
Company.................. 32

Knot Springs 22

Lille Boutique...........27

Missionary
Chocolates................38

Palace 47

Providore
Fine Foods................34

Redux 26

Sweet Jayne 19

COFFEE & QUICK BITES

Compass Coffee
Roasting.....................1

Cup and Bar 24

Eb & Bean................16

Henry Higgins
Boiled Bagels 30

Pix Patisserie 48

DINING

Altabira City
Tavern......................14

Cadillac Cafe 18

City State Diner........52

Dove Vivi 39

Epif............................41

Güero 44

Hak...........................15

Han Oak 36

Laurelhurst
Market 43

Navarre....................53

Noble Rot 28

Ox Restaurant 9

Pambiche..................40

People's Pig 2

Sammich..................46

Screen Door 49

The Sudra 35

Tails & Trotters........37

Toro Bravo 8

BARS & NIGHTLIFE

Capitol 17

Church......................33

Culmination
Brewing 31

Ex Novo
Brewing 7

Game Knight
Lounge 3

Hale Pele 21

LABrewatory 6

LaurelThirst
Public House 42

Reverend Nat's
Hard Cider...............11

Sandy Hut 29

Swift Lounge 20

White Eagle Saloon....5

PERFORMING ARTS

Laurelhurst
Theater....................50

Moda Center.............13

Wild Roots Spirits

In a contemporary tasting room just across the Burnside Bridge from Downtown and Old Town, sample this local distiller's vodkas infused with pear, marionberry, dark sweet cherry, and other Oregon-grown fruits; there's even a cucumber-grapefruit gin. The location is at the northern end of the Central Eastside's Distillery Row, so a good place to begin or end a sipping tour of that district. ⊠ *77 N.E. Grand Ave., Central East Side* ☎ *971/254–4617* ⊕ *www.wildrootsspirits.com* 🖃 *Free.*

Shopping

Alma Chocolate

What began as a modest table at Portland's farmers' market has grown into a nationally celebrated artisan chocolate shop that takes great pride is sourcing just about every ingredient but the cacao locally, from the almonds and fruit in the fig-marzipan candies to the nuts and sea salt in the vegan hazelnut pralines. In the flagship shop on Northeast 28th, you can also munch on fresh-baked cookies and cakes, pick up jars of house-made caramel, and sip tea, espresso, and drinking chocolates. ⊠ *140 N.E. 28th Ave., East Burnside/28th Ave.* ☎ *503/517–0262* ⊕ *www.almachocolate.com.*

★ Beam & Anchor

Set on a busy street corner several blocks from the North Side's trendy North Mississippi strip, this once-dilapidated warehouse houses an upstairs workshop for makers of artisanal goods and an inspiring downstairs retail space where you'll find a carefully curated selection of lifestyle goods for every room in the home, many of them produced locally—some as local as upstairs. Among the hipster treasures, look for warm and soft camp blankets and Navajo rugs with vibrant prints, women's jewelry in a variety of simple-but-beautiful styles, Portland Apothecary bath salts and soaps, and quite a few larger pieces of distinctive furniture. ⊠ *2710 N. Interstate Ave., North Mississippi Ave.* ☎ *503/367–3230* ⊕ *www.beamandanchor.com.*

★ Cosube

It might surprise you just how popular surfing is among Portlanders, but a visit to any of the major wave-producing beaches along the Oregon Coast—such as Oswald West State Park and Pacific City—will show you otherwise. This well-stocked shop inside one of Portland's most architecturally noteworthy new buildings carries everything you need for a day of cold-water surfing, plus stylish beach apparel, sunglasses, and skin lotions. You can also rent boards, wetsuits, and gear, or take a lesson on how to shape your own board. Even if you're not looking for gear, stop by the shop's hip cafe, which serves Coava coffee, plus teas and light snacks. ⊠ *111 N.E. Martin Luther King Blvd., Central East Side* ☎ *971/229–4206* ⊕ *www.cosube.com.*

Creo Chocolate

Drop by one of Portland's most acclaimed artisan bean-to-bar chocolate shops for a tour, or just a taste. Free—and fascinating—factory tours and "make a bar" classes are offered for a fee (sign up on the website), and a small café doles out chocolates as well as brownies, hot chocolate, and even chocolate soda. ⊠ *122 N.E. Broadway, Lloyd District/Convention Center* ☎ *503/477–8927* ⊕ *www.creochocolate.com* ☉ *Closed Sun.–Mon.*

Jasmine Pearl Tea Company

This discerning importer of small-batch, often hard-to-find loose-leaf teas distributes its high-grade oolongs, chais, and herbal and breakfast blends to some of Portland's top restaurants, but everything is also available retail in this spacious shop in a quiet industrial area. The aromatic shop also sells hot and iced teas to go, as well as tea-brewing equipment and colorful pots, cups, and tea sets. ⊠ *724 N.E. 22nd Ave., Kerns* ☎ *503/236–3539* ⊕ *www.thejasmine-pearl.com.*

Knot Springs

You can work out in the state-of-the-art gym, take yoga classes, and book a variety of body and skin-care treatments in this gorgeous, contemporary day spa on the ground floor of a luxury condo in the Burnside Bridgehead development. But this hip, self-proclaimed "social club" is especially appreciated for its soaking pools and water treatments, which include an exfoliation shower, warm and hot tubs, a cold plunge, and sauna and steam rooms. Nonmembers are welcome, but reservations are advised, even just for using the soaking pools. You'll save money by visiting during the day or midweek. Some Portland hotels also offer discount access. ⊠ *The Yard, 33 N.E. 3rd Ave., Suite 365, Central East Side* ☎ *503/222–5668* ⊕ *www.knotsprings.com.*

Lille Boutique

You'll find an exceptional selection of lingerie, from Stella McCartney bodysuit teddies to Samantha Chang silk camisoles, at this woman-owned boutique that also carries swimwear and bath and beauty products. ⊠ *1007 E. Burnside St., Central East Side* ☎ *503/232–0333* ⊕ *www.lilleboutique.com.*

Missionary Chocolates

Portland's appreciation of artisan chocolates and veganism comes together at this community-supportive shop. These allergy-friendly treats are made without nuts and gluten and come in alluring flavors like spicy cinnamon chipotle, Meyer lemon explosion, and Earl Grey. A favorite since Oregon legalized marijuana: Missionary's CBD truffles. ⊠ *2712 N.E. Glisan St., East Burnside/28th Ave.* ☎ *503/206–8439* ⊕ *www.missionarychocolates.com* ☉ *Closed Sat.*

Palace

At this eclectic lifestyle shop that also carries bright and whimsical women's outerwear, vintage threads, jewelry, and accessories, you'll find a smartly curated mix of playful gifts and goods for the home—everything from recycled-bamboo tableware to colorful baskets, totes, and notebooks. It's a fun place to kill time while waiting for a table at any of the nearby restaurant hot spots, such as the Screen Door. ⊠ *2205 E. Burnside St., East Burnside/28th Ave.* ☎ *503/517-0123* ⊕ *www.palacestore.com.*

Providore Fine Foods

This sleek gourmet market features the artisan and local fare of several notable Portland purveyors, including Little T Baker, Rubinette Produce, Flying Fish Company and Oyster Bar, Arrosto (which turns out delicious Mediterranean-style rotisserie chicken), and Pastaworks, plus a lovely flower shop. It's a terrific source for picnic supplies, and there's table seating. ⊠ *2340 N.E. Sandy Blvd., Kerns* ☎ *503/232-1010* ⊕ *www.providorefinefoods.com.*

Redux

The team behind this jewelry boutique and art gallery carries the work of more than 300 mostly local artists, with a particular emphasis on creations that use recycled materials and repurposed objects. You'll find hand-painted gift cards and mugs, wall art, earrings, and more, and at a wide range of prices. Receptions and rotating shows take place every other month. ⊠ *811 E. Burnside St., Central East Side* ☎ *503/231-7336* ⊕ *reduxpdx.com.*

Sweet Jayne

With much of its clothing, jewelry, clutches, and accessories created by Portland artists, this unpretentious women's boutique near Lloyd Center mall celebrates the local but also stocks hip national brands like Aakaa dresses and Bamboo vegan suede boots. ⊠ *1914 N.E. Broadway, Lloyd District/Convention Center* ☎ *503/281-1366* ⊕ *www.sweetjayne. net* ☺ *Closed Sun.*

 Coffee and Quick Bites

Compass Coffee Roasting

$ | Café. This crop-to-cup coffeehouse in the lower end of the North Williams corridor carefully trains its baristas and roasts its beans in small batches. The care and attention to detail shows in the rich, complex flavors of the cold brew and espresso drinks. **Known for:** small selection of excellent baked goods;

several varieties of chai tea; high-quality, small-batch roasted coffee beans (available to go, too). *Average main: $5 ⊠ 3290 N. Vancouver Ave., North Williams Ave.* ☎ *888/723-2007* ⊕ *www.compasscoffeeroasting.com* ☾ *No dinner.*

Cup and Bar

$ | Café. This collaborative cafe showcases the superior products of two Portland makers: Trailhead Coffee Roasters and Ranger Chocolates. In this spacious storefront with handcrafted wooden furniture, you can sip cappuccino or hot chocolate, naturally, but you'll also want to explore the delectable food offerings, like avocado and lemon-ricotta toast and brie and jam baguettes. **Known for:** chocolate factory tours offered every other Saturday afternoon; heavenly pastries and cakes featuring Ranger Chocolate; extensive savory and sweet toast selection. *Average main: $6 ⊠ 118 N.E. Martin Luther King Jr. Blvd., Central East Side* ☎ *503/206-8924* ⊕ *www.cupandbar.com* ☾ *No dinner.*

★ Eb & Bean

$ | Café. Choosing your flavor of silky, premium frozen yogurt at this hip dessert cafe is relatively easy, as there are only a few flavors offered at any given time, unique though they often are (honey-grapefruit and mango lassi, for example). It's the formidable list of toppings that may leave you overwhelmed, albeit happily so, highlights of which include coconut-pecan

cookie, organic sour fruity bears, marionberry compote, cold-brew bourbon sauce, and nondairy peanut butter magic shell. **Known for:** inventive dairy-based and vegan flavors; seasonal fruit toppings (figs, blueberries, etc.); made-from-scratch waffle cones. *Average main: $5 ⊠ 1425 N.E. Broadway St., Lloyd District/Convention Center* ☎ *503/281-6081* ⊕ *www.ebandbean. com.*

Henry Higgins Boiled Bagels

$ | Bakery. Stop by this unpretentious bakery in the Kerns neighborhood for some of the best traditional boiled bagels in the city, available in classic flavors like onion, pumpernickel, and everything. Order one toasted with a schmear of honey-almond or scallion cream cheese, or go for one of the substantial sandwiches, such as open-face lox, cream cheese, and capers, and the hot corned-beef Reuben. **Known for:** fresh, chewy boiled bagels; lox and whitefish salad bagel sandwiches; egg and cheese breakfast sandwiches. *Average main: $8 ⊠ 523 N.E. 19th Ave., Kerns* ☎ *503/327-1844* ⊕ *www.hhboiledbagels.com* ☾ *No dinner.*

Pix Patisserie

$ | Café. In a handsome café and bar with a small patio along East Burnside Street, Pix is famous for its sweet treats, including passion-fruit macarons and dark-chocolate truffles. The adjoining Bar Vivant serves authentic Spanish tapas and has one of the most impressive selections of Champagne in the country. **Known for:** huge Champagne list; late-night desserts; complete tea service with sandwiches and sweets on weekends afternoons (reservation only). *Average main: $8* ⊠ *2225 E. Burnside St., East Burnside/28th Ave.* ☎ *971/271-7166* ⊕ *www.pixpatisserie. com* ⊗ *No lunch weekdays.*

🍴 Dining

Altabira City Tavern

$$ | American. Located on the top floor of the sleek Eastlund Hotel, this mod interpretation of a neighborhood bar and grill is best known for its sweeping panoramas of downtown Portland—when the weather is nice, enjoy these vistas from a table on the spacious terrace, which is heated and has a retractable roof. Popular for lunch and dinner, Altabira specializes in comfort fare with novel twists, and also features 16 local beers on tap and a commendable wine and cocktail list. **Known for:** generous happy hour; dramatic skyline views; house-made ice creams and sorbets. *Average main: $21* ⊠ *1021 N.E. Grand Ave., Lloyd District/ Convention Center* ☎ *503/963-3600* ⊕ *www.altabira.com* ⊗ *No lunch weekends.*

Cadillac Cafe

$ | American. Classic car memorabilia, including a fully operational 1961 pink Cadillac convertible, are on display in this family-friendly

For a superb view of the Downtown skyline, with the Willamette River in the foreground and the West Hills beyond, snag a table on the terrace of Altabira City Tavern, on the top floor of the Hotel Eastlund, or on the rooftop patio of Noble Rot wine bar.

 Share your photo with us! @FodorsTravel #FodorsOnTheGo

breakfast and lunch spot in the Lloyd District. The breakfasts, served in slightly ridiculous portions, are particularly good and reveal a discernible Southern influence—note the Cajun catfish and eggs and biscuits and gravy. **Known for:** French custard toast with bananas, cranberries, and hazelnuts; art deco aesthetic and colorful car memorabilia; French dip sandwiches. *Average main: $12* ⊠ *1801 N.E. Broadway St., Lloyd District/ Convention Center* ☎ *503/287-4750* ⊕ *www.cadillaccafepdx.com* ⊗ *No dinner.*

City State Diner

$ | Diner. In the cluster of buzzy restaurants along 28th Avenue near Burnside Street, this chatter-filled space with large windows that open on warm days and sidewalk seating serves elevated breakfast and lunch fare—along with fresh baked goods—throughout the day. The hefty servings of eggs Benedict (choose from nine varieties), burgers, crab hash, and house-smoked salmon salad will keep you sated for a day of exploring the neighborhood. **Known for:** Reuben sandwiches; eggs Benedict; sour cream coffee cake. *Average main: $13* ⊠ *128 N.E. 28th Ave., East Burnside/28th Ave.* ☎ *503/517-0347* ⊕ *www.citystatediner.com* ⊗ *No dinner.*

Dove Vivi

$ | Pizza. The easygoing neighborhood pizza spot stands out for its cornmeal-crust pies, which are deceptively filling—these generously topped 12-inch beauties are served in cast-iron pans and can feed two or three diners. With a few exceptions, including a delicious sausage-and-peppers pie, most of these pizzas are vegetarian, and a couple have vegan crusts as well. **Known for:** the chef choice: six slices, each with a different topping; the corn-cashew vegan pizza with smoked tomatoes; house-pickled jalapeño can be added to any pie. *Average main: $14* ⊠ *2727 N.E. Glisan St., East Burnside/28th Ave.* ☎ *503/239-4444* ⊕ *www.dovevivipizza.com* ⊗ *No lunch.*

Epif

$ | Peruvian. Run by an amiable couple who formerly operated a restaurant in Chile, this lively neighborhood bistro—cleverly decorated with repurposed church pews and other distinctive elements—serves an entirely vegan menu of Andean-inspired dishes and boasts the best pisco selection in town. The hearts of palm and mushroom ceviche, sunflower-seed-pesto empanadas, and other South America treats pack plenty of flavor and are reasonably priced. **Known for:** creative pisco-based cocktails; friendly and unpretentious vibe; passionfruit cheesecake with chocolate sauce. *Average main: $15* ⊠ *404 N.E. 28th Ave., East Burnside/28th Ave.* ☎ *971/254-8680* ⊕ *www.epifpdx. com* ⊗ *Closed Sun.–Mon. No lunch.*

Güero

$ | Mexican. This casual but inviting counter-service Mexican eatery decorated with leafy plants and green-and-white Talavera tiles specializes in hefty tortas stuffed generously with chicken pibil, braised beef, carnitas, and plenty of flavorful accoutrements like habanero slaw and pickled onions. If you'd rather go breadless, you can customize a "cart bowl" using most of the torta ingredients. **Known for:** excellent mezcal and tequila list; esquites (corn sautéed chile and garlic and topped with lime mayonesa and cotija cheese); several vegetarian and vegan choices. *Average main: $12* ⊠ *200 N.E.*

28th Ave., East Burnside/28th Ave.
☎ 503/887-9258 ⊕ www.guerotortas.
com.

Hak

$$ | Korean. A step above most of
the city's Korean restaurants both
in quality and authenticity, this
simple yet sleek space with light-
wood tables and retractable garage
windows serves lip-smacking good
spicy brisket noodle soup along with
well-prepared renditions of kimchi
stew and stonepot be bim bob. Try
chasing down your food with a glass
of *makgeolli*, a fermented, lightly
bubbly grain-alcohol beverage that's
fairly hard to find outside the Korean
Peninsula. **Known for:** beef brisket
noodle soups; kimchi and seafood
scallion pancake appetizers; bo
ssam (thinly sliced pork belly boiled
in spices). *Average main: $16* ✉ *914
N.E. Broadway St., Lloyd District/
Center* ☎ *503/208-2172* ⊕ *www.hak-
restaurant.business.site* ☉ *Closed
Sun.*

★ Han Oak

$$$ | Korean. Begun as a pop-up
and still with somewhat limited
hours, this clean and contemporary
space lined with shelves of beautiful
plates, glassware, and cookbooks
produces some of the most exciting
Korean fare on the West Coast. The
carefully plated food is arranged
as artful vignettes, and everything
bursts with flavor, from hand-
cut noodle soups to Korean fried
chicken wings. **Known for:** fresh-
fruit "slushy" cocktails; communal
seating (that's expanded to outside

in summer); pork-and-chive dumplings. *Average main: $26* ✉ *511 N.E.
24th Ave., Kerns* ☎ *971/255-0032*
⊕ *www.hanoakpdx.com* ☉ *Closed
Tues.–Thurs. No lunch.*

Laurelhurst Market

$$$ | Steakhouse. With an artisanal
butcher shop anchoring the right
side of the building, Laurelhurst
Market offers some of the best
meaty fare in Portland—think
Wagyu steak with charred-green-
onion sauce and pork ribeye with
grilled apricots for dinner, and
prodigious sandwiches during
the casual order-at-the-counter
lunch service in the butcher shop
section. The candlelit dining room is
comfortable and sophisticated and
the stainless steel kitchen along the
back wall underneath the beef cuts
diagram illustrates what this place
is all about: the preparation and
serving of outstanding meat. **Known
for:** delicious sandwiches; exhibition
kitchen that's fun to watch while
dining; surprising amount of meat-
free side dishes and salads. *Average
main: $29* ✉ *3155 E. Burnside St.,
East Burnside/28th Ave.* ☎ *503/206-
3097* ⊕ *www.laurelhurstmarket.com.*

★ Navarre

$$$ | Spanish. It's easy to miss this
intimate storefront space whose
kitchen produces stellar Spanish,
French, and Italian food, but don't
miss it. The menu changes daily
and specials are written in red ink
on the front window and always
include some sensational seasonal
dishes, from a simple summery

radish-and-sweet-pea salad to foie gras on cumin toast. **Known for:** more than 50 wines by the glass; sourcing many ingredients from a local CSA; western Mediterranean cuisine, often with Basque influences. *Average main: $24 ⊠ 10 N.E. 28th Ave., East Burnside/28th Ave. ☎ 503/232-3555 ⊕ www.navarreportland.com ⊗ No lunch weekdays.*

Noble Rot

$$$ | Wine Bar. Perched atop a four-story building on the Central East Side, this polished wine bistro offers expansive views of the river and Downtown skyline from its outdoor patio and large south- and west-facing windows, an extensive wine list, and creative food prepared by celebrated chef-owner Leather Storrs. Many of the produce and herbs used in creative salads and grills are raised in the restaurant's rooftop garden. **Known for:** impressive patio view of Downtown and the West Hills; extensive list of both regional and international wines; regularly changing menu of seasonal Northwest cuisine. *Average main: $27 ⊠ 1111 E. Burnside St. , 4th fl., Central East Side ☎ 503/233-1999 ⊕ www.noblerotpdx. com ⊗ No lunch.*

★ Ox Restaurant

$$$$ | Argentine. Specializing in "Argentine-inspired Portland food," Ox is all about prime cuts of meat— along with flavorful garden-fresh side dishes—prepared to perfection. In a dimly lit dining room with hardwood floors, exposed brick walls, and a bar against the front window, the flannel-shirt-and-white-apron clad waitstaff serves beef, lamb, pork, and fish dishes cooked over flames in a large, hand-cranked grill. **Known for:** the asado Argentino platter (lots of amazing meaty grills); creative side dishes, a few of which could make a full meal; vanilla tres leches cake dessert. *Average main: $36 ⊠ 2225 N.E. Martin Luther King Blvd., Lloyd District/ Convention Center ☎ 503/284-3366 ⊕ www.oxpdx.com ⊗ No lunch.*

Pambiche

$$ | Cuban. Painted in bright purples, pinks, and greens, this festive spot offers traditional Cuban fare: slow-roasted meats, tropical root vegetables, hearty stews, rice, and beans. The meat plates— featuring slow-roasted pork, oxtail, shredded beef, rubbed chicken, or giant prawns—with various rich and saucy accompaniments, are all tasty and best enjoyed with a side of fried plantains. **Known for:** sangria with fresh fruit; empanadas with several types of fillings; guava cheesecake.

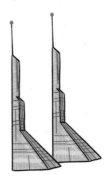

Average main: $17 ✉ 2811 N.E.
Glisan St., East Burnside/28th Ave.
☎ 503/233–0511 ⊕ www.pambiche.
com.

People's Pig

$$ | Barbecue. This pork-centric purveyor sells smoked meats by the pound as well as mouthwatering platters and sandwiches. It operates out of an appropriately funky down-home space in the shadows of the many sleek new apartment buildings on North Williams. **Known for:** classic Southern barbecue side dishes; any two meats and two sides for $25; the full rack of ribs. *Average main: $16 ✉ 3217 N. Williams Ave., North Williams Ave. ☎ 503/282–2800 ⊕ www.peoplespig.com.*

★ Sammich

$ | Deli. You'll need both hands to get a handle on the mammoth Chicago-style sandwiches that have been celebrated on the Food Network and in numerous food publications. This Portland outpost of the original in Ashland, Oregon, can get crowded at lunchtime, but regulars are willing to wait for the "wet and dipped" Italian beef with peppers or the Cubbie Cobb salad with house-smoked bacon, turkey, and ham. **Known for:** the Pastramie Zombie; house-smoked and -brined meats; mural of the Chicago skyline on one inside wall. *Average main: $11 ✉ 2137 E. Burnside St., East Burnside/28th Ave. ☎ 503/477–4393 ⊕ www.sammichrestaurants.com.*

★ Screen Door

$$ | Southern. The line that forms outside this Southern cooking restaurant during weekend brunch and dinner is as epic as the food itself, but you can more easily score a table if you come for weekday breakfast or lunch. A large, packed dining room with canned pickles and peppers along the walls, this Portland hot spot does justice to authentic Southern cooking, especially when it comes to the crispy buttermilk-battered fried chicken with creamy mashed potatoes and collard greens cooked in bacon fat. **Known for:** fried chicken (with waffles at breakfast or brunch); seasonal side dishes, from praline bacon to spiced zucchini fritters; banoffee pie with shortbread-pecan crust. *Average main: $20 ✉ 2337 E. Burnside St., East Burnside/28th Ave. ☎ 503/542–0880 ⊕ www.screendoor-restaurant.com.*

The Sudra

$ | Indian. This popular, reasonably priced restaurant that relocated to a cute storefront in the 28th and Burnside area in 2019 serves some of the best vegan *and* Indian food in town. The kitchen here makes no claim of authenticity, and indeed, many dishes—like turmeric-roasted Brussels sprouts with hazelnuts and lemon or the kale-infused dosas stuffed with black-eyed peas, pickled Anaheim chiles, collards, and potato masala—take a fusion approach, but everything is delicious and nicely seasoned. **Known for:** kofta and dosa plates and bowls; jackfruit vindaloo; colorful cocktails and mocktails. *Average main: $12* ⊠ *28 N.E. 28th Ave., East Burnside/28th Ave.* ☎ *971/302-6002* ⊕ *www.thesudra.com.*

Tails & Trotters

$ | Deli. Carnivores can't seem to get enough of the glorious guanciale, Sardinian sausages, applewood-smoked ham, and other fine meats and charcuterie sold at this high-quality butcher with a popular sandwich counter. You'll find a nice range of hot and cold dishes at lunch, including the ethereal Doug Fir, with sliced smoked pork loin, Gruyère, and sweet-mustard-seed aioli, plus salads and charcuterie boards. **Known for:** cured and custom-butchered meats to go; the porchetta with marinated, boneless pork belly loin; the butcher salad with an assortment of prime meats and greens. *Average main: $11* ⊠ *525 N.E. 24th Ave., Kerns* ☎ *503/477-8682* ⊕ *www.tailsandtrotters.com* ⊙ *Closed Sun. No dinner.*

★ Toro Bravo

$$ | Tapas. The success of this wildly popular and impressively authentic Spanish tapas bar has spawned a popular cookbook and helped spur chef-owner John Gorham to create a restaurant empire in Portland. This bustling spot with closely spaced tables and a lively vibe turns out sublime, share-friendly dishes like fried Spanish anchovies with fennel and lemon, and Ibérico sausage and braised cuttlefish in ink. **Known for:** "chef's choice for the table" menu; molten chocolate cake and other rich desserts; extensive sherry list. *Average main: $21* ⊠ *120 N.E. Russell St., North Williams Ave.* ☎ *503/281-4464* ⊕ *www.torobravopdx.com* ⊙ *No lunch.*

 Bars and Nightlife

Capitol

The Lloyd District is short on notable nightspots, but this contemporary space with clean geometric lines and one big kaleidoscopic wall of jewel tones to balance out the otherwise restrained wood and glass aesthetic feels at once posh and playful. The cocktail program is first rate, the kitchen doles out interesting vegetarian food, and groups of friends can reserve the private karaoke room. ⊠ *1440 N.E. Broadway, Lloyd District/Convention Center* ⊕ *www.capitolpdx.com.*

Church

The "Eat, Drink, Repent" sign inside this lightheartedly blasphemous bar is your first clue that you've entered a decidedly nontraditional church setting. Also note the huge neon cross and other vaguely liturgical decorative elements while you sip a Rosemary's Baby gin cocktail and feast on well-prepared burgers, mac and cheese, and other bar favorites (everything can be prepared vegan or gluten-free). ⊠ *2600 N.E. Sandy Blvd., Kerns* ☎ *503/206-8962* ⊕ *www.churchbarpdx.com.*

Culmination Brewing

A bit cozier and neighborhood-y than many of Portland's brew-pubs, Culmination is set inside a sustainably designed building with a dog-friendly patio in the Kerns neighborhood. It's a favorite of serious beer aficionados, always featuring at least 20 taps of often creative limited-release brews, including barrel-aged sours, heady barleywines, and beers produced in collaboration with other craft labels around town. ⊠ *2117 N.E. Oregon St., Kerns* ☎ *971/254–9114* ⊕ *www. culminationbrewing.com.*

★ Ex Novo Brewing

What began as a humble Portland homebrew operation in 2012 has blossomed into a highly esteemed craft-beer producer with brewpubs in Oregon and New Mexico. You can quaff the company's hops-focused classics and distinctive seasonal one-off beers here at the original location, which also serves quite good bar fare, such as deviled eggs with pork belly burnt ends and pimento mac and cheese. ⊠ *2326 N. Flint Ave., North Williams Ave.* ☎ *503/894–8251* ⊕ *www.exnovobrew. com.*

★ Game Knight Lounge

You certainly don't need a competitive personality to enjoy your visit to what the owners describe as Oregon's "first board game lounge," but a little fire in your belly won't hurt. Pay the $5 cover, and you and your friends can order from the considerable beer, cocktail, and pub-food menu, and play any of the more than 800 board games available in the bar's astoundingly vast library. You'll find four versions of Risk, three kinds of Sorry!, and such intriguing options as Kittens in a Blender and Terror in Meeplecity. ⊠ *3037 N. Williams Ave., North Williams Ave.* ☎ *503/236–3377* ⊕ *www.pdxgameknight.com.*

Hale Pele

The riotously colorful lighting and kitschy retro-Polynesian decor of this island-inspired tiki bar creates the ideal ambience for sipping tropical cocktails like the fruity Volcano Bowl (which serves two to three) or the potent Zombie Punch. The crab rangoon dip and lumpia spring rolls are highlights among the small plates. ⊠ *2733 N.E. Broadway, Lloyd District/Convention Center* ☎ *503/662–8454* ⊕ *www. halepele.com.*

LABrewatory

This malty wonderland of beer experimentation and innovation is nirvana for beer geeks. The owners of this nanobrewery, which also features great Mexican food from Tamale Boy along with chewy pretzels and single-origin coffee, invites renowned guest brewers from around the world to concoct novel ales and lagers on-site. The result: a constantly changing rotation of beers you won't find elsewhere. Brewery tours are also available. ⊠ *670 N. Russell St., North Mississippi Ave.* ☎ *971/271–8151* ⊕ *www.labrewatory.com.*

LaurelThirst Public House

Regulars crowd this chatter-filled brewpub to sip well-crafted beers, sit in cozy red booths, and listen to folk, jazz, country, or bluegrass music on its tiny stage. There are pool tables in an adjoining room. ⊠ *2958 N.E. Glisan St., East Burnside/28th Ave.* ☎ *503/232-1504* ⊕ *www.laurelthirst.com.*

★ Reverend Nat's Hard Cider

The ambitious mission of this beloved cidery and taproom is to "handcraft the most unusual ciders that no one else will make." Whatever the weird factor, the final products are complex and delicious, and it's especially worth checking out what's on tap seasonally—maybe the mandarin orange and chamomile cider available around Chinese New Year, or the limited-release Br'er Rabbit with fermented carrot and apple juices. The cheerful taproom shares a building with Pine State Biscuits and Sizzle Pie pizza, and you're welcome to bring their food in to dine while sampling ciders. ⊠ *1813 N.E. 2nd Ave., Lloyd District/Convention Center* ☎ *503/567-2221* ⊕ *www.reverend-natshardcider.com.*

Sandy Hut

This triangular 1923 dive bar with a glass-brick facade and a wood-paneled interior has legions of fans, old and young, who appreciate its stiff drinks, pinball and video poker machines, and hulking platters of old-fashioned pub grub. It's one of the few original buildings along this commercial stretch that's now a forest of mostly bland modern apartment buildings. Here's hoping it never disappears. ⊠ *1430 N.E. Sandy Blvd., Kerns* ☎ *503/235-7972.*

Swift Lounge

The bird-themed Swift Lounge, an endearingly dive-y hipster hangout, offers a menu of Mason-jar cocktails, including the Guilty Sparrow (citrus vodka, lemongrass, and house limoncello) and the Stoned Finch (cucumber-infused vodka and house elderflower syrup). You can order the drinks in two sizes—the 32-ounce "Fatty" or the 16-ounce "Sissy." The weekend "hangover brunch" is quite the scene. ⊠ *1932 N.E. Broadway, Lloyd District/Convention Center* ☎ *503/288-3333* ⊕ *www.swiftloungepdx.com.*

White Eagle Saloon

This ivy-covered redbrick saloon, music club, and hotel—it still rents out cute and cheap rooms with shared baths—is a storied member of the McMenamins pub and lodging family. Opened in 1905, the White Eagle has hosted countless rockers over the years (and is supposedly home to a ghost or two). There's still live music a few times a week, and the funky bar and outdoor patio with firepits are lively spots to strike up a conversation. ⊠ *836 N. Russell St., North Mississippi Ave.* ☎ *503/282-6810* ⊕ *www.mcmenamins.com/white-eagle-saloon-hotel.*

Performing Arts

Laurelhurst Theater

With a huge classic neon sign out front, the 1920s-era Laurelhurst Theater serves beer and pizza and shows first-run movies, often tending toward indie cinema. ✉ *2735 E. Burnside St., East Burnside/28th Ave.* ☎ *503/232–5511* ⊕ *www.laurelhursttheater.com.*

Moda Center

This 20,000-seat facility is home to the Portland Trail Blazers basketball team and the site of other sporting events and rock concerts. It's right on the MAX light-rail line, just across from Downtown. ✉ *1 N. Center Ct., Lloyd District/Convention Center* ☎ *503/235–8771* ⊕ *www.rosequarter.com.*

VANCOUVER, WA

NORTH

NORTHWEST

NORTHEAST

SOUTHWEST

SOUTHEAST

Sightseeing ★★★★☆ | Shopping ★★★★★ | Dining ★★★★★ | Nightlife ★★★★☆

The city's Southeast quadrant, and especially the "inner" section covered in this chapter and closest to the Willamette River—extending from Powell Boulevard north to Burnside Street—comprises several of Portland's hottest and hippest neighborhoods. The closest-in section (from about the river to 12th Avenue) is known as the Central East Side and was historically an industrial tract of warehouses and factories but is now an ultra-trendy hub of food and retail that also contains a number of top-quality artisanal distilleries, urban wineries, craft brewers, and coffee roasters.—*by Andrew Collins*

Farther east (this chapter covers the blocks extending as far as 30th Avenue), the area is dominated by middle- to upper-middle class residential blocks with shade trees, Craftsman-style houses, and backyard chicken coops. You'll encounter vibrant pockets of foodie-driven restaurants—as well as bars, coffeehouses, markets, food-cart pods, and boutiques—along east–west running Division, Hawthorne, Belmont, Stark, and Burnside Streets, making Inner Southeast a Portland cultural must-see. Other Southeast highlights include the Eastbank Esplanade on the Willamette River (which connects with Downtown via several historic bridges), the kid-focused Oregon Museum of Science and Industry (OMSI), the sleek Tilikum Crossing Bridge, and the beautiful park at Mt. Tabor, an inactive volcanic cinder cone. For coverage of businesses east of 30th Avenue and south of Powell Boulevard, see the Outer Southeast chapter.

Central East Side

 Sights

★ Central East Side

This expansive 681-acre tract of mostly industrial and commercial buildings was largely ignored by all but local workers until shops, galleries, and restaurants began opening in some of the neighborhood's handsome, high-ceilinged buildings beginning in the 1990s. These days, it's a legitimately hot neighborhood for shopping and coffeehouse-hopping by day, and dining and bar-going at night, and a slew of high-end apartment buildings have added a residential component to the Central East Side. The neighborhood lies just across the Willamette River from Downtown—it extends along the riverfront from the Burnside Bridge south to the Oregon Museum of Science and Industry (OMSI) and Division Street, extending east about a dozen blocks to S.E. 12th Avenue. Businesses of particular note in these parts include urban-chic coffeehouses (Water Avenue, Coava), breweries (Base Camp Brewing, Cascade Brewing Barrel House, Modern Times, Wayfinder Beer), shops and galleries, and restaurants (Kachka, Le Pigeon, Revelry, Afuri). In the past few years, a number of acclaimed craft distilleries and urban wineries have joined the mix. This is a large neighborhood, and some streets are a bit desolate (though still quite safe). If you're coming by car, street parking is becoming tougher with all the new development but still possible to find, especially on quieter side streets. ⊠ *Willamette River to S.E. 12th Ave. from Burnside to Division Sts., Central East Side* ⊕ *reachable via the East Side Streetcar, walking from Downtown, or taking any of several buses across the Hawthorne or Burnside bridges. Street parking is becoming tougher with all the new development but still possible to find, especially on quieter side streets* ⊕ *www.ceic.cc.*

Freakybuttrue Peculiarium and Museum

Portland doesn't get much weirder than this oddball museum packed full of macabre kitsch, science-fiction ephemera, and handmade exhibits on such oddities as zombie brains and alien autopsies. You're encouraged to come in costume (free entry if your outfit impresses the cashier) and snap plenty of selfies. In the shop, peruse gag gifts and tacky souvenirs, and wave farewell to the giant Bigfoot statue

GETTING HERE

Just across from Downtown via the Tilikum Crossing, Hawthorne, Morrison, and Burnside bridges—which you can walk, bike, ride the bus, or drive (except for Tilikum Crossing) across—Inner Southeast is easy to reach. It's also traversed north to south by the Portland Streetcar. Parking has become steadily harder to find with increased development, but with a little persistence it's still not hard to find a spot on the street.

on your way out. ⊠ *640 S.E. Stark St., Central East Side* ☎ *503/227–3164* ⊕ *www.peculiarium.com* ☜ *$5* ⊗ *Closed Tues.*

Kidd's Toy Museum

Unusually, you need to knock to gain admission to this toy museum (it's open regularly only on Thursdays and Fridays, but you can visit other times by appointment). Once inside, there are oodles of antique toys—from cars and trains to dolls and teddy bears—and banks. It's a quiet place, obviously the beloved compilation of a dedicated collector, namely Frank Kidd. There are some more recent die-cast items, but the toys range mostly from 1869 to 1939; be aware that these older toys can be shockingly racist as was customary during that time period and would never be produced today. Keep in mind that younger kids may not find the museum atmosphere especially kid-friendly; it's better suited to older kids and vintage-toy

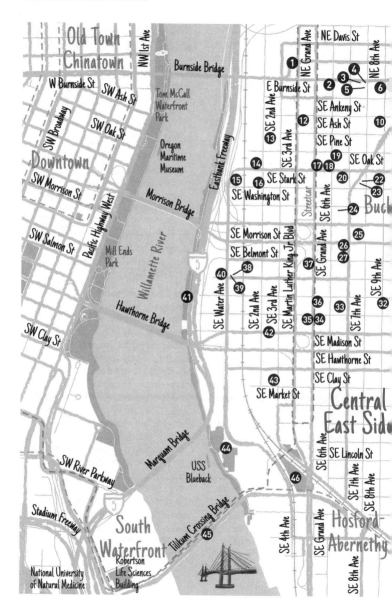

Map labels

Buckman Field
Kerns
NE 11th Ave
NE Sandy Blvd
SE Sandy Blvd
SE 12th Ave
SE 14th Ave
St. Francis Park
SE Stark St
SE Alder St
kman
SE Morrison St
SE Belmont St
Col. Summers Park
SE 10th Ave
SE 11th Ave
SE 12th Ave
SE 14th Ave
SE 16th Ave
SE Holly St
SE Ladd Ave
SE Poplar Ave
SE 12th Ave
SE 10th Ave
Ladd's Addition
SE Spruce Ave
SE Elliott Ave
SE Orange Ave
SE Ladd Ave
SE Hickory St
SE 11th Ave
SE Division St
Light Rail

250 m
500 ft

enthusiasts. ✉ *1301 S.E. Grand Ave., Central East Side* ☎ *503/233-7807* ⊕ *www.kiddstoymuseum.org* ⊗ *Closed Sun.–Wed.*

New Deal Distillery

One of the top spirits makers in Southeast Portland's Distillery Row, New Deal has become nationally regarded for its eponymous vodka, which also comes in several flavored varieties, including Hot Monkey Pepper and Mud Puddle Bitter Chocolate. Visitors to the tasting room can sample limited releases and seasonal products as well as other New Deal standards, like aromatic gin and coffee liqueur made with beans from nearby Water Avenue Coffee. ✉ *900 S.E. Salmon St., Central East Side* ☎ *503/234-2513* ⊕ *www.newdealdistillery.com* ⊗ *Closed Mon.–Tues.*

★ Oregon Museum of Science and Industry *(OMSI)*

Hundreds of engaging exhibits draw families to this outstanding interactive science museum, which also contains the Empirical Theater (featuring Portland's biggest screen), and the Northwest's largest planetarium. The many permanent and touring exhibits are loaded with enough hands-on play for kids to fill a whole day exploring robotics, ecology, rockets, animation, and outer space. Moored in the Willamette River as part of the museum is a 240-foot submarine, the USS *Blueback,* which can be toured for an extra charge. OMSI also offers some very cool event programming for adults, including the hugely popular monthly OMSI After Dark nights, where "science nerds" can enjoy food, drink, and science fun, and the twice-monthly OMSI Science Pub nights, where local and national experts lecture on a wide range of topics in the museum's Empirical Theater. ■TIP➔ OMSI's excellent restaurant, Theory, open for lunch, offers great views of the Willamette River and Downtown skyline, and Empirical Café is a great stop for a light bite or drink. ✉ *1945 S.E. Water Ave., Central East Side* ☎ *503/797-4000, 800/955-6674* ⊕ *www.omsi.edu* ✎ *Museum $15, planetarium $7.50, Empirical Theater Show $8.50, submarine $7.50, parking $5* ⊗ *Closed Mon. early Sept.–early Mar.*

Oregon Rail Heritage Center

Train-history buffs aren't the only ones who'll appreciate the three steam-driven locomotives on display here. The center, which runs mostly on donations, also plays host to diesel locomotives, historic passenger cars, and other nuggets of train days gone by. The ORHC offers hugely popular, family-oriented "Holiday Express" excursions on weekends between Thanksgiving and mid-December, departing from the station at Oaks Amusement Park. ✉ *2250 S.E. Water Ave., Central East Side* ☎ *503/233-1156* ⊕ *www.orhf.org* ✎ *Free* ⊗ *Closed Mon.–Wed.*

Produce Row Mural

In 2019, the Portland Street Art Alliance (PSAA) launched the Viaduct Arts project to transform the former industrial zone of Central East Side with colorful murals. Many works have been completed, including the Produce Row Mural, which covers the old Coast Auto Supply building with larger than life depictions of local produce. ■TIP➜ You can download the Central East Side mural guide from the PSAA website to find other murals like those covering the remains of the old Taylor Electrical Supply Company building. ⊠ *S.E. 2nd Ave. and S.E. Stark St., Central East Side* ⊕ *PDXStreetArt.org.*

★ Tilikum Crossing Bridge

Downtown Portland's collection of striking bridges gained a new member in 2015 with the opening of this sleek, cable-stayed bridge a few steps from Oregon Museum of Science and Industry (OMSI). Nicknamed "the Bridge of the People," the Tilikum is unusual in that it's the largest car-free bridge in the country—it's open only to public transit (MAX trains, buses, and streetcars), bikes, and pedestrians. The 1,720-foot-long bridge connects Southeast Portland with the South Waterfront district and rewards those who stroll or cycle across it with impressive skyline views. ⊠ *Tilikum Crossing, Southeast* ⊹ *Eastbank Esplanade just south of OMSI on the East Side, and S.W. Moody Ave. in South Waterfront.*

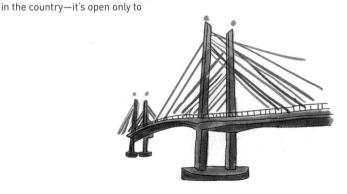

Vera Katz Eastbank Esplanade

A stroll along this 1½-mile pedestrian and cycling path across from Downtown is one of the best ways to experience the Willamette River and Portland's bridges close-up. Built in 2001, the esplanade runs along the east bank of the Willamette River between the Hawthorne and Steele bridges, and features a 1,200-foot walkway that floats atop the river, a boat dock, and public art. Pedestrian crossings on both bridges link the esplanade to Tom McCall Waterfront Park, making a 3-mile loop. ⊠ *S.E. Water Ave. between Hawthorne Bridge and Steel Bridge, Central East Side* ⊕ *www. portlandoregon.gov/parks*.

★ Westward Whiskey

One of the stalwarts of Distillery Row, this highly respected outfit (formerly known as House Spirits) opened in 2004 and now occupies this spacious 14,000-square-foot facility. It's earned international acclaim for its Aviation American Gin (which it has since sold to Davos Brands) and Krogstad Festlig Aquavit. Other favorites include Westward American Single Malt Whiskey made with locally sourced barley, and Casa Magdalena Rum. In the cozy tasting room, you can also browse a fine selection of barware, books, and other booze-related gifts. Tours are offered every afternoon, but weekends are busy so best to reserve a spot in advance. There's an additional tasting room at Portland International Airport.

Distillery tasters take note! Located in the Central East Side neighborhood, Distillery Row is a group of about a dozen craft spirits producers that include Eastside Distilling, New Deal Distillery, Westward Whiskey, as well as Bull Run and Aria in the Northwest. You can view a map of the cluster of distilleries at the group's website (⊕ *www.distilleryrowpdx.com*) and order a Distillery Row Passport—also available in print from participating distilleries or online as an app—which costs $20 but includes a credit toward tastings and tours at the 12 distilleries, as well as discounts at a number of restaurants, hotels, and shops around the city.

■**TIP**→ If you plan to check out a few of the spots on Distillery Row, be sure to order a Distillery Row Passport or download the app, which gives credit toward tastings and tours and discounts at a number of restaurants, hotels, and shops around the city. ⊠ *65 S.E. Washington St., Central East Side* ☎ *503/235-3174* ⊕ *www.westward-whiskey.com*.

 Shopping

First Friday Art Walk

One of the best times for experiencing the Central East Side's growing gallery scene is during these monthly First Friday strolls, during which about two-dozen galleries stay open until 9 pm, often serving refreshments and debuting new exhibitions. From April through October, there are also outdoor art exhibits. Although focused heavily on the Central East Side, many of the participating galleries are located elsewhere through Southeast, from Hawthorne to Sellwood. ✉ *Central East Side, Central East Side* ⊕ *www.firstfri-daypdx.org*.

★ Jacobsen Salt Co.

Established in 2011 on the Oregon Coast, this artisan saltworks has become wildly successful and prolific, and you can sample its carefully balanced finishing salts as well as Portland-made Bee Local Honey in this handsome gourmet shop. There's also a wide selection of salty treats—salted caramels, black licorice, and other goodies. ✉ *602 S.E. Salmon St., Central East Side* ☎ *503/719-4973* ⊕ *www.jacobsensalt.com*.

Machus

This small, somewhat under-the-radar, upscale, men's clothier carries one of the best selections of fashion-forward, emerging labels in the city. In addition to Machus's own private-label dress shirts and tees, check out threads by A.P.C., Ksubi, and Purple Brand Denim. You won't find many—or any—pastels or bright prints in here; expect clean classics, with lots of blacks, grays, and whites. ✉ *542 E. Burnside St., Central East Side* ☎ *503/206-8626* ⊕ *www.machusonline.com* ♥ *Closed Tues*.

Next Adventure Sports

It's all about the gear here. Next Adventure Sports carries new and used sporting goods, including camping gear, snowboards, kayaks, and mountaineering supplies. Kayak classes and Outdoor School provide plenty of opportunities to get out and enjoy Oregon like a local. They also operate Portland Paddle Sports Center, just a few blocks southeast at 624 S.E. 7th Avenue. ✉ *426 S.E. Grand Ave., Central East Side* ☎ *503/233-0706* ⊕ *www.nextadventure.net*.

Spartan Shop

As the name suggests, the aesthetic at this trendy lifestyle shop is on the clean and spare side, all the better for browsing the natty selection of muted-tone housewares and accessories. There's a notable selection of bath and apothecary products, plus jewelry, wallets, and other intriguing goods you never knew you needed. ✉ *1210 S.E. Grand Ave., Central East Side* ☎ *503/360-7922* ⊕ *www.spartan-shop.com*.

★ Una

The fashion-minded devotees of this chic, upscale women's boutique swear by its staff's discerning eye for international jewelry and clothes. Creations by dozens of vaunted designers are displayed here—hammered sterling silver link collars from Annie Costello Brown, Japanese wool and flax dresses from Vlas Blomme, and Italian leather bags from Massimo Palomba, plus enticing home accessories. ✉ *922 S.E. Ankeny St., Central*

East Side ☎ *503/235–2326* ⊕ *www. unanegozio.com.*

★ Urbanite

In this huge warehouse packed with both vintage and contemporary furniture and accessories, you'll find wares from about 40 different designers and sellers. You could easily lose yourself in here for a couple of hours, admiring the antique signs and containers, mid-century lamps, cushy armchairs, industrial tables and drawers, and curious knickknacks. ⊠ *1005 S.E. Grand Ave., Central East Side* ☎ *971/801–2361* ⊕ *www.urbanitepdx. com.*

☕ Coffee and Quick Bites

★ Coava Coffee Roasters

$ | Café. The light and open, bamboo wood–filled flagship location of Coava Coffee Roasters offers some of the highest-quality single-origin, pour-over coffees in the city. There's a second branch in Hawthorne, and a separate coffee bar a few blocks away on S.E. **Known for:** honey lattes; coffee roasted to the most exacting standards; sustainable sourcing and production processes. *Average main: $5* ⊠ *1300 S.E. Grand Ave., Central East Side* ☎ *503/894–8134* ⊕ *www.coavacoffee.com* ☉ *No dinner.*

Crema Bakery + Cafe

$ | Café. If you're seeking a comfy spot serving great local coffee brands and exceptional baked goods—both savory and sweet—consider this light-filled bakery-café in the bustling Burnside and 28th section of Buckman. Drawing young families, laptop-toting freelancers, and hoodied hipsters, the kitchen turns out delicious breakfast sandwiches with candied bacon in the morning, and a wide range of sandwiches at lunchtime. **Known for:** honey-vanilla lattes; an oft-changing selection of tarts, custards, cakes, and cookies; plenty of sidewalk seating. *Average main: $8* ⊠ *2728 S.E. Ankeny St., East Burnside/28th Ave.* ☎ *503/234–0206* ⊕ *www.cremabakery.com* ☉ *No dinner.*

★ Water Avenue Coffee

$ | Café. Coffee aficionados serious about single-origin beans favor this Central East Side roastery, which sources from top growers in Colombia, Ethiopia, and Indonesia, roasts on custom-built machines, and provides its house-roasted coffees to many restaurants and cafés around town. The attractive, high-ceilinged cafe also serves delicious toasts, bowls, and burritos until 2 pm daily. **Known for:** the spicy avocado egg sandwich on a Lauretta Jean's English muffin; well-balanced coffee house blends; decadent s'mores lattes. *Average main: $8* ⊠ *1028 S.E. Water Ave., Central East Side* ☎ *503/808–7084* ⊕ *www.wateravenuecoffee.com* ☉ *No dinner.*

🍴 Dining

★ Afuri Ramen

$$ | Ramen. When the acclaimed Japanese ramen chain Afuri decided to open an outpost in the United States in 2016, it chose this modern, high-ceilinged dining room in food-obsessed Portland in part because the exacting culinary team appreciated the city's pristine, glacially fed water supply, which plays a significant part in the steaming, savory portions of *yuzu shio* (with chicken broth, yuzu citrus, shimeji mushrooms, seasoned egg, chashu, endive, and nori), one of a half dozen deeply satisfying ramen bowls. The kitchen also turns out flavorful skewers of shishito peppers and chicken thighs, pork dumplings, sushi, and other izakaya-style fare, all of it consistently exceptional. **Known for:** authentic Japanese ramen; meat and veggie skewers; flights of premium sake. *Average main: $18 ⊠ 923 S.E. 7th Ave., Central East Side ☎ 503/468-5001 ⊕ www. afuri.us.*

Baker's Mark

$ | Deli. Overstuffed hot and cold subs on fresh-baked Italian rolls are the draw at this cheerful shop with skylights, tall wooden counters and tables, and outside picnic tables. Go for one of the classics, like the Godfather with Italian cold cuts and cheeses or the hot meatball sub with house-made marinara, or try the innovative beet-tuna. **Known for:** short list of excellent salads; lots of customizable side options (bacon, avocado, pepper salad); open daily until 6. *Average main: $10 ⊠ 1126 S.E. Division St, Division/Clinton ☎ 971/279-4225 ⊕ www.thebakers-mark.com ⊗ No dinner.*

Bunk

$ | American. Focusing on both craft cocktails and the exceptionally delicious sandwiches that Portland's local Bunk chainlet has become justly known for, this trendy spot in the Central East Side has an industrial vibe with soaring ceilings, exposed ducts, and concrete beams. It's a great lunch option by day, and more of a drinking spot in the evenings, when you might also catch live bands playing, but anytime you visit you can sink your teeth into a pork-belly Cubano, fried chicken, or double cheeseburger. **Known for:** excellent cocktails; creative extra-stuffed sandwiches; live music some evenings. *Average main: $12 ⊠ 1028 S.E. Water Ave., Central East Side ☎ 503/328-2865 ⊕ www.bunk-sandwiches.com ⊗ No dinner.*

Clarklewis

$$$$ | Pacific Northwest. In a former warehouse between the Willamette River and the train tracks in the industrial Central East Side, this upscale restaurant serves up inventive, farm-fresh, modern-American cuisine and has an excellent happy hour. The daily changing menu features beautifully plated cheese and charcuterie platters and entrées like fire-grilled leg of lamb with heirloom tomato tapenade, and king salmon with farro, purple cabbage, and a charred tomatillo sauce. **Known for:** family-style $60 prix-fixe menu option; great happy-hour specials on food and drink; light and airy space in great old industrial building. *Average main: $32 ⊠ 1001 S.E. Water Ave., Central East Side ☎ 503/235–2294 ⊕ www.clarklewispdx.com ⊗ No lunch weekends.*

★ Hey Love
$$ | Asian Fusion. The food-and-drink component of the stylish Jupiter Next hotel has quickly become one of the East Side's hottest destinations for hobnobbing over drinks and creative bar fare, much of it—salmon poke, wagyu steak fajitas—framed around Asian and Latin American elements. The space is adorned with hanging and potted greenery and Oriental rugs, which provide a decidedly funky aesthetic. **Known for:** fried chicken chow mein; late-night dining and people-watching; a cast-iron macadamia nut–white chocolate cookie with coconut caramel and sea-salt ice cream. *Average main: $19 ⊠ 920 E. Burnside St., Central East Side ☎ 503/206–6223 ⊕ www.heylovepdx. com.*

★ Kachka
$$ | Russian. This Central East Side establishment decorated to resemble a *dacha* (a Russian country/vacation house) turns out wonderfully creative and often quite light Russian fare, including plenty of shareable small plates, like crispy beef tongue with sweet onion sauce, orange, and pomegranate; panfried sour-cherry *vareniki* (Ukranian dumplings), and—of course—caviar with blini and all the usual accompaniments. Another crowd-pleaser on the menu is the classic chicken Kiev, prepared the old-fashioned way, oozing with butter. **Known for:** extensive craft vodka list; the cold "zakuski" assorted appetizer experience ($30 per person); hearty Ukranian dumplings. *Average main: $22 ⊠ 960 S.E. 11th Ave., Central East Side ☎ 503/235–0059 ⊕ www. kachkapdx.com.*

★ Le Pigeon
$$$$ | French. Specializing in adventurous Northwest-influenced French dishes of extraordinary quality, this cozy and unassuming restaurant consistently ranks among the city's most acclaimed dining venues. The menu changes regularly but often features items like beef-cheek bourguignon, chicken and oxtail with semolina gnocchi, and seared foie gras with chestnut, raisins, bacon, and cinnamon toast (especially exceptional). James Beard award–winning chef Gabriel Rucker also operates Canard, next door, which serves lighter and less pricey breakfast, lunch, and dinner fare. **Known for:** open kitchen in which diners at the counter can interact with chefs; one of the best burgers in town; grilled dry-aged pigeon with a seasonally changing preparation. *Average main: $34 ⊠ 738 E. Burnside St., Central East Side ☎ 503/546–8796 ⊕ www.lepigeon.com ⊗ No lunch.*

Normandie

$$$ | Modern American. An understated elegance prevails in this classy, contemporary neighborhood bistro with tall windows, high ceilings, exposed air ducts, and tightly spaced tables. The standout here is the elegantly plated contemporary European food, such as steamed mussels with bouillabaisse broth and grilled flat-iron steak with fingerling potatoes and horseradish sauce. **Known for:** broiled oysters with miso butter; a well-curated international wine list; house-made ice cream and sorbet. *Average main: $26 ⊠ 1005 S.E. Ankeny St., Central East Side ☎ 503/233–4129 ☉ No lunch.*

★ Olympia Provisions

$$$ | Modern American. The flagship restaurant of one of the country's leading sources of artisanal charcuterie, such as smoked chorizo, pepper-coated capicola, and pork-pistachio pâté, Olympia Provisions serves gorgeous platters of meats and cheeses along with more eclectic seasonal American fare like eggplant a la plancha with pine nuts and lemon vinaigrette, and pan-roasted black cod with stewed chickpeas. The setting is a smartly designed warehouse space and features a glowing "Meat" sign which quite simply says it all. **Known for:** lively happy hours; deeply flavorful charcuterie; interesting cocktail selection. *Average main: $26 ⊠ 107 S.E. Washington St., Central East Side ☎ 503/954–3663 ⊕ www.olympiaprovisions.com.*

Pepper Box Cafe

$ | Southwestern. Portlanders flock to this cute and simple breakfast and lunch spot to get their New Mexico food fix with dishes like sopaipillas stuffed with eggs, potatoes, and cheddar and topped with red or green chile, and Albuquerque turkey-avocado-bacon sandwiches on a flour tortilla featured on the menu. The build-your-own chile bowl is a good way to go if you're feeling indecisive. **Known for:** red and green sauces made with New Mexico chiles; smothered breakfast burritos; no alcohol license, but there's good coffee. *Average main: $9 ⊠ 932 S.E. Morrison St., Central East Side ☎ 503/841–5004 ⊕ www.pepperboxpdx.com ☉ Closed Tues. No dinner.*

Revelry

$$ | Korean Fusion. Seattle's renowned Relay Korean restaurant group operates this stylish, industrial-chic restaurant in Portland's white-hot Central East Side. Open late and serving stellar food to a soundtrack of clubby lounge music, Revelry is both a dinner and drinks spot (soju cocktails are a specialty)—noteworthy dishes from the Korean-fusion menu include kimchi pancakes with pork belly, Szechuan bolognese with lap cheong sausage, and rice bowls with grilled prawns and crushed-pineapple tabbouleh. **Known for:** house-made fudgesicles with banana glaze for dessert; soju cocktails; dinner till midnight on weekends. *Average main: $16 ⊠ 210*

S.E. Martin Luther King Blvd., Central East Side ☎ *971/339-3693* ⊕ *www.relayrestaurantgroup.com* ⊘ *No lunch.*

Stacked Sandwich Shop

$ | Deli. A worthy contestant in Portland's ongoing battle for the best sandwich shop honors, this modern industrial space offers not only sensational lunch fare but also well-conceived cocktails. It's hard to decide which of these overstuffed 'wiches is the most amazing, but you can't go wrong with the braised oxtail French dip with cast-iron-charred onions, or the Cubano with pineapple jalapeño relish. **Known for:** generous daily afternoon happy hour from 2 to 5 pm; weekend brunch with fried chicken and waffles; five-cheese truffle mac and cheese. *Average main: $13* ☒ *1643 S.E. 3rd Ave., Central East Side* ☎ *971/279-2731* ⊕ *www.stackedsandwichshop.com* ⊘ *No dinner.*

Taqueria Nueve

$ | Modern Mexican. This bright, colorful space serves excellent wild boar, cochinita pibil, and other authenticity prepared tacos, and it offers one of the better happy hours on the Central East Side. More substantial fare is offered, too, including skirt steak with a smoky Oaxacan pasilla chile sauce, and there's an impressive cocktail list. **Known for:** Caesar salad topped with ceviche; encyclopedic selection of fine mezcals and tequilas; pleasant sidewalk seating. *Average main: $15* ☒ *727 S.E. Washington St.,*

Central East Side ☎ *503/954-1987* ⊕ *www.taquerianueve.com* ⊘ *Closed Mon. No lunch.*

Bars and Nightlife

Base Camp Brewing

An East Side mainstay that turns out robustly flavored brews, Base Camp draws a decidedly outdoorsy crowd of hiking, biking, and camping enthusiasts. Decorated with canoes, gear, and outdoorsy photos of hiking dogs, the cavernous beer tasting room and adjoining beer garden are inviting spots to sip the crisp PCT Days Hazy Pale and toasty S'more Stout. ☒ *930 S.E. Oak St., Central East Side* ☎ *503/477-7479* ⊕ *www.basecampbrewingco.com.*

Bossanova Ballroom

Revelers take to this converted historic theater for different events, including blues and jazz, EDM/dance, and burlesque shows as well as the legendary LGBTQ party, Blow Pony, held the last Saturday of every month. There's a massive dance floor and a stage, and upstairs is a quieter lounge overlooking the festivities below. ☒ *722 E. Burnside St., Central East Side* ☎ *503/206-7630* ⊕ *www.bossanovaballroom.com.*

★ Cascade Brewing

This laid-back brewpub and pioneer of the Northwest sour-beer movement is a good place for friends and sour-beer lovers to share tart flights of several varieties, including Blackcap Raspberry, Kriek, and potent (10.1% ABV) Sang Noir. You'll find 24 rotating taps, small plates and sandwiches to complement the sour beers, and ample outdoor seating. ⊠ *939 S.E. Belmont St., Central East Side* ☎ *503/265-8603* ⊕ *www.cascadebrewingbarrelhouse. com.*

Century Bar

This energetic sports bar contains the usual features: large TV monitors airing major games and tiered stadium-style seating. But the main draw is the expansive roofdeck with views of the Downtown skyline, and the cozier side patio with a firepit. ⊠ *930 S.E. Sandy Blvd., Central East Side* ⊕ *www.centurybarpdx.com.*

★ Coopers Hall

Part of the Central East Side's burgeoning wine scene, this urban winery and taproom is set inside a dramatic and spacious Quonset-hut structure, which was once home to an auto-repair shop. Order any of the outstanding wines produced on-site, or delve into the happily esoteric menu of unusual wines from all over the West Coast, with a few French varieties in the mix. The kitchen turns out seriously good food, too. The only drawback here is that Coopers Hall is closed to the public on weekends, when it's booked solid with events. ⊠ *404 S.E. 6th St., Central East Side* ☎ *503/719-7000* ⊕ *www.coopershall.com.*

Doug Fir Lounge

Part retro diner and part log cabin, the Doug Fir serves food and booze and hosts DJs and live rock shows from both up-and-coming and established bands most nights

of the week. It adjoins the trendy Hotel Jupiter. ⊠ *830 E. Burnside St., Central East Side* ☎ *503/231-9663* ⊕ *www.dougfirlounge.com.*

Holocene

Hosting DJ dance nights that range from indie-pop dance parties to LGBTQ hip hop nights and poetry slams, the 5,000-square-foot former auto-parts warehouse pulls in diverse crowds. It's sometimes closed early in the week; check the online calendar before you visit. ⊠ *1001 S.E. Morrison St., Central East Side* ☎ *503/239-7639* ⊕ *www. holocene.org.*

Loyal Legion

A handsome spot with leather booths and a long central wooden bar, this Central East Side pub carries an eye-opening 99 ales on draft, from local standards to seasonally changing oddballs that delight beer geeks like the Block 15 barley wine, a Ross Island Brewing–Loyal Legion collaboration rice lager. Hefty burgers, Austrian-style wood-smoked pork sausages, and chili-cheddar-smothered fries are among the delicious pub-food accompaniments. ⊠ *710 S.E. 6th Ave., Central East Side* ☎ *503/235-8272* ⊕ *www.loyallegionpdx.com.*

Modern Times Beer

It's a quick hop from downtown to this spacious Central East Side taproom that features the well-crafted ales and lagers of this Southern California craft brewer. You'll also find well-prepared vegetarian pub fare. ⊠ *630 S.E. Belmont*

St., Central East Side ☎ *503/420–0799* ⊕ *www.moderntimesbeer.com.*

Rum Club

This diminutive neighborhood spot doesn't look like much from the outside, but inside you'll find a horseshoe-shaped wood bar and spirits connoisseurs devoted to the bar's exceptional, typically tropical fruit cocktails. Half the menu is, as the bar's name more than hints, devoted to rum-based concoctions, including the best daiquiris in town (never too sweet, and made with high-quality, aged spirits). ⊠ *720 S.E. Sandy Blvd., Central East Side* ☎ *503/265–8807* ⊕ *www.rumclubpdx. com.*

Scotch Lodge Whisky Bar

This debonair basement space has an elegant marble bar, dark-wood paneling, and a beautiful back-lit bar. The specialty here, as the name suggests, is whiskey—in both cocktail and sipping form. And there's superb bar food to boot. ⊠ *215 S.E. 9th Ave., basement, Central East Side* ☎ *503/208–2039* ⊕ *www.scotchlodge. com.*

Wayfinder Beer

This esteemed Central East Side craft brewer occupies a strikingly designed mod-industrial space with high ceilings, exposed wooden rafters, and brick walls. Wayfinder's beer-making approach is decidedly international, with a spicy über-alt-esque lager and a chocolaty London-style porter among the standouts. The bar food is excellent, too, especially the addictive Wagyu

skirt steak asada fries and prodigious burgers. ⊠ *304 S.E. 2nd Ave., Central East Side* ☎ *503/718–2337* ⊕ *www.wayfinder.beer.*

Performing Arts

Imago Theatre

One of Portland's most outstanding innovative theater companies, the Imago specializes in movement-based work for both young and old. ⊠ *17 S.E. 8th Ave., Central East Side* ☎ *503/231–9581* ⊕ *www.imagotheatre.com.*

★ Milagro Theatre Group

This well-established nonprofit company in the Central East Side showcases the region's vibrant, and growing, Latino voice through theatrical performances, featuring everything from classic dramas and musicals to experimental works and world premieres. ⊠ *525 S.E. Stark St., Central East Side* ☎ *503/236–7253* ⊕ *www.milagro.org.*

Theatre Vertigo

Founded in 1997 and presenting largely experimental and often provocative works at its intimate black-box home venue, the Shoebox Theater near Ladd's Addition, Vertigo has even commissioned its own works. ⊠ *2110 S.E. 10th Ave., Central East Side* ☎ *503/482–8655* ⊕ *www.theatrevertigo.org.*

Inner Division, Hawthorne, and Belmont

Sights

Ladd's Addition

One of the city's prettiest residential neighborhoods, this close-in quadrant of tree-lined streets that converge upon a grassy, landscaped traffic circle (Ladd Circle) of flowering trees is a favorite spot for strolling and cycling. A highlight when roses are in bloom—usually April through October, with peak times in June and September—are the four diamond-shaped rose gardens north, east, south, and west of Ladd Circle. Most of the homes here were built from around 1900 to 1930, making the neighborhood a lovely walking tour for fans of early 20th-century residential architecture, from Tudor to Mission Revival to Arts and Crafts, everything from three-story mansions to cozy bungalows. The neighborhood is framed to the north by Hawthorne Boulevard and to the south by Division Street, both of which are lined with cafés and bars. ⊠ *Between S.E. 12th and S.E. 20th Aves. from S.E. Hawthorne Blvd. to S.E. Division St., Hawthorne.*

Lone Fir Cemetery

Portland's most historic cemetery is a tranquil, undulating slice of greenery that's a joy to stroll through when you're in the Belmont or 28th and Burnside areas. You'll find headstones and several impressive monuments dating to the 1850s, paved walkways leading through this hilly 30-acre plot that are shaded by large deciduous trees, and a handful of benches. Guided tours ($10) are given twice a month, and the Portland Actors Ensemble occasionally performs Shakespeare-in-the-Park here. ⊠ *S.E. 26th Ave. at S.E. Stark St., Belmont* ⊕ *www.friendsoflonefircemetery.org.*

Shopping

Black Star Bags

Leave it to an entrepreneur in one of the country's wettest cities to come up with a brand of messenger bags and backpacks that are both great looking and fully waterproof. Also check out Black Star's canvas and leather dopp kits, bike polo packs, and hip pouches. ⊠ *2033 S.E. Hawthorne Blvd., Hawthorne* ☎ *503/284-4752* ⊕ *www.black-star-bags.myshopify.com* ⊗ *Closed Sun. and Mon.*

Books with Pictures

As the name hints, this terrific little shop on inner Division Street specializes in comics, and of virtually every subgenre: limited-release self-published titles, LGBTQ, family-friendly, and cult classics. ⊠ *1403 S.E. Division St., Division/Clinton* ⊕ *www.bookswithpictures.com.*

Herbivore Clothing

An animal-rights-minded shop in the Central East Side, Herbivore is a terrific resource if you're seeking clothing and accessories—from cotton-rayon tees and sweaters to braided canvas belts and wallets

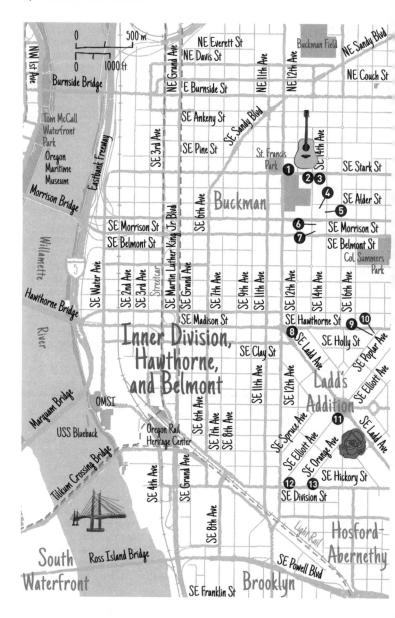

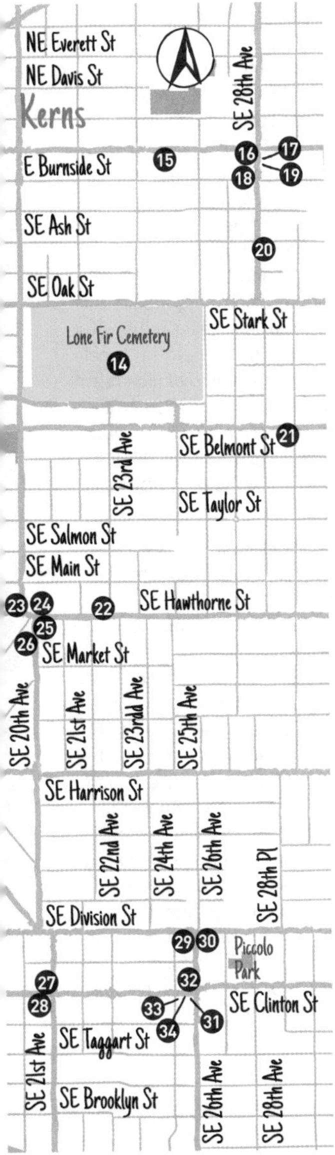

NE Everett St
NE Davis St
Kerns
SE 28th Ave
E Burnside St
SE Ash St
SE Oak St
Lone Fir Cemetery
SE Stark St
SE Belmont St
SE 23rd Ave
SE Taylor St
SE Salmon St
SE Main St
SE Hawthorne St
SE Market St
SE 20th Ave
SE 21st Ave
SE 23rdd Ave
SE 25th Ave
SE Harrison St
SE 22nd Ave
SE 24th Ave
SE 26th Ave
SE 28th Pl
SE Division St
Piccolo Park
SE Clinton St
SE Taggart St
SE 21st Ave
SE Brooklyn St
SE 26th Ave
SE 28th Ave
14
15
16
17
18
19
20
21
22
23
24
25
26
27
28
29
30
31
32
33
34

SIGHTS

Ladd's Addition 11
Lone Fir Cemetery... 14

SHOPPING

Black Star Bags 24
Books with Pictures 13
Herbivore Clothing 1
Magpie 26
Zenana Center for Wellbeing................. 28

COFFEE & QUICK BITES

Fifty Licks Ice Cream 16
Little T Baker 30
New Cascadia Traditional 29

DINING

Broder...................... 34
Castagna Restaurant 9
Delores 5
Farm Spirit 7
The Goose................ 18
Jacqueline 27
Jam On Hawthorne............... 22
Ken's Artisan Pizza 20
Langbaan................. 19
La Moule.................. 33
Lardo.......................... 8
Magna Kusina 32
Maruti 23
Nimblefish............... 25
Nodoguro................. 21
Nostrana.................... 4
OK Omens............... 10
PaaDee 17
Tusk 15

BARS & NIGHTLIFE

Crush 6
Double Dragon 12
ENSO Winery 3
Revolution Hall 2

PERFORMING ARTS

Clinton Street Theater 31

fashioned out of reclaimed bike and truck tubes—that have been created without the harm or use of animals. There's also a great selection of books on veganism, plus food, health-care products, and gifts. ⊠ *1211 S.E. Stark St., Central East Side* ☎ *503/281–8638* ⊕ *www. herbivoreclothing.com.*

Magpie

For funky vintage garb that dates from the 1950s through the 1990s, look no further than this colorful nest of fashion treasures. Jewelry, shoes, dresses, coats, and even rhinestone tiaras can be found here. ⊠ *1960 S.E. Hawthorne Blvd., Hawthorne* ☎ *503/946–1153.*

Zenana Center for Wellbeing

In a charming section of Clinton-Division, this attractive holistic day spa offers a wide range of treatments to help you restore your balance or perhaps heal your sore muscles following a day of hiking in the Gorge or skiing at Mt. Hood. Services include organic facials, a variety of massage and body treatments, and complete self-care packages. You can also book acupuncture and naturopathic sessions. ⊠ *2024 S.E. Clinton St., Division/Clinton* ☎ *503/238–6262* ⊕ *www.zenana-spa.com* ☏ *Closed Sun.*

🍵 Coffee and Quick Bites

Fifty Licks Ice Cream

$ | Café. An enticing go to for a sweet treat after a movie across the street at Laurelhurst Theater, this inviting parlor doles out fun flavors of satisfyingly rich ice cream. Thai rice pudding with pandan, ancho chile-mango, and challah French toast with cinnamon and maple are among the standouts. **Known for:** several luscious vegan options; affogato-style cafe Cubano with a scoop of ice cream; unusual toppings, such as bee pollen. *Average main: $6* ⊠ *2742 E. Burnside St., East Burnside/28th Ave.* ☎ *503/395–3333* ⊕ *www.fifty-licks. com.*

★ Little T Baker

$ | Bakery. Set in an airy, high-ceilinged space on the ground floor of the architecturally noteworthy Clinton Condominiums building, this sleek operation serves delectable breakfast and lunch sandwiches and sweets that are nearly impossible to pass up, like the lemon-curd-and-currant scones and sea-salt chocolate brownies. **Known for:** tantalizing pastries and sweets; house-cured lox on spelt and other breakfast sandwiches; savory breads, including a delectable olive slab. *Average main: $9* ⊠ *2600 S.E. Division St., Division/Clinton* ☎ *503/238–3458* ⊕ *www.littletbaker. com* ☏ *No dinner.*

New Cascadia Traditional

$ | Bakery. This long-running bakery moved into the Geode building on Division Street in 2019 but continues to produce delicious savory and sweet gluten-free pastries and breads. It's a great spot for breakfast and lunch, serving chewy bagel sandwiches, turkey club sandwiches, and pizzas by the slice. **Known for:** brioche French toast (during Sunday brunch only); gluten-free baked goods; vegan cupcakes. *Average main: $10* ✉ *2512 S.E. 25th Ave., Division/Clinton* ☎ *503/546-4901* ⊕ *www.newcascadiatraditional.com* ⊘ *No dinner.*

🍴 Dining

★ Broder

$ | Scandinavian. This adorable neighborhood café—one of the most outstanding brunch spots in town—serves fresh and delicious Scandinavian food with fun-to-pronounce names like *friterade applen* (apple fritter) and *aebleskivers* (Danish pancakes). All of the food—the hashes, *lefse* potato crepes, the baked egg scrambles, the Swedish breakfast boards—is delicious, with the Swedish meatballs in sherry cream sauce and salmon fish cakes with carraway vinaigrette being especially tasty among the midday choices. **Known for:** light-filled dining room with rustic-modern furniture; often long waits for a table, especially for breakfast; the largest selection of aquavit in the western United

States. *Average main: $13* ✉ *2508 S.E. Clinton St., Division/Clinton* ☎ *503/736-3333* ⊕ *www.broderpdx.com* ⊘ *No dinner.*

Castagna Restaurant

$$$$ | Pacific Northwest. Enjoy artful Pacific Northwest cuisine—like squid with burnt-onion jus, and fermented plum with shiso—at this sophisticated Hawthorne restaurant. Chef Justin Woodward's lavish 10-course tasting menu runs for $165 per guest; opt for the superb wine pairings for an additional $85. **Known for:** artfully prepared modern fare; outstanding wine pairings; less-pricey smaller tasting menus offered throughout the year. *Average main: $165* ✉ *1752 S.E. Hawthorne Blvd., Hawthorne* ☎ *503/231-7373* ⊕ *www.castagnarestaurant.com* ⊘ *Closed Sun.–Tues. No lunch.*

★ Delores

$$ | Polish. Former Top Chef contestant BJ Smith, who established himself as one of Portland's premier barbecue chefs, runs this modern take on Polish food—a tribute to his late mom, for whom the restaurant is named. Many of the artfully plated dishes here showcase Smith's talent for grilling, including smoked kielbasa hash (a brunch favorite) and chicken-fried rabbit with mustard cream, but you'll also discover ethereal plates of stuffed cabbage rolls and *kopytka* (Polish gnocchi with corn puree and pickled shallots). **Known for:** duck-confit pierogis; Monday family-style ($25 per person)

Marczewski Night with polka and traditional Polish food (named in honor of the owner's grandmother); weekend brunch. *Average main: $20* ✉ *1401 S.E. Morrison St., Belmont* ☎ *503/231–3609* ⊕ *www.delorespdx. com* ⊘ *Closed Mon. No lunch weekdays* Ⓜ *97214.*

★ Farm Spirit

$$$$ | **Vegetarian.** Dinners at this chef-driven vegan restaurant are truly an event—in fact, admission to these several-course repasts, which you can experience at your own table in the dining room or at a lively communal counter (this choice is a bit pricier but includes more courses) overlooking the kitchen, is by advance ticket purchase only. The highly inventive menu changes daily but utilizes about 95% Northwest ingredients and might feature delicata squash with smoked pumpkin seed or fire-roasted plums with oat cream and rosemary. **Known for:** interesting wine, beer, and juice flights; no-tipping policy; nut- and gluten-free menus by advance notice. *Average main: $89* ✉ *1403 S.E. Belmont St., Belmont* ☎ *971/255–0329* ⊕ *www.farmspiritpdx.com* ⊘ *Closed Sun.–Tues. No lunch.*

The Goose

$ | **Southwestern.** This festive tribute to the food of the Southwest has wooden booths and a long tile bar, along with turquoise Zia symbols and cow-skull wall sconces that speak to the restaurant's mix of New Mexican, Texas, and interior Mexican recipes. Fire-roasted green chilies from Hatch, New Mexico, are used in several dishes like the spicy smoked-chicken flautas and the hearty beef brisket tacos, and there's an extensive list of margaritas and local drafts to help cool your taste buds. **Known for:** smoked chicken wings with chili-lime butter; margaritas; stacked chicken tinga, pork, and beef brisket enchiladas. *Average main: $13* ✉ *2725 S.E. Ankeny St., East Burnside/28th Ave.* ☎ *503/235–2222* ⊕ *www.thegoosepdx. com* ⊘ *Closed Sun. and Mon. No lunch.*

Jacqueline

$$$ | **Seafood.** This sophisticated but unfussy neighborhood restaurant on a quiet corner of Clinton Street presents a nightly changing menu of superb small and large plates, with an emphasis on seafood. Oysters on the half shell and yellowtail crudo are typically stellar raw-bar offerings, while you might find Dungeness crab toast with saffron hollandaise or sea scallops with a lime leaf-coconut curry elsewhere on the menu. **Known for:** raw oysters ($1 each at happy hour) sourced exclusively from the Pacific Northwest; Monday-night fish fries; family-style supper option ($60 per person). *Average main: $27* ✉ *2039 S.E. Clinton St., Division/Clinton* ☎ *503/327-8637* ⊕ *www.jacquelinepdx.com* ⊘ *Closed Sun. No lunch.*

Jam on Hawthorne

$ | **American.** The name of this chatter-filled brunch spot refers to the house-made jams that appear on the table (and are available by the jar) and go perfectly with everything from lemon ricotta pancakes to coconut-almond French toast (note as well that there's often a wait for a table at this jam-packed spot). The extensive menu showcases plenty of savory creations, too, including wild smoked salmon eggs Benedict and corned-beef breakfast sandwiches. **Known for:** mimosas and breakfast cocktails; cool art for sale on the walls; enormous portions. *Average main: $10* ⊠ *2239 S.E. Hawthorne Blvd., Hawthorne* ☎ *503/234–4790* ⊕ *www. jamonhawthorne.com* ⊗ *No dinner.*

Ken's Artisan Pizza
$ | Pizza. Douglas-fir beams, old wine barrels, and hungry crowds surround the glowing, beehive-shaped wood oven in the open kitchen of this thin-crust pizza joint. Ken Forkish, also of Ken's Artisan Bakery, uses fresh, organic ingredients for the dough, sauces, and toppings of his pies, which include a margherita with arugula, a hand-pressed fennel sausage with onion, and a soppressata with basil. **Known for:** terrific salads and vegetable sides; classic margherita pizza with arugula; solid wine list. *Average main: $15* ⊠ *304 S.E. 28th Ave., East Burnside/28th Ave.* ☎ *503/517–9951* ⊕ *www.kensartisan.com* ⊗ *No lunch.*

★ Langbaan
$$$$ | Thai. Guests reach this tiny, wood-paneled, 24-seat gem with an open kitchen by walking through the adjoining PaaDee restaurant and pushing open a faux bookshelf that's actually a door. Of course, you won't even get this far unless you've called ahead to reserve a table; the restaurant serves the most interesting and consistently delicious Southeast Asian food in Portland via a weekly changing 10-course, $95 tasting menu that features unusual dishes like duck breast and tongue skewer wih duck yolk jam and fermented fish suace, or turmeric broth with Arctic char and clams. **Known for:** some of the most inventive Thai food in the country; a carefully curated wine list; wonderfully creative and flavorful desserts. *Average main: $95* ⊠ *6 S.E. 28th Ave., East Burnside/28th Ave.* ☎ *971/344–2564* ⊕ *www.langbaanpdx. com* ⊗ *Closed Mon.–Wed. No lunch.*

La Moule
$$ | Seafood. Along quaintly hip Clinton Street, in a fanciful red-roof building, cozy La Moule specializes in the dish for which it's named: Totten Inlet (Washington) mussels with several interesting preparations, such as Korean-inspired with ginger and kimchi or with a cilantro-lime salsa verde sauce. But, there's also steak frites, spätzle, and other French-Belgian specialties. **Known for:** braised-oxtail waffles at brunch; an outstanding Belgian beer list; a generous happy hour menu. *Average main: $22* ⊠ *2500 S.E. Clinton St., Division/Clinton* ☎ *971/339–2822* ⊕ *www.lamoulepdx.com* ⊗ *No lunch weekdays.*

★ Lardo
$ | American. One of several spots around Portland that has become known for advancing the art of sandwich making, Lardo offers

a steady roster of about a dozen wonderfully inventive variations, plus one or two weekly specials, along with no-less-impressive sides like maple carrots and escarole Caesar salads. Sandwiches of particular note include the tender Korean-style braised pork shoulder with kimchi, chili mayo, cilantro, and lime, and grilled mortadella with provolone, marinated peppers, and mustard aioli. **Known for:** inviting covered outdoor seating area; excellent craft-beer and cocktail selection; "dirty fries" topped with pork scraps, marinated peppers, and Parmesan. *Average main: $12 ⊠ 1212 S.E. Hawthorne Blvd., Hawthorne ☎ 503/234-7786 ⊕ www. lardosandwiches.com.*

Magna Kusina

$$ | Philippine. This cozy and colorfully decorated corner space, which opened in 2019, has quickly developed a near-fanatical following for flavorful Filipino-fusion food prepared by the restaurant's renowned classically trained chef-owner. Expect creative, artfully prepared renditions of classics like squid-ink crab-fat noodles with peppers and corn, pork-skin cracklings with spiced coconut vinegar, and tender pork adobo. **Known for:** a loud and intimate dining room; hearty main dishes featuring beef, lamb, pork, and other meaty fare; tupig (coconut sticky rice with condensed milk) for dessert. *Average main: $19 ⊠ 2525 S.E. Clinton St., Division/Clinton ☎ 503/395-8542 ⊕ www.magnapdx. com ☯ Closed Sun.–Mon. No lunch.*

Maruti

$$ | Indian. This sophisticated little spot with two levels of seating and ornate mandala symbols decorating the walls serves vegetarian Indian food from the healthful Ayurvedic tradition—vegan and gluten-free diets are enthusiastically accommodated. The menu is fairly traditional, with chickpea samosas, organic mushroom biryani, and paneer tikka masala among the house specialties, but the use of fresh and local ingredients adds bold flavor to every dish. **Known for:** Ayurvedic yellow split lentil daal with sweet mango chutney; naan in a wide variety of flavors; good beer, wine, and mocktail selection. *Average main: $16 ⊠ 1925 S.E. Hawthorne Blvd., Hawthorne ☎ 503/236-0714 ⊕ www. maruti-restaurant.com ☯ Closed Tues. No lunch.*

Nimblefish

$$$$ | Sushi. Expect some of the finest nigiri sushi in the city at this intimate, stylish Japanese restaurant, but also prepare to pay top dollar for it. The multi-course omakase feasts are the best way to sample the kitchen's top offerings, but you can also work your way through a menu of à la carte items, such as big-eye Hawaiian tuna, chopped amberjack with yuzu sauce, and braised shiitake mushroom. **Known for:** fantastic list of Japanese whiskeys; elaborate but spendy omakase menus; a spare artfully designed dining room. *Average main: $32 ⊠ 1524 S.E. 20th Ave., Hawthorne ☎ 503/719-4064 ⊕ www.nimble-fishpdx.com ☯ No lunch.*

★ Nodoguro

$$$$ | Japanese. A nightly changing selection of exquisitely plated, imaginative Japanese cuisine is served in this small, sophisticated dining room on an otherwise unpretentious stretch of Belmont Street. The 15- to 25-course omakase menus are available exclusively by advance-ticket purchase, and pairings featuring fine sakes and natural wines are available. **Known for:** elaborate 2½-hour feasts; an emphasis on sublime fish and shellfish; knowledgeable and gracious service. *Average main: $125 ⊠ 2832 S.E. Belmont St., Belmont ⊕ www. nodoguropdx.com ⊗ Closed Mon.– Tues. No lunch.*

Nostrana

$$ | Modern Italian. This smart but informal restaurant delivers delicious wood-grilled meats and seafood from the large brick oven, as well as superb thin-crust pizzas that carry an assortment of high-quality toppings; the Funghi Verde pizza—topped with shiitake and maitake mushrooms with house mozzarella and garlic—is one of the best. Good bets among the pastas and grills are the ravioli filled with braised-beef short rib and beef sugo, and wood-grilled Idaho trout with chanterelles. **Known for:** terrific happy hour deals; smoked rotisserie chicken; drinks and lighter fare next door in Enoteca Nostrana. *Average main: $22 ⊠ 1401 S.E. Morrison St., Belmont ☎ 503/234–2427 ⊕ www.nostrana. com ⊗ No lunch weekends.*

OK Omens

$$ | Wine Bar. Natural wines from around the world and well-chosen bistro fare are the focus of this charming little neighborhood spot on the edge of historic Ladd's Addition. Shiso-wrapped ahi tartare, Spanish cheeses, and grilled steak with foie gras are representative of the European-inspired but regionally sourced cuisine. **Known for:** spicy spaghetti with Thai chiles and taleggio cheese; the "kinda like a McFlurry" dessert of vanilla ice cream, Butterfingers, and chocolate; an extremely interesting selection of natural wines. *Average main: $18 ⊠ 1758 S.E. Hawthorne Blvd., Hawthorne ☎ 503/231–9939 ⊕ www.okomens.com ⊗ Closed Mon. No lunch.*

★ PaaDee

$ | Thai. Adjoining the more celebrated, reservations-only sister restaurant Langbaan, PaaDee serves some of the freshest, most flavorful Thai food in town, and at remarkably fair prices given the complexity of the cooking, the warmth of the staff, and the attractiveness of the dining room, which is on the ground floor of a contemporary condo building at the restaurant-blessed intersection of 28th and Burnside. The kitchen here specializes in traditional Thai comfort fare: grilled squid skewers with chili-lime sauce; wild-caught prawns with lemongrass, scallions, ground rice, and a spicy lime dressing; and sautéed pork belly with basil, chili, green beans, and a fried egg rank among the most

ECO FRUIT OF THE VINE: ORGANIC WINE

Portland is globally recognized for the sustainability practices of its dining scene. Another trend putting this region in the spotlight is the production of organic wine. Although Oregon has only about 34,000 acres of wine grapes compared to California's 925,000-plus acres, nearly 50% of Oregon's vineyards are certified sustainable or organic compared to about 25% in California.

The goal of organic wine production is to protect both the farmer and the environment by reducing reliance on synthetic chemicals and fertilizers. Finding ways to preserve wine without adding sulfites is perhaps the biggest roadblock in making organic wine. Though yeast naturally produces sulfites during the fermentation process, adding more goes against certification standards.

People with allergies, including sulfite sensitivities, often seek out organic wines. The FDA requires warning labels for wines with sulfites more than 10 parts per million (ppm). Most red wines contain approximately 40 ppm sulfite. There's also the term "no detectable sulfite," which means that wine constitutes less than 1 milligram per liter. Many wineries create wine made from organic grapes and label it as such, so long as the detectable sulfite level remains below 100 ppm.

Because the preservation and storage challenges still conflict with the strict certification requirements, 100% certified-organic wine labels are still uncommon. However, many of the wineries in Portland as well as in the nearby Willamette Valley and Columbia Gorge are turning new soil on what they believe are best practices for farming—and cultivating highly respected wine in the process.

---

popular dishes. **Known for:** Issan-style Thai food; daily-changing fish entrée, always with a creative preparation; interesting cocktails and well-chosen local wines and beers. *Average main: $15 ⊠ 6 S.E. 28th Ave., East Burnside/28th Ave. ☎ 503/360-1453 ⊕ www.paadeepdx. com.*

Tusk
$$$ | Middle Eastern. With its clean lines and whitewashed walls, Tusk provides a setting to show off its colorful, beautifully presented modern Middle Eastern fare like flatbread with salmon roe, squash, mustard oil, and yogurt, or grilled sweet potato with hazelnut tahini and dukka. Many of the dishes here are meatless, but you'll also find some pork, lamb, beef, and seafood grills, including a delicious pork schnitzel with carrot-mustard and ancho cress. **Known for:** extensive selection of vegetarian small plates; family-style chef's choice feasts ($60 per person); savory grilled flatbreads with house-made toppings. *Average main: $27 ⊠ 2448 E. Burnside St., East Burnside/28th Ave. ☎ 503/894-8082 ⊕ www.tuskpdx. com ⊗ No lunch weekdays.*

🍸 Bars and Nightlife

★ Crush

A favorite LGBTQ hangout in the Central East Side, Crush serves up tasty pub grub, strong cocktails, and DJ-fueled dance parties. The front section is mellow and good for conversation, while the back area contains a small but lively dance floor. ⊠ *1400 S.E. Morrison St., Belmont* ☎ *503/235–8150* ⊕ *www. crushbar.com.*

Double Dragon

Drop by this festive, low-lit bar for its sassy cocktails, such as the Burnt Reynolds (bourbon, Lapsang souchong honey, lemon, and orange bitters), scene-y crowd, and karaoke parties. Stay for the delish Asian bar food, including the 12-hour-braised pork-belly banh mi sandwiches and curried-coconut ramen with chicken and pork. ⊠ *1235 S.E. Division St., Division/Clinton* ☎ *503/230–8340* ⊕ *www.doubledragonpdx.com.*

★ ENSO Winery

Based in a large garage-like space in Southeast Portland's trendy Buckman neighborhood, ENSO is the creation of young and talented winemaker Ryan Sharp, who sources grapes from Washington, California, and Oregon to produce superb wines that are quickly earning notice in the national wine press. Notable varietals include Petite Sirah, Malbec, Dry Riesling, and the especially popular L'American blend of Zinfandel, Petite Sirah, and Mourvèdre. The high-ceilinged, industrial-chic tasting lounge—with exposed air ducts, a timber-beam ceiling, and a wall of windows (open on warm days)—has become one of the neighborhood's favorite wine bars, serving local Olympia Provisions charcuterie, Woodblock chocolates, Steve's Cheese Bar cheeses, and Little T Baker breads, plus local microbrews and a few wines, mostly from other Portland producers. ⊠ *1416 S.E. Stark St., Central East Side* ☎ *503/683–3676* ⊕ *www.ensowinery.com.*

★ Revolution Hall

Southeast Portland's stately early 1900s former Washington High School building has been converted into a state-of-the-art concert hall, featuring noted pop and world-beat music acts and comedians, from Steve Earle to Tig Notaro, plus film festivals and other intriguing events. There are two bars on-site, including a roof deck with great views of the Downtown skyline. ⊠ *1300 S.E. Stark St., Central East Side* ☎ *503/288–3895* ⊕ *www.revolutionhall.com.*

Performing Arts

Clinton Street Theater
Even among Portland's many
indie neighborhood cinemas, this
intimate theater that opened in
1915—making it one of the oldest
on the West Coast—stands out for
its decidedly old-school ambience
and idiosyncratic programming.
Every Saturday night at 11:30 pm,
an animated bunch pile in to watch
the *Rocky Horror Picture Show*, while
other nights you might catch an
indie documentary or some rarely
screened Hollywood cult classic.
⊠ *2522 S.E. Clinton St., Division/
Clinton* ☎ *503/238–5588* ⊕ *www.
cstpdx.com.*

Outer North Portland

VANCOUVER, WA

NORTH

NORTHWEST

NORTHEAST

SOUTHWEST

SOUTHEAST

Sightseeing ★★☆☆☆ | Shopping ★★★★☆ | Dining ★★★★☆ | Nightlife ★★★★☆

Northward Portland has come into its own in recent years, as the comparatively low cost of real estate has made its generally middle-income neighborhoods popular with young entrepreneurs, students, and other urban pioneers. Identified strongly with the Kenton neighborhood's 31-foot-tall statue of the strapping lumberman Paul Bunyan, North Portland occupies the peninsula formed by the confluence of the Willamette River (to the west) and the Columbia River (to the north), extending east to North Williams Avenue. For the purposes of this book, we've divided North Portland into two sections, with this "outer" chapter encompassing everything north of Fremont Street. See the Inner North and Northeast chapter for the portions of North Portland closer to Downtown.—*by Andrew Collins*

Outer North Portland contains about a half-dozen distinct neighborhoods, some of which—Overlook, Arbor Lodge, Portsmouth, and University Park (home to the private Catholic university, the University of Portland)—are primarily residential. At the far northern tip, port-side St. Johns is a working-class district that feels a bit like a separate town. In its compact commercial center, old-school barbershops and hardware stores sit alongside a steadily growing mix of cool but unpretentious shops, restaurants, and cafés. Aforementioned Kenton has a similarly welcoming, old-school but becoming ever slightly more trendy vibe. The area's star attraction among visitors is the neighborhood historically known as but rarely referred to today as Boise, which contains parallel North Mississippi and North Williams Avenues. These corridors are about 10 short blocks apart and claim some of the hottest food, drink, and music venues in the entire city.

St. Johns

⊙ Sights

★ Cathedral Park

Whether it's the view of the imposing and stunning Gothic St. John's Bridge, which rises some 400 feet above the Willamette River, or the historic significance of Lewis and Clark having camped here in 1806, this 23-acre park is divine. Though there's no church, the park gets its name from the picturesque arches supporting the bridge. It's rumored that the ghost of a young girl haunts the bridge, and that may be true, but if you're told that it was designed by the same man who envisioned the Golden Gate Bridge, that's just a popular misconception. Dog lovers, or those who aren't, should take note of the off-leash area. ⊠ *N. Edison St. and N. Pittsburg Ave., St. Johns* ⊕ *www.portland-oregon.gov/parks.*

Kelley Point Park

There is but one spot in this river-centric metropolis where you can view both the mighty Willamette and the even mightier Columbia, and that's the northern tip of this 105-acre park situated in a relatively isolated section of the city. It's named for one of the state's earliest boosters, an eccentric settler named Hall Jackson Kelley who tried without success to establish a prosperous community at the confluence of the region's two big rivers. You can walk along a number of wooden, for the most part lightly trod, paved and dirt trails in this underrated recreation area that also offers picnic tables, but swimming is prohibited due to the tricky currents. It's a great spot from which to watch massive freighters from all over the world make their way into the bustling Port of Portland, which is several miles downstream along the Willamette. ⊠ *N. Kelley Point Park Rd. and N. Lombard St., St. Johns* ☎ *503/823–2525* ⊕ *www.portland-oregon.gov/parks.*

St. Johns

As the city's more central neighbor-hoods have become more expensive and densely developed, a growing number of folks have moved into this far-northern district on a bluff overlooking the Willamette River and the evergreen-dotted hills of Forest Park (which you can easily

GETTING HERE

A car is helpful, and free street parking abundant, in North Portland, which is bisected by Interstate 5 and encompasses neighborhoods that are 5 to 8 miles from Downtown. The MAX light rail yellow line parallels Interstate 5 and is handy for visiting North Mississippi and North Williams as well as Kenton. Without a car, however, getting to other parts of North Portland will require long rides by bus or ride-hailing services.

access via the handsome St. Johns suspension bridge). For now at least, rents are lower and the pace feels roughly akin to that of a mid-size town. The walkable neighborhood center, which is bisected by lively North Lombard Street, supports a healthy concentration of inexpensive cafes, unpretentious brewpubs, and prosaic shops, plus the funky old St. Johns Cinema, with its colorfully restored neon sign. ⊠ *St. Johns.*

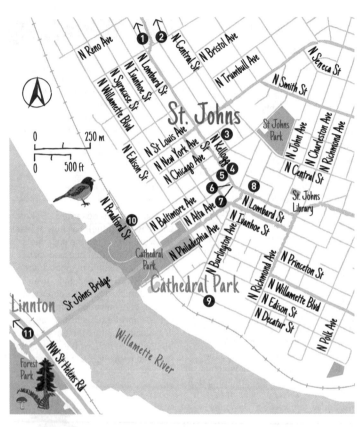

★ Sauvie Island

If it's a day to take advantage of gorgeous weather, then drive about a half hour northwest of Downtown, or 15 minutes north of St. Johns, to Sauvie Island. The largely agrarian 33-square-mile piece of paradise in the Columbia River has a wildlife refuge, three beaches (including Collins Beach, which is clothing-optional), superb biking and hiking trails, and several farms offering seasonal "u-pick" bounty (and one, Bella Organic, offering an autumn pumpkin patch and corn maze). One excellent hike, and one of the few with free parking, is the Wapato Greenway, which is just 3 miles north of the bridge onto the island. The trail leads through a white oak savannah and around a pond, and you may see green horned owls, nuthatches, and deer. Part of the trail leads to a peaceful dock on the Multnomah Channel, where you can tie a boat or kayak. To get to the beaches, after crossing the Sauvie Island bridge, turn right; follow N.W. Sauvie Island Road to Reeder Road and follow signs. There's plenty of parking at the beaches, but a permit is required ($10 for a one-day permit, $30 annual, available at the general store at the base of the bridge). Keep in mind that visitors are banned from bringing alcohol onto the island from May to September. ⊠ *N.W. Sauvie Island Rd., Sauvie Island* ✛ *Take U.S. 30 north from Portland to the Sauvie Island Bridge* ⊕ *www.sauvieisland.org.*

Dining

Gracie's Apizza

$ | Pizza. A Connecticut native with an inside knowledge of and adulation for New Haven–style pizza first opened a still-operating food truck and then this lively brick-and-mortar joint in 2019. The coal-fired pizzas with charred, blistered crusts are individual-sized and layered with robustly flavored toppings like castelvetrano olives and fennel salami, and you can add a side of kicky calabrian chili to any order. **Known for:** large patio shared with the Garrison craft cocktail bar; a short but excellent salad list; made-from-scratch dough, sauces, and mozzarella. *Average main: $11* ⊠ *8737 N. Lombard St., St. Johns* ☎ *971/328–1672* ⊕ *www.graciesapizza. com* ⊗ *Closed Mon. No lunch.*

Homegrown Smoker

$ | Vegetarian. A seemingly unlikely cross-pollination between two of Portland's most popular food categories, this ultra-casual eatery serves an entirely vegan menu of richly smoked barbecue, along with sides like "macnocheese" and sweet-potato fries. Smoked soy curls, nori-crusted tofu po'boys, and tempeh or seitan burgers are among the meat-free specialties, and you'll find a good selection of kombucha, beer, and wine. **Known for:** a good variety of mild to spicy barbecue sauces; fried pickles with ranch dip; gluten-free options. *Average main: $10* ⊠ *8638*

N. Lombard St., St. Johns ☎ 503/477-7274 ⊕ www.homegrownsmoker.com ⊘ Closed Mon.–Tues.

Mark's on the Channel

$$ | American. Although this low-key waterfront restaurant is technically outside of Portland city limits, it's a terrific and relatively nearby dining option if you've spent the day on Sauvie Island, which is located just across Multnomah Channel (it's a 10-minute drive north of Sauvie Island Bridge). Grab a seat on the deck, and tuck into platters of local oysters gratin, Oregon rockfish and chips, and pasta with seafood. **Known for:** great views of Multnomah Channel and Sauvie Island; Sunday brunch; live music on Friday and Saturday nights in summer. *Average main: $19* ⊠ 34326 Johnson's Landing Rd., Scappoose ☎ 503/543-8765 ⊕ www.marksonthechannel.com ⊘ Closed Tues.

Paiku

$ | American. The aroma of freshly prepared sweet and savory pies, pan-baked banana-nut pancakes, and buckwheat crepes tempt all who enter this unfussy St. Johns cafe that serves food throughout the day but is especially popular for breakfast and weekend brunch. Beyond the baked goods, Paiku offers rustic omelets, pan-fried hashes, venison shepherd's pie, and bountiful salads. **Known for:** savory and sweet pies; sandwiches and burgers made with wild boar, venison, and elk; stellar breakfast and brunch fare. *Average main: $11*

⊠ 7425 N. Leavitt Ave., St. Johns ☎ 503/860–4773 ⊕ www.paikupdx.com ⊘ Closed Mon. No dinner Sun.

Tienda Y Taqueria Santa Cruz

$ | Mexican. In the back of this unprepossessing Mexican grocery on the main drag in St. Johns, a fluorescent-lighted counter-service restaurant doles out delicious and authentic street food. You really can't go wrong with any of them, but favorites include chorizo, lengua, and carne asada, available in burritos, tacos, and tortas. **Known for:** caldo de camaron; chorizo con huevo tortas; incredibly low prices. *Average main: $6* ⊠ 8630 N. Lombard St., St. Johns ☎ 503/286–7302 ⊕ www.tiendasantacruz.com.

🍸 Bars and Nightlife

The Garrison

One of the friendliest cocktail and craft-beer bars in North Portland, this handsome little watering hole with timber beams and a spacious patio (shared with Gracie's Apizza restaurant) is also a pleasant hangout for meeting locals and watching games on TV. ⊠ 8773 N. Lombard St., St. Johns ☎ 503/780–6914.

Occidental Brewing

Steps from beautiful Cathedral Park in St. Johns, this respected brewer specializes in Kölsch, Dunkel, Maibock, and other classic Eastern European ales. In the roomy taproom and beer garden with views of St. Johns Bridge, you can play board games and munch on German sausages and pretzels. ■TIP→ 21 and over only; dogs are allowed in the outdoor space. ⊠ 6635 N. Baltimore Ave., St. Johns ☏ 503/719-7102 ⊕ www.occidentalbrewing.com ⊙ Closed Mon.–Tues.

Kenton

Sights

Disjecta Contemporary Art Center

This grass-roots-supported gallery in a nondescript former bowling alley has been a cornerstone of Kenton's ongoing neighborhood renaissance. Since 2010, the 20,000-square-foot space has hosted the increasingly prestigious Portland Biennial, which showcases the work of both visual and performing artists "who are defining and advancing Oregon's contemporary art landscape." And other times, curators-in-residence present edgy, provocative shows that generally run for six to eight weeks. There's also an annual art auction every November. ⊠ 8371 N. Interstate Ave., Kenton ☏ 503/286-9449 ⊕ www.disjecta.org ☑ Free ⊙ Closed Mon.–Thurs.

Kenton

One of the northernmost neighborhoods in Portland, Kenton had for many years been a fairly predictable and prosaic "company town," having been developed in 1907 by the Swift meatpacking plant to house its employees and their families. Back in the day, you could watch workers herd cattle down North

Portland International Raceway sits on the site of Vanport, a city hastily built during World War II to house some 40,000 workers (and their families) at the nearby Kaiser shipbuilding yards. Although a devastating Columbia River flood completely destroyed the shoddily constructed community in 1948, Vanport—which was about 40% African American—did ultimately help diversify Oregon, whose laws had been notoriously racist and exclusionary right up until the war. Many displaced residents relocated elsewhere in the city, especially in North Portland.

Denver Avenue—now Kenton's primary commercial drag—to one of the West Coast's largest slaughterhouses. The neighborhood is well known for its 31-foot-tall statue of Paul Bunyan (cradling a giant axe and clad in a red-checkered shirt, blue jeans, and work boots), which was installed at the corner of North Denver and North Interstate Avenues in 1959 during the Centennial Exposition and International Trade Fair (a celebration of Oregon's 100th birthday). Although a cluster of mostly indie retailers and eateries have sprung up over the past 20 years along North Denver and adjoining blocks, Kenton feels decidedly less hipsterized and more typical of pre-gentrification Portland than much of the city, and it retains a loyal following and proudly embraced identity on the part of its residents. ⊠ Kenton ⊕ Although nearly 7 miles north of

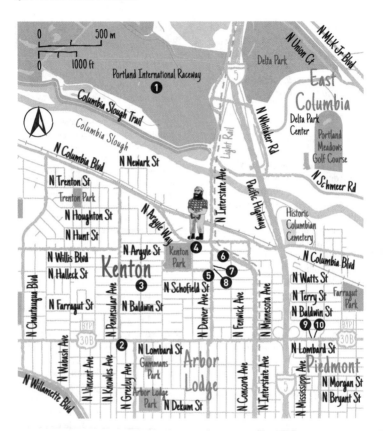

SIGHTS

Disjecta Contemporary Arts Center 6

Kenton 3

Portland International Raceway 1

SHOPPING

Mantel 8

Speck's Records & Tapes 7

DINING

Casa Zoraya 9

King Burrito 2

Swift and Union 5

BARS & NIGHTLIFE

Eagle Portland 10

Parkside 4

Downtown, Kenton is easily reached via the yellow lines of TriMet's MAX light rail ⊕ www.historickenton.com/.

Portland International Raceway

The region's premier autoracing and motorcross venue hosts dozens of prominent drag races, motorcross, motorcycle, and auto racing events throughout the year, including two biggies, the IndyCar Series Grand Prix of Portland and the Pirelli World Challenge Rose Cup Races. ⊠ *1940 N. Victory Blvd., Kenton* ☎ *503/823-5896* ⊕ *www.portlandraceway.com.*

Shopping

★ Mantel

Set along North Kenton's bustling Denver Avenue strip, this splendid shop run by a former ceramics teacher carries pedestal vases, textured-glaze stoneware mugs, clay hanging planters, and other both artful and utilitarian household items designed mostly by local Portland artists. The aesthetic tends toward clean, simple lines and muted colors. You'll also discover glassware, jewelry, vegan soaps, and other items for the contemporary urban home. ⊠ *8202 N. Denver Ave., Kenton* ☎ *503/289-0558* ⊕ *www.mantelpdx.com.*

Speck's Records & Tapes

Hard-core audiophiles frequent this record and cassette shop in Kenton whose owner is truly passionate about vinyl and is constantly adding new merchandise. Looking to unload that Abba *Waterloo* or Marvin Gaye *What's Going On* album? Look no further—Speck's is always eager to buy. ⊠ *8216 N. Denver Ave., Kenton* ☎ *971/544-7158* ⊕ *www.specksrecords.com.*

Dining

Casa Zoraya

$$ | Peruvian. A warm and welcoming Peruvian American family runs this superb—and reasonably priced—Latin American restaurant that occupies a pretty little house on an otherwise bland commercial street in North Portland. The beautifully plated food bursts with flavor and complexity, from classic causas and ceviches packed with seasonal vegetables, Peruvian chiles, and fresh shellfish to stick-to-your-ribs fish, lamb, and steak grills. **Known for:** plenty of vegetarian options; ceviche with a flavorful ají limo leche de tigre sauce; bright and refreshing pisco cocktails. *Average main: $20* ⊠ *841 N. Lombard St., Woodlawn/Concordia* ☎ *503/384-2455* ⊕ *www.casazorayapdx.com* ⊗ *Closed Mon. No lunch.*

King Burrito

$ | Mexican. This hole-in-the-wall fast-food spot is a reliable and affordable option for well-prepared street tacos, burritos smothered in spicy red-chile sauce, chorizo-potato breakfast burritos, and other Mexican and Southwestern favorites. Arrive hungry if you're planning to indulge in the carne asada fries, which are doused in beans, cheese, avocado, and sour cream. **Known for:** carne asada fries;

Jarritos-brand Mexican soft drinks; no-frills, counter-service dining room. *Average main: $5 ⊠ 2924 N. Lombard St., Overlook/Arbor Lodge ☎ 503/283-9757.*

Swift and Union

$ | American. This quintessential "where everybody knows your name" neighborhood tavern in Kenton draws a mix of young transplants and local old-timers for convivial banter and above-average pub fare. Fried fish tacos with mango salsa, smoked corn fritters with spicy honey, and steamed banh mi sandwiches reflect the kitchen's eclectic approach, and there's an impressive menu of beers, wines, and well-poured cocktails. **Known for:** friendly and welcoming neighborhood vibe; weekend brunch; globally inspired comfort fare. *Average main: $15 ⊠ 8103 N. Denver Ave., Kenton ☎ 503/206-4281 ⊕ www. swiftandunion.com.*

 Bars and Nightlife

Eagle Portland

The least centrally located LGBTQ bar in Portland draws a sizable crowd of both locals and others willing to trek north to the Piedmont neighborhood in order to partake of such renowned festivities as amateur underwear contests, classic disco parties, and leather-uniform events. Expect the kinds of guys you might spy on your Scruff dating app, but all styles are warmly welcomed. ⊠ *835 N. Lombard St., Woodlawn/Concordia ☎ 503/283-9734 ⊕ www.eagleportland.com.*

Parkside

After a stroll through Kenton's quirky retail district or amid the greenery of Kenton Park, drop by this spiffy but unpretentious corner bar for a well-poured cocktail or a bite to eat. The Parkside Plate with aged cheeses and housemade charcuterie pairs well with the mostly Italian reds by the glass, or a selection from the thoughtfully curated local beer list. ⊠ *2135 N. Willis Blvd., Kenton ☎ 503/719-6826 ⊕ www.portlandparkside.com.*

North Mississippi and North Williams

 Sights

Mocks Crest Park

One of Portland's little gems, this slightly out-of-the-way slice of greenery on a bluff in North Portland offers a view of the city that captures both its rugged industrial past and its increasingly contemporary future. In the foreground, you can see Swan Island with its freighter terminals as well as a broad swath of commercial rail tracks, but just beyond is the Willamette River, the Pearl District's sleek skyline, and beyond that Downtown and the gently climbing West Hills. ⊠ *2206 N. Skidmore Ct., Overlook/Arbor Lodge ☎ 503/823-7529 ⊕ www.portlandoregon.gov/parks.*

★ North Mississippi Avenue

One of North Portland's strips of indie retailers, the liveliest section of North Mississippi Avenue stretches for several blocks and includes a mix of old storefronts and sleek new buildings that house cafés, brewpubs, collectives, shops, music venues, and an excellent food-cart pod, Mississippi Marketplace. Bioswale planter boxes, found-object fences, and café tables built from old doors are some of the innovations you'll see along this eclectic thoroughfare. At the southern end of the strip, stop by the ReBuilding Center, an outlet for recycled building supplies that has cob (clay-and-straw) trees and benches built into the facade. ⊠ *N. Mississippi Ave., North Mississippi Ave.* ✛ *Between N. Fremont and N. Skidmore Sts.* ⊕ *www.mississippiave. com.*

North Williams Avenue

About a 10-minute walk east and running parallel to North Mississippi, the bike-friendly North Williams corridor is a much more recently developed area of almost entirely new, eco-friendly buildings and condos rife with trendy restaurants, nightspots, and boutiques. Highlights here include Eem, JinJu Patisserie, Vendetta, the People's Pig Barbecue, XLB, and Hopworks BikeBar, a branch of Hopworks Urban Brewery in Outer Southeast. ⊠ *N. Williams, from N. E. Monroe St. to N. E. Going St., North Williams Ave.* ✛ *To get here on MAX light rail, get off at the Albina/Mississippi station* ⊕ *williamsdistrict.com.*

Peninsula Park & Rose Garden

The "City of Roses" moniker started here, at this park that harks back to another time. The city's oldest (1913) public rose garden (and the only sunken one) houses about 5,000 plantings of roses. The daunting task of deadheading all these flowers is covered in classes taught to volunteers. The bandstand is a historic landmark, and the last of its kind in the city. This 16-acre North Portland park also contains an ornate historic fountain, Italian villa–inspired community center, playground, wading pool, tennis and volleyball courts, and picnic tables. ⊠ *700 N. Rosa Parks Way, Overlook/ Arbor Lodge* ⊕ *www.penrosefriends. org.*

 Shopping

Ink & Peat

Inside this handsomely outfitted lifestyle shop that occupies a row of eateries and food shops, you'll find a noteworthy selection of cookbooks and bowls and other odds and ends for the kitchen, plus throw pillows, scented candles, casual women's wear, and beautiful brass-bell windchimes. ⊠ *3808 N. Williams Ave., North Williams Ave.* ☎ *503/282–6688* ⊕ *www.inkandpeat.com.*

Land Gallery

At this creatively inspired two-story along lively North Mississippi Avenue, the upstairs gallery shows a variety of works by mostly Pacific Northwest talents—new shows are held about once a month. On

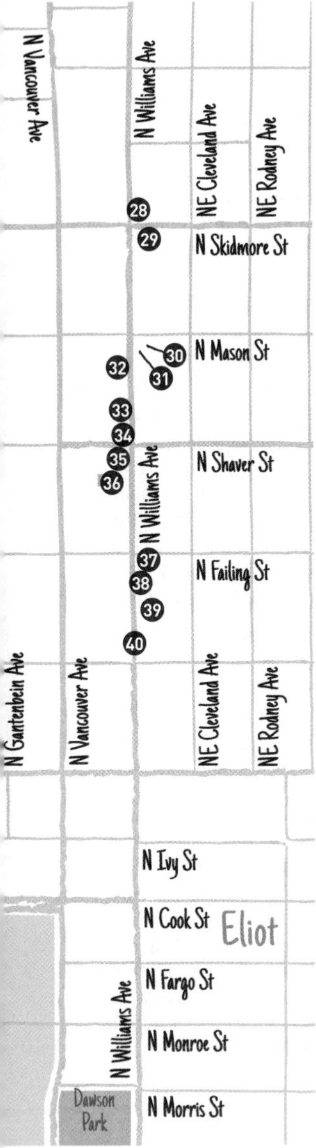
N Vancouver Ave
N Williams Ave
NE Cleveland Ave
NE Rodney Ave
28
29
N Skidmore St
30
31
32
N Mason St
33
34
35
36
N Shaver St
N Williams Ave
37
38
39
40
N Failing St
N Gantenbein Ave
N Vancouver Ave
NE Cleveland Ave
NE Rodney Ave
N Ivy St
N Cook St
Eliot
N Fargo St
N Williams Ave
N Monroe St
Dawson Park
N Morris St

SIGHTS

Mocks Crest Park 1
North Mississippi Avenue 20
North Williams Avenue 40
Peninsula Park & Rose Garden............... 4

SHOPPING

Ink & Peat................. 38
Land Gallery............. 18
The Meadow. 22
Ori Gallery 13
Paxton Gate 10
Pistils Nursery......... 21
Queen Bee Creations 36
Rebuilding Center........................ 25
She Bop 23
SpielWerk Toys 39
Workshop Vintage.... 33
Worn Path................. 14

COFFEE & QUICK BITES

Blend Coffee............... 3
Dos Hermanos 31
Either/Or Cafe.......... 34
JinJu Patisserie 32

DINING

Eem.......................... 37
Interurban 11
Lovely's Fifty Fifty.... 12
Matt's BBQ 9
milk glass mrkt.......... 2
Prost! Marketplace 7
Radar 16
Sweedeedee 5
Wolf and Bear's 19
XLB........................... 30

BARS & NIGHTLIFE

Alibi Tiki Lounge 15
The Box Social 35
Ecliptic Brewing....... 27
Mississippi Studios...................... 17
Prost! 8
Psychic Bar 26
Shine Distillery & Grill 29
StormBreaker Brewing 24
Tulip Shop Tavern......................... 6
Vendetta 28

the ground floor, there's a gift shop packed with paper goods, cards, books, and crafts designed and handcrafted by more than 100 artists—you'll find items at just about every price point in this section. ✉ *3925 N Mississippi Ave., North Mississippi Ave.* ☎ *503/451–0689* ⊕ *www.landpdx.com.*

★ The Meadow

Food writer Mark Bitterman (not to be confused with food writer Mark Bittman—he's written popular books on the subject, and he's the owner of this tiny purveyor of gourmet finishing salts, some of them smoked or infused with unusual flavors, like cherry and plums, or saffron. At this flagship location (there's a second Meadow in Nob Hill, and others in Manhattan and Tokyo) you can also purchase the additional magical touches you might need to create the perfect dinner party, from Oregon and European wines and vermouths, to fresh-cut flowers, aromatic cocktail bitters, and high-quality, single-origin chocolates. ✉ *3731 N. Mississippi Ave., North Mississippi Ave.* ☎ *503/974–8349* ⊕ *www. themeadow.com.*

Ori Gallery

The sign above this gallery along North Mississippi, an avenue that's emblematic of both the good and the bad that comes with rapid gentrification, says a good bit about its mission: "How many black families were displaced so you could be here today?" Founders Maya Vivas and Leila Haile host rotating exhibits throughout the year as well as free or low-cost classes and workshops geared toward creative-minded people who otherwise may lack access to and resources to further pursue their passions. The gallery also strives to serve as an exhibit and meeting space for queer and trans artists of color. ✉ *4038 N. Mississippi Ave., North Mississippi Ave.* ⊕ *www.oriartgallery.com.*

★ Paxton Gate

Here, science and biology mix with whimsy and imagination. You'll find everything from taxidermied scorpions and baby goats to ostrich eggs and ceramic chimes. It's a fascinating and strangely beguiling mix of goods, although not for the faint of heart. ✉ *4204 N. Mississippi Ave., North Mississippi Ave.* ☎ *503/719–4508* ⊕ *www.paxtongate.com.*

Pistils Nursery

Even if you're traveling from afar and won't be buying any of the gorgeous plants on display, it's a joy to explore this beautiful shop's fragrant garden, and explore the plant-minded gifts (balsam fir incense, tree-bark-inspired mugs), horticulture books, and decorative items for your home and garden. A favorite feature is the DIY terrarium bar, where you'll find a kaleidoscope of sands, pebbles, and accessories to build your own indoor Garden of Eden. ✉ *3811 N. Mississippi Ave., North Mississippi Ave.* ☎ *503/288–4889* ⊕ *www.pistilsnursery.com.*

Queen Bee Creations

Since 1996, this stalwart along the rapidly developing North Williams strip has been creating fairly priced products to help you carry and organize your stuff in style. Many of these items—which include honeybee faux-leather messenger bags, canvas weekenders, and convertible tote-backpacks—are waterproof or water resistant, and everything is handcrafted in Portland. Wallets, eyeglass cases, notebooks, and other useful accessories are also available. ⊠ *3961 N. Williams Ave., North Williams Ave.* ☎ *503/232-1755* ⊕ *www.queenbee-creations.com.*

★ Rebuilding Center

Although much of the recycled and repurposed merch at this eco-minded building materials clearing-house is too big and bulky to carry back home (especially if you flew to Portland), this massive nonprofit facility is worth checking out if for no other reason than to acquire some remodeling know-how and inspiration. The 50,000-square-foot ReBuilding Center teaches more than 200 DIY classes and diverts more than 1,800 tons of materials from the "waste stream." It's fascinating to walk through the building and view the aisles of well-priced appliances, doors, bathtubs, tiles, and all sorts of interesting decorative hardware, trim, and lighting. ⊠ *3625 N. Mississippi Ave., North Mississippi Ave.* ☎ *503/331-1877* ⊕ *www.rebuildingcenter.org.*

She Bop

With locations here on North Mississippi and in Southeast on Division Street, She Bop has long been Portland's premier women-owned sex-positive boutique for nontoxic toys, harnesses, lubricants and safer-sex supplies, BDSM gear, and other products to help you explore your sexuality. The staff helpfully answers questions and dispenses advice, and workshops on a wide range of topics are offered. ⊠ *909 N. Beech St., North Mississippi Ave.* ☎ *503/473-8018* ⊕ *www.shebop-theshop.com.*

SpielWerk Toys

This colorful, cheerful toy shop eschews mass-produced, big-brand-name products in favor of games and playful items that have been hand-made and often locally designed. The style here is more wooden building blocks, whimsical dolls, kid-friendly musical instruments, and old-fashioned marbles. There's a fine selection of kids books, too. ⊠ *3808 N. Williams Ave., North Williams Ave.* ☎ *503/282-2233* ⊕ *www.spielwerktoys.com.*

Workshop Vintage

This funky boutique carries accessories and gifts created by local makers, as well as women's floral dresses, quilted prairie jackets, and other vintage wear. Goods for the home include hand-made cards, and retro glassware and lamps—the sorts of offbeat pieces you've been looking for to put the final touches on your living room or kitchen nook. ⊠ *4011 N. Williams*

PORTLAND'S FOOD CARTS

Throughout Portland, more than 500 food carts dish up steaming plates of everything from Korean bibimbap to brick-oven pizza to Texas-style barbecue to Oaxacan *tlayudas* (flatbread with toppings). The food-cart scene that's become a fixture in countless North American cities owes much of its popularity to Portland, which fervently embraced the movement in the 1990s.

Brightly colored and mostly stationary, the carts tend to cluster in former parking lots in pods ranging from 3 to nearly 60 establishments, oftentimes ringing a cluster of picnic tables or a covered awning. The city's rampant boom has led to the closure or reloca-tion of some key cart pods, but other pods have opened, often farther from the city center, where land costs less; there's always a handful of notable carts at the town's farmers' markets. Arguably the city's most famous pod, downtown's S.W. 9th and Alder cart community shut down in 2019 to make way for an impending Ritz-Carlton hotel development, but as of this writing, it's slated to reopen at some point along the North Park Blocks on the edge of the Pearl District and Old Town.

With plate prices averaging $7 to $10, cart fare provides a quick, inexpensive, and delicious alternative to traditional sit-down restaurants. It's also an easy way to sample Portland's extensive ethnic food offerings.

Visit **Food Carts Portland** (⊕ *www. foodcartsportland.com*) and its corre-sponding apps for up-to-date informa-tion on the city's food cart scene.

Some Top Pods

Prost! Marketplace (4233 N. Missis-sippi Ave.): A snug encampment of about 15 pods that's adjacent to the excellent German-beer hall **Prost!** (where you'll also find restrooms), this fixture along North Mississippi contains some of the city's most vaunted carts, including the smoky Texas-style chopped brisket of **Matt's BBQ,** exceptional Mexico City–style street tacos from **Little Conejo,** and two-fisted smoked-meat sandwiches from **Pastrami Zombie.** There's also an expansive (and covered) beer garden with taps from some of the Pacific Northwest's best craft brewers.

Southeast, Portland Mercado (S.E. 73rd Avenue and Foster Road): A convivial collection of some 40 busi-nesses, including food carts and crafts and gift vendors, the Mercado is devoted to Latin culture and heritage. Feast on *ropa vieja* (braised beef) and other Cuban delicacies at **Que Bolá?;** Venezuelan egg and sweet-pepper arepas at **La Arepa**; and Oaxacan mole blue-corn enchiladas at **Tierra del Sol.**

The Bite on Belmont (4255 S.E. Belmont): There are just 9 or 10 carts at this cozy but festive cart colony in Southeast, but the variety and quality is right up there with city's the best. **Viking Soul Food** has delectable Norwegian meatballs and house-smoked-salmon wraps. There are also gooey-good casseroles with plenty of mix-in ingre-dients available (bacon, jalapenos) at **Herb's Mac & Cheese,** bulgogi chees-esteak sandwiches and Hawaiian plate lunches at **Namu,** and pints of local beer at **Hindsight Tap Cart.**

Ave., North Williams Ave. ☎ 503/206–
5813 ⊕ www.workshopvintage.com
⊘ Closed Mon.

Worn Path

The motto of this hip outdoor-gear
shop is "Be Outside." To help you
achieve this aim, come inside and
browse the vast array of camp
lanterns, backpacks, surfboards,
tents, books, and everything else
you could possibly need to plan
and undertake an expedition into
the great outdoors surrounding
Portland. ✉ 4007 N. Mississippi Ave.,
North Mississippi Ave. ☎ 971/331-
8747 ⊕ www.worn-path.com ⊘ Closed
Mon.

🍵 Coffee and Quick Bites

Blend Coffee

$ | Café. Among just a handful of
destination-worthy dining options
in the laid-back Overlook neighborhood, Blend has a loyal legion
of fans who appreciate its focus
on sustainability and community
giving, but also its extensive selection of well-prepared espresso
and tea drinks, including the honey
badger latte, which is produced
with Portland's own Bee Local
honey. Food options include pastries
from Pearl Bakery, bagels from
Henry Higgins, and a few breakfast
snacks. **Known for:** a light-filled
seating area that's great for getting
work done; breakfast sandwiches;
flavored coffee drinks. *Average
main: $5* ✉ 2710 N. Killingsworth St.,
Overlook/Arbor Lodge ☎ 503/473-
8616 ⊕ www.blendcoffeepdx.com
⊘ No dinner.

Dos Hermanos

$ | Bakery. A pair of brothers
from Mérida, Mexico, with a gift
for savory and sweet breads run
this simple artisan bakery located
inside a slick modern building on
North Williams Avenue. Many items
have a Mexican bent, including
concha pastries, baguettes with
habanero and pumpkin seeds,
and single-serving pies with ham,
cheese, and jalapeños. **Known
for:** hearty sandwiches; traditional
Mexican pastries; baguettes baked
with delicious flavorings. *Average
main: $6* ✉ 4082 N. Williams Ave.,
North Williams Ave. ☎ 971/266–8348
⊕ www.doshermanosbakery.com
⊘ No dinner.

Either/Or Cafe

$ | Café. The name of this high-
ceiling, vaguely industrial-chic
space reflects its dual personality as a either java-focused cafe
during the day or a hip cocktail bar
(complete with a DJ some evenings)
at night. Whenever you visit, you
can count on a short menu of
excellent Chinese-influenced food,
including Shandong-style noodle
bowls with tofu or sausage and
vegan fried "chicken" sandwiches
with sriracha aioli. **Known for:** rice
and noodle bowls; alcohol-free
coffee mocktails; generously priced
twice-daily happy hours. *Average
main: $11* ✉ 4003 N. Williams Ave.,
North Williams Ave. ☎ 971/266–8348
⊕ www.eitherorpdx.com.

★ JinJu Patisserie

$ | Café. Dessert isn't the only
offering at this modish East-meets-
West patisserie, but these opulent

treats—matcha-yuzu mousse tarts, fig–and–red wine chocolates, red velvet whoopie pies—are unquestionably JinJu's raison d'etre. For a more substantial breakfast or lunch experience, tuck into a five-grain Korean bulgogi bowl or a curried-chicken panini. **Known for:** exquisitely crafted pastries and cakes; artisan chocolates; savory and sweet breakfast croissants. *Average main: $12 ⊠ 4063 N. Williams Ave., North Williams Ave. ☎ 503/828–7728 ⊕ www.jinjupatisserie.com ⊘ Closed Tues.–Wed. No dinner.*

¶¶ Dining

★ Eem

$$ | **Thai.** This impossibly delicious mash-up of Thai street food and Texas barbecue, a collaboration between the talents behind locally renowned restaurants Langbaan and Matt's BBQ, excels in both its playful approach and smoking-good execution. Potted plants and hanging basket lamps impart a subtle, relaxed beach bar vibe, perfect for enjoying tiki-esque cocktails with inspired names like Arranged Marriage and Act of God. **Known for:** colorful tropical drinks; chopped barbecue-fried rice with shishito peppers; rich curries with smoked brisket, lamb shoulder, and other barbecue staples. *Average main: $16 ⊠ 3808 N. Williams Ave., North Williams Ave. ☎ 971/295–1645 ⊕ www.eempdx.com.*

★ Interurban

$ | **Modern American.** A laid-back North Mississippi gastropub with an L-shaped indoor bar and a bi-level back patio with lush landscaping and a shaded pergola, Interurban is both a convivial drinkery and a fine spot for affordable, well-crafted American fare served from midafternoon until 2 am (hours start earlier on weekends, with brunch kicking off at 10 am). The kitchen creates consistently good and creative food, such as steak tartare and smoked-trout BLT sandwiches, and there's an extensive selection of cocktails and microbrews. **Known for:** terrific afternoon and late-night happy hour menu; salted-caramel French toast at brunch; pretty back patio. *Average main: $15 ⊠ 4057 N. Mississippi Ave., North Mississippi Ave. ☎ 503/284–6669 ⊕ www.interurbanpdx.com ⊘ No lunch weekdays.*

★ Lovely's Fifty-Fifty

$ | **Pizza.** This unpretentious and airy neighborhood spot with wooden booths and whimsical fire-engine-red chairs is really two delicious dining options in one: the dining room serves inventively topped, crisp, wood-fired pizzas, and a small takeout counter dispenses homemade hard and soft-serve organic ice cream with flavors like hazelnut toffee and candied kumquat. Among the pizzas, you can't go wrong with the pie layered in shaved-and-roasted potatoes, sage, taleggio, and pancetta, and topped with an egg. **Known for:** innovative flavors of house-made ice cream; perfectly crispy wood-fired pizzas; beautiful seasonal salads with local greens. *Average main: $15* ✉ *4039 N. Mississippi Ave., North Mississippi Ave.* ☎ *503/281-4060* ⊕ *www.lovelysfiftyfifty.com* ◷ *Closed Mon. No lunch.*

★ Matt's BBQ

$ | Barbecue. Located in the Prost! Marketplace on North Mississippi, you'll often have to stand in line (it's worth it!) to experience the top food-cart *and* (Texas-style) barbecue joint in Portland. **Known for:** the hotmess sandwich (with brisket, sausage, jalapeños, and slaw); combo platters featuring brisket, ribs, sausage, pulled pork, and sides; outstanding craft-beer offerings elsewhere in this cart pod. *Average main: $10* ✉ *Prost! Marketplace, 4233 N. Mississippi Ave., North Mississippi Ave.* ☎ *503/504-0870* ⊕ *www.mattsbqpdx.com.*

milk glass mrkt

$ | Modern American. From the chandeliers to the floral vases on the angular wooden tables, vintage milk glass informs the vintage-cool style of this cozy breakfast and lunch spot located in a relatively off-the-beaten-path NoPo neighborhood. The kitchen sources locally to create sublime smoked-trout plates, runny egg–and–prosciutto breakfast sandwiches, Oregon albacore and miso-sesame noodle bowls, and Middle Eastern mezze boards. **Known for:** bubbly and brunchy cocktails featuring house-made shrubs; fresh-baked tartines, bread puddings, danishes, and other flaky pastries; locavore-driven sandwiches and bowls. *Average main: $13* ✉ *2150 N. Killingsworth St., Overlook/ Arbor Lodge* ☎ *503/395-4742* ⊕ *www. milkglassmrkt.com* ◷ *Closed Mon. No dinner.*

Prost! Marketplace

$ | Eclectic. The former Mississippi Marketplace regained its glory when the owners of Prost! beer hall bought the Prost building and lot that bordered their outdoor space. Today, the food pod is open daily with 10 food carts that range from Persian (Caspian Kabob) and Indian fusion (Desi PDX) to sandwiches and burgers (Pastrami Zombie) and barbecue (Matt's BBQ). **Known for:** one of the original food pod locations; great food and beer; North Mississippi Avenue location. *Average main: $7* ✉ *4237 N. Mississippi Ave., North Mississippi Ave.* ☎ *503/954-2674.*

Radar

$$ | Modern American. A long, narrow storefront space on the lively North Mississippi strip, this convivial restaurant with exposed-brick walls, a long bar, and high timber ceilings is appreciated as a drinking hole and source of reasonably priced, well-crafted modern American fare. Sip an inventive cocktail and order a few of the shareable small plates, such as smoked-bluefish pâté or summer squash sweet corn risotto. **Known for:** weekend brunch; impressive craft cocktail list; moules or steak frites. *Average main: $20* ✉ *3951 N. Mississippi Ave., North*

Mississippi Ave. ☎ 503/841–6948
⊕ www.radarpdx.com ⏲ No lunch
Mon.–Thurs.

Sweedeedee

$ | Modern American. Although
this modest white-brick storefront
on a quiet street doesn't look like
anything special from the outside,
it produces some of the most
memorable breakfast and lunch
fare in North Portland, including
savory bacon-lettuce-beet sandwiches on cornmeal molasses bread
and sweet porridge with fruit and
cardamom yogurt. This Southern-
inspired eatery also offers up flaky-
crust marionberry, salted-honey,
and other delectable pies. **Known
for:** seasonal fruit pies; hearty but
fresh Southern breakfast fare; sandwiches on unusual house-baked
breads. *Average main: $13* ⊠ 5202
N. Albina Ave., North Mississippi Ave.
☎ 503/946–8087 ⊕ www.sweedeedee.
com ⏲ No dinner.

★ Wolf and Bear's

$ | Middle Eastern. This hallowed
Portland food cart—with two locations—has fantastic vegetarian
Middle Eastern food prepared from
scratch with local and organic
ingredients. Every item on the short
menu can be prepared as a bowl
or pita sandwich, from the fluffy
falafel with grilled eggplant to the
Sabich, an Iraqi-Jewish breakfast dish chock-full of hummus,
mango pickle, hard-boiled egg,
and potatoes. **Known for:** offering a
wide range of add-ons—eggplant,
labneh—that add pop to each dish;
they carry locally brewed Lion Heart

Kombucha; vegan- and gluten-free
versions of most dishes. *Average
main: $9* ⊠ 3925 N. Mississippi
Ave., North Mississippi Ave.
☎ 503/453–5044.

XLB

$ | Chinese. In this bright, modern
space with comfy booth and counter
seating and colorful Chinese zodiac
wallpaper, the hands-down specialties are dumplings and buns (the
pork-filled Shanghai *bao* with ginger
and garlic are especially tasty). XLB
has excellent happy hours both late
at night and in the early evening,
and the kitchen is also adept with
several other tasty dishes, including
five-spice popcorn chicken and cold-
sesame (tofu or chicken) noodles.
Known for: buns and dumplings;
late-night dining; the "two bao and
a beer" happy-hour special. *Average
main: $12* ⊠ 4090 N. Williams Ave.,
North Williams Ave. ☎ 503/841–5373
⊕ www.xlbpdx.com.

Bars and Nightlife

Alibi Tiki Lounge

The camp factor is sky high in
this aggressively kitschy tropical-
themed bar that's known for its
enthusiastic karaoke scene and big,
colorful drinks. Although divey and
unexceptional food-wise, it's a fun
place to while away a boozy night
of sipping and singing with friends.
⊠ 4024 N. Interstate Ave., Overlook/
Arbor Lodge ☎ 503/287–5335 ⊕ www.
alibiportland.com.

The Box Social

Aptly located in a boxy glass-and-steel contemporary building in the trendy North Williams Corridor, this low-keyed, self-proclaimed "drinking parlor" stands out in particular for its nicely balanced whiskey cocktails. Note the extensive use of house-made, sometimes barrel-aged, bitters, and the long list of premium whiskeys and small-batch bourbons. ✉ *3971 N. Williams Ave., North Williams Ave.* ☎ *503/288-1111* ⊕ *www.bxsocial.com.*

★ Ecliptic Brewing

Fans of boldly flavored brews flock to this spacious, airy brewery and pub at the south end of the Mississippi strip, which also has a spacious patio that's abuzz with revelers on summer afternoons. Founder John Harris is as obsessed with astronomy as he is with beer, hence the cosmic names of beers, which include Quasar Pale Ale and Phobos Single Hop Red Ale. ■TIP→ Brewery tours are offered at noon three times a week. ✉ *825 N. Cook St., North Mississippi Ave.* ☎ *503/265-8002* ⊕ *www.ecliptic-brewing.com.*

★ Mississippi Studios

An intimate and inclusive neighborhood music venue, with a seated balcony and old Oriental rugs covering the standing-room-only floor, community-oriented Mississippi Studios offers high-quality live music performances every night of the week in a wide range of genres. Between sets, you can jump back and forth from the adjacent BarBar, a hip, comfortable bar serving delicious burgers and vegan fare and a covered back patio. ✉ *3939 N. Mississippi Ave., North Mississippi Ave.* ☎ *503/288-3895* ⊕ *www.mississippistudios.com.*

Prost!

At the northern end of the hip North Mississippi retail and restaurant strip, Prost! is an airy, amber-lit, contemporary bar specializing in old-school German beers like Spaten Lager, Franziskaner Weissbier, and Erdinger Dunkel Weisse. Nosh on Bavarian pretzels and other Euro snacks or venture next door to one of the city's best food-cart pods, Prost! Marketplace. The owners also operate the excellent German pub Stammtisch, on NE 28th Avenue. ✉ *4237 N. Mississippi Ave., North Mississippi Ave.* ☎ *503/954-2674* ⊕ *www.prost-portland.com.*

Psychic Bar

Set in an eye-catching Victorian house with neon signage befitting a séance parlor, this playfully eerie cocktail bar is run by a trio of Portland film-industry veterans. Most of the nicely balanced drinks have mystical names (Marfa Lights, New Age Aunt), and the delish bar snacks—tandoori chicken tacos, massaman curry snacks—will put you in the mood for a Bollywood movie. ✉ *3560 N. Mississippi Ave., North Mississippi Ave.* ☎ *503/206-5343* ⊕ *www.psychicbarpdx.com.*

Shine Distillery & Grill

The city's first craft distillery with a full-service restaurant and bar, Shine provides the opportunity to sample house-made gin and vodka in cocktail form, and enjoy a commendable selection of comfort victuals, such as smoked and rum-cured hot wings and blackened-shrimp po'boys. One standout feature, especially in warm weather, is the spacious roofdeck, but the street-level interior dining room is also a stunner, with its chic postindustrial design. ⊠ *4232 N. Williams Ave., North Williams Ave.* ☎ *503/825-1010* ⊕ *www.shinedistillerygrill.com.*

★ StormBreaker Brewing

Choose from either North Portland location of this popular brewpub. There's one just off North Mississippi with an enormous beer garden and picnic tables as well as a handsome interior with hops-shaped lamps, and a smaller satellite branch in St. John's that's notable for its outdoor mural of St. John's Bridge (which is depicted as morphing surrealistically into a stream of golden lager). ⊠ *832 N. Beech St., North Mississippi Ave.* ☎ *971/703-4516* ⊕ *www.stormbreakerbrewing.com.*

Tulip Shop Tavern

A cute and eclectic neighborhood bar that's a good stop if you're between the Mississippi and Alberta districts, the Tulip Shop is run by a couple with extensive experience at a number of notable Portland bars and restaurants. Eastern European-centric tavern fare and a beer menu that's remarkably well curated even by Portland standards are among the highlights, and there's ample seating on the enclosed patio out

back. ⊠ *825 N. Killingsworth St., North Mississippi Ave.* ☎ *503/206-8483* ⊕ *www.tulipshoptavern.com.*

Vendetta

This friendly neighborhood bar stands out in particular for one fantastic feature: a big leafy patio with picnic tables and umbrellas, bench seating, and shuffleboard—it's a refreshingly old-school space compared with many of the glitzy newcomers that line the North Williams corridor. Bar snacks lean toward Mexican street food, with flat-iron steak quesadillas and pulled-pork street tacos. ⊠ *4306 N. Williams Ave., North Williams Ave.* ☎ *503/288-1085* ⊕ *www.vendettapdx.com.*

GO FOR

**20th-century
architecture**

Arts districts

**Easygoing,
artsy vibe**

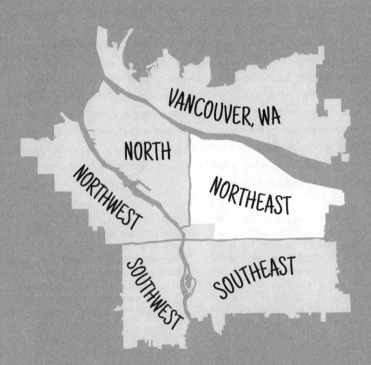

VANCOUVER, WA

NORTH

NORTHWEST

NORTHEAST

SOUTHWEST

SOUTHEAST

C ontaining the trendy Alberta Arts District as well as an eclectic mix of both residential and commercial neighborhoods, Northeast Portland is one of the city's largest quadrants and also the location of Portland International Airport, which occupies a large strip of land near the Columbia River. Northeast is diverse, containing the epicenter of the city's relatively small—compared with comparably sized U.S. cities—African American community, but many areas have slowly gentrified over the last half century, leading to challenging questions about how to balance new development with the inevitable toll of displacement and neighborhood identity shifts. In this book, we've divided Northeast Portland into two sections. This "outer" chapter includes the area north of Fremont Street and east of Martin Luther King Jr. Boulevard, and additionally everything east of 33rd Avenue and north of Burnside Street. Northeast Portland continues all the way to the city border with the suburbs of Fairview and Gresham, but there are few attractions or businesses east of Interstate 205. See the Inner North and Northeast chapter for the areas of Northeast Portland closer to Downtown.—by Andrew Collins

Lined with many excellent—and generally affordable—restaurants, bars, galleries, and boutiques, Alberta Street has become one of the city's trendiest neighborhoods. Generally referred to locally as the Alberta Arts District or just Alberta, it also hosts a bustling street art fair the last Thursday of every month (primarily between 12th and 31st Avenues). Just north of Alberta, the presence of notable dining and nightlife spots has grown considerably in the adjoining Woodlawn and Concordia neighborhoods. Immediately south of Alberta, the Sabin and Alameda districts contain few businesses but are lovely to stroll through as Alameda, in particular, contains hilly, tree-shaded streets dotted with grand early-20th-century homes. Two neighborhoods worth exploring that lie east of 33rd Avenue are Beaumont-Wilshire, which has an increasingly interesting commercial strip along Fremont Street (from about 38th to 57th Avenues), and Hollywood, a dense and historic hub of retail and dining centered at the junction of Broadway Street, Sandy Boulevard, and Cesar E. Chavez Boulevard.

Alberta, Concordia, and Woodlawn

◉ Sights

★ Alberta Arts District

Arguably the first of Portland's several hipster-favored East Side neighborhoods to earn national attention, the Alberta Arts District (aka Alberta) has morphed from a downcast commercial strip into an offbeat row of hippie-driven counterculture and then more recently into a considerably more eclectic stretch of both indie arts spaces and downright sophisticated bistros and galleries. Favorite stops include Pine State Biscuits, Salt & Straw ice cream, the Bye and Bye bar, Tin Shed Garden Cafe, Aviary restaurant, Bollywood Theater restaurant, Urdaneta restaurant, Proud Mary coffeehouse, Ampersand art gallery and books, PedX shoes, and Grayling jewelry. Extending a little more than a mile, Northeast Alberta offers plenty of one-of-a-kind dining and shopping; you'll find virtually no national chains along here. The area is also home to some of the best people-watching in Portland, especially during the Last Thursday (of the month) art walks, held from 6 pm until 9 pm. The Alberta Street Fair in August showcases the neighborhood's offerings with arts-and-crafts displays and street performances. ■TIP→ Northeast Alberta is about a mile from the smaller but similarly intriguing North Mississippi and North Williams corridors; fans of indie dining and shopping could easily spend a full day strolling or biking among both areas. ⊠ N.E. Alberta St. between N.E. Martin Luther King Jr. Blvd. and N.E. 30th Ave., Alberta Arts District ⊕ www.albertamainst.org.

Concordia

This largely working-class neighborhood in northern Northeast Portland is mostly residential, along with being home to the 13-acre campus of Concordia University. But the area's relatively low, though climbing, housing costs have helped attract many of the artists, students, and young entrepreneurs who have been priced out of more central areas, and this influx of residents has helped to spur the development of increasingly buzzy dining and nightlife districts. Much of the action is around the intersection of NE Killingsworth Street and 30th Avenue. But you'll also find growing restaurant-bar rows along NE 42nd Avenue, which forms Concordia's border with the up-and-coming

GETTING HERE

As with the rest of outlying Portland, it's easiest to explore Outer Northeast if you have a car—there's plenty of free street parking in most areas, and distances can be considerable. However, TriMet's MAX light rail blue, green, and red lines stop in Hollywood and several points farther east (the red line continues to the airport). To reach the other neighborhoods covered extensively in this chapter, including Alberta, buses are your best option if you don't have a car.

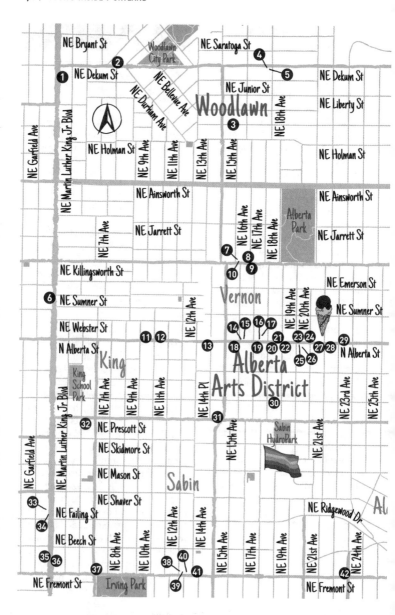

Map labels:
NE Lombard St
NE Dekum St
Concordia University
NE Rosa Parks Way
NE 31st Ave
NE 33rd Ave
NE 35th Ave
Concordia
NE Simpson St
NE 27th Ave
NE Killingsworth St
NE 27th Ave
NE 29th Ave
NE 31st Ave
NE 33rd Ave
NE 35th Ave
NE Skidmore St
Wilshire Park
NE Mason St
Alameda
NE Bryce St
NE Dunckley St
NE Hamblet St
NE 33rd Ave
NE Alameda St
500 m
1000 ft

SIGHTS

Alberta Arts District	30
Concordia	43
Woodlawn	3

SHOPPING

Alberta Street Gallery	21
Ampersand Gallery & Fine Books	51
Backyard Bird Shop	41
collage annex	14
Community Cycling Center	19
Common Ground Wellness Co-Operative	55
Crafty Wonderland	25
Darling Distraction	18
EcoVibe Home	22
Grayling Jewelry	15
Last Thursdays on Alberta	27
Monograph Bookwerks	50
pedX Shoe Shangri-la	23
Rerun	37
Tumbleweed	20

COFFEE & QUICK BITES

Barista	16
Bushel & Peck Bakeshop	34
Guilder	42
Proud Mary	26
Salt & Straw Ice Cream	24
Seastar Bakery	7

DINING

Acadia	38
Akadi PDX	35
Aviary	17
Beast	45
Dame	44
DOC	46
Firehouse Restaurant	2
Grain & Gristle	31
Hat Yai	10
Kargi Gogo	53
Ned Ludd	33
Pine State Biscuits	28
Podnah's Pit BBQ	8
Ranch Pizza	4
Tamale Boy	5
Tiffin Asha	9
Tin Shed Garden Cafe	13
Urdaneta	54
Verdigris	39

BARS & NIGHTLIFE

The Bye and Bye	11
Expatriate	47
Free House	40
Jinx	48
The Knock Back	29
Local Lounge	36
Radio Room	12
Retro Game Bar	1

PERFORMING ARTS

Alberta Rose Theatre	52
Curious Comedy Theater	6
Kennedy School Theater	49
Portland Playhouse	32

Cully neighborhood, and just a little farther west, around NE Killingsworth and 16th, which is also close to grassy, tree-shaded Alberta Park. Note that Concordia's southern end officially overlaps a bit with the eastern end of the Alberta Arts District. ✉ *From N.E. 22nd Ave. east to N.E. 42nd Ave., between N.E. Prescott St. and N.E. Columbia Blvd., Woodlawn/Concordia.*

Woodlawn

A northerly neighborhood that adjoins Alberta and Concordia and is just east of North Portland, laid-back and middle-class Woodlawn contains a growing strip of fun eateries and bars along Dekum Street, especially along the strip between Northeast 6th Avenue and verdant Woodlawn City Park—this area is also known as Dekum Triangle. ✉ *From N.E. Martin Luther King Blvd. east to N.E. 22nd Ave., between N.E. Ainsworth St. and N.E. Columbia Blvd., Woodlawn/Concordia.*

 Shopping

Alberta Street Gallery

This outstanding collective gallery—which launched in 2004 and moved into its current, much larger home in 2018—helped establish the neighborhood's reputation as a creative hub. Peruse the superb and diverse works of the 30 resident artists, much of it quite reasonably priced. ✉ *1829 N.E. Alberta St., Alberta Arts District* ☎ *503/954-3314* ⊕ *www. albertastreetgallery.com.*

Ampersand Gallery & Fine Books

Part art gallery, part media store, this minimalist white-wall space on Alberta Street has monthly shows featuring edgy, contemporary art, and stocks a fascinating trove of photography and art books, vintage travel brochures, curious photography, pulp-fiction novels, and other printed materials of the sort you might find in a chest in a mysterious neighbor's attic. The owners also operate the cute Cord boutique next door, which stocks artfully designed household goods, from handcrafted soaps to aerodynamic coffeepots. ✉ *2916 N.E. Alberta St., Alberta Arts District* ☎ *503/805-5458* ⊕ *www. ampersandgallerypdx.com* ⊗ *Closed Mon.-Tues.*

Backyard Bird Shop

You'll find everything for the bird lover here, including bird feeders, birdhouses, a huge supply of bird seed, and colorful bird-theme gifts ranging from wind chimes to stuffed animals. There are several other locations in the Portland metro area. ✉ *1419 N.E. Fremont St., Irvington* ☎ *503/445-2699* ⊕ *www. backyardbirdshop.com.*

collage annex

This colorful shop is the gift locale of a chainlet of thoughtfully curated art supply stores with branches a few doors away on Alberta Street as well as on Southeast Division and in Sellwood. It's easy to lose yourself for an hour here browsing the clever greeting cards, bold-print umbrellas, illustrated books, logo'd mugs, and the like. ✉ *1607 N.E. Alberta St., Alberta Arts District*

PORTLAND'S BORING VOLCANOES

With several breathtaking mountain peaks visible from much of the city, Portland's setting is anything but dull. The two most prominent mountains are just 50 miles away: 11,250-foot Mt. Hood and 8,363-foot Mt. St. Helens, which famously—and violently—erupted in 1980, destroying 230 square miles of forestland and killing 57 people.

Portland itself lies in the center of the 1,500-square-mile Boring Volcanic Field, which is named for the small, nearby town of Boring (which took its name from its founder), around which many of the field's roughly 90 cinder cones and small shield volcanoes are located. Within Portland's city limits, there are four extinct cinder cones: Mt. Tabor, Kelly Butte, Powell Butte, and Rocky Butte. The slopes of all of these urban volcanoes are easy to explore—each is home to a public park. And you needn't worry about any imminent eruptions, as the entire Boring Volcanic Field has slept silently for more than 50,000 years.

Keep your eyes on the Northwest's biggest peaks, however. Mt. St. Helens still ranks as the second-most dangerous volcanic threat in the United States, with Mt. Rainier—about 100 miles north of Portland, as the crow flies—ranking third. Some geologists are concerned that this 14,411-foot monolith could blow its top in our lifetime and cause unprecedented damage, albeit primarily to the Seattle metro area. There's certainly nothing boring about that.

☎ 503/432-8163 ⊕ www.collagepdx. blogspot.com.

Community Cycling Center

This nonprofit space with a huge, colorful mural on one exterior wall is an excellent bike and gear shop and a helpful source of advice on the best Portland places to pedal, especially in North and Northeast. The center also runs bike camps, organizes a holiday bike drive, and develops other programs geared toward introducing biking to lower-income kids and families. ✉ 1700 N.E. Alberta St., Alberta Arts District ☎ 503/287-8786 ⊕ www.community-cyclingcenter.org.

Common Ground Wellness Co-Operative

At this beautifully designed wellness co-op in Concordia, nonmembers can pay a slightly higher fee to enjoy sessions in the clothing-optional outdoor communal soaking pools and dry-cedar sauna, or book from an extensive menu of body and skin therapies, including several types of massage, naturopathy, acupuncture, skin care, and spiritual guidance. Prices are quite reasonable, and there are different times when the soaking pools are available exclusively for visitors who identify as female, male, transgender/genderqueer, or BIPoC (black, indigenous, and people of color). ✉ 5010 N.E. 33rd Ave., Woodlawn/Concordia ☎ 503/238-1065 ⊕ www.cgwc.org.

⭐ Crafty Wonderland

Although the Alberta branch of this whimsically named arts and crafts gallery is smaller than the original Downtown location, it still showcases the handmade cards, books, apparel, jewelry, household goods, and toys of more than 60 carefully selected makers. Crafty Wonderland also hosts two huge annual markets, featuring works by about 250 artists, in May and December at the Oregon Convention Center. ✉ *2022 N.E. Alberta St., Alberta Arts District* ☎ *503/281–4616* ⊕ *www.craftywonderland.com.*

Darling Distraction

The staff at this jewelry and beauty boutique would love nothing more than happily distracting customers by pointing out colorful and quirky candles, acrylic hair clips, berets, totes, hoop earrings, lip gloss, and other baubles and tchotchkes. The vibe is decidedly youthful and free-spirited. ✉ *1524 N.E. Alberta St., Alberta Arts District* ☎ *971/279–2943* ⊕ *www.darlingdistraction.com.*

EcoVibe Home

This stylish, green-conscious lifestyle shop—a sister to EcoVibe Apparel, just down the street—is filled with gorgeous accents for your home and garden: bamboo planters, horticulture coffee-table books, throw pillows, laser-cut greeting cards, soy candles, modern jewelry, and dozens of actual houseplants. EcoVibe makes a lot of its own apparel and accessories and also carries noted sustainability-focused brands like Ética Denim

---

ART IN THE WILD

The Alberta Arts District boasts one of the city's largest collections of street art, with remarkably detailed, often riotously colorful murals covering numerous walls along about 25 blocks of Alberta Street. At ⊕ *PDXStreetArt.org,* you can download a PDF guide to the most significant murals, but also be sure to watch for less conspicuous examples, like the cheeky painting of a little girl standing over a bowl with a little pig in it, above the front door of Boxer Ramen.

---

and Corkcicle kitchenwear. ✉ *1906 N.E. Alberta St., Alberta Arts District* ☎ *503/266–9538* ⊕ *www.ecovibestyle.com.*

⭐ Grayling Jewelry

All of the locally made pieces at this friendly boutique have been carefully and exquisitely designed with sensitive skin in mind—every piece is nickel-free. The simply elegant lariat necklaces, chain-cuff earrings, and wrap rings are done mostly in silver and gold and displayed in a clean, unobtrusive storefront on Alberta Street. ✉ *1609 N.E. Alberta St., Alberta Arts District* ☎ *503/548–4979* ⊕ *www.graylingjewelry.com.*

⭐ Last Thursdays on Alberta

The Alberta Arts District hosts an arts walk on the last Thursday of each month. This quirky procession along 15 blocks of one of the city's favorite thoroughfares for browsing art galleries, distinctive boutiques, and hipster bars and restaurants features street performers and buskers, crafts makers, and food vendors. During the three summer events, from June through August, the street is closed to traffic from 6 to 9 pm, and many more arts and crafts vendors show their work. ⊠ N.E. Alberta St. and N.E. 22nd Ave., Alberta Arts District.

Monograph Bookwerks

The fascinating, idiosyncratic selection of art books and ephemera at this cozy shop just off Alberta reveals the thoughtful eye of its owner. You'll find long-out-of-print art and graphic design books, rare small-press editions, and issues of highly collectible discontinued magazines, along with literary-minded objets d'art, from bookends to a priceless NYC subway drawing by Keith Haring. ⊠ 5005 N.E. 27th Ave., Alberta Arts District ☎ 503/284–5005 ⊕ www.monographbookwerks.com ☉ Closed Mon.–Thurs.

pedX Shoe Shangri-La

The fashion-savvy owners of this cool footwear emporium in a sleek contemporary showroom on Alberta opened in 2003 with a mission to bring urbane women's shoes and accessories to outer Northeast Portland. Here you'll find sturdy boots, sensible flats, and swanky pumps from brands like Camper, El Naturalista, Miz Mooz, and Vagabond, plus an extensive selection of jewelry, sunglasses, handbags, and other accents. ⊠ 2005 N.E. Alberta St., Alberta Arts District ☎ 503/460–0760 ⊕ www.pedxshoes.com.

Rerun

Treasures, some of them bargain-priced, await at this 2,000-square-foot, eco-minded resale and consignment shop that specializes in antique and not-so-old furniture, clothing, movies, music, toys, and collectibles. There's a second branch farther out on Northeast Sandy Boulevard. ⊠ 707 N.E. Fremont St., Irvington ☎ 503/517–3786 ⊕ www.portlandrerun.com ☉ Closed Tues.

Tumbleweed

Carrying fun and stylish designer clothing, you might describe Tumbleweed as "country chic," for the woman who likes to wear flirty feminine dresses with cowboy boots. There's also baby and toddler clothing in their children's shop next door, Grasshopper. ⊠ 1812 N.E. Alberta St., Alberta Arts District ☎ 503/335–3100 ⊕ www.tumbleweed-boutique.com.

☕ Coffee and Quick Bites

Barista

$ | Café. If you're looking to test-drive some of the country's top beans, this café with other locations Downtown, in the Pearl, and in Nob Hill is a great option, offering brews from Sightglass, Intelligentsia, and other noted roasters as well as their own house coffees. In this high-ceilinged café with ample indoor and outdoor seating, you'll also find a few craft beers and a small selection of high-quality chocolates and desserts. **Known for:** daily-changing specialty coffee drinks; mochas with Valrhona chocolate; locations in several popular neighborhoods. *Average main: $5* ⊠ *1725 N.E. Alberta St., Alberta Arts District* ☎ *503/208–2568* ⊕ *www.baristapdx.com* ⊗ *No dinner.*

Bushel & Peck Bakeshop

$ | Bakery. As much a coffee-house—serving first-rate espresso drinks that feature locally roasted Trailhead beans—as a bakery, this charming hole-in-the-wall café serves rave-worthy pastries, like blueberry-lavender muffins, three-cheese asparagus-and-basil scones, and roasted-pear–gingerbread coffee cake. The daily chalkboard selection of breakfast and lunch sandwiches is absolutely worth a look, too. **Known for:** unusual muffin and pastry flavors; breakfast biscuit sandwiches; limited, partially communal, seating. *Average main: $6* ⊠ *3907 N.E. Martin Luther King Jr. Blvd., North Williams Ave.* ☎ *503/206–8953* ⊕ *www.bushelandpeckpdx.com* ⊗ *No dinner.*

Guilder

$ | Café. Clean lines, natural light, and angular, modern tables (some communal) define the Scandinavian aesthetic of this bi-level café in the mostly residential—and quite pictur-esque—Alameda neighborhood, close to Beaumont's commercial strip. Drop by to work or socialize over cappuccinos or "freelancer" cocktails (espresso and fernet), or dig into a bowl of porridge, a fried egg and avocado sandwich, or a salad of roasted beets with a dill-chive yogurt dressing. **Known**

for: tartines and sandwiches; a well-chosen mix of espresso drinks and cocktails; spacious, airy dining rooms well-suited to work or conversation. *Average main: $9* ⊠ *2393 N.E. Fremont St., Beaumont* ☎ *503/841–6042* ⊕ *www.guildercafe. com.*

★ Proud Mary

$ | Australian. Launched in 2009 in Melbourne, Australia, this third-wave coffeehouse that sources its beans sustainably from around the world opened a U.S. location on Alberta Street in 2017. In this light-filled post-industrial space, you can savor perfectly prepared espresso drinks alongside tasty breakfast and lunch fare, such as Singapore chili crab omelets and grilled croissant brioches with cured ham, blackened corn, and poached egg. **Known for:** avocado and other breakfast toasts; healthy, inventive salads; flat whites. *Average main: $12* ⊠ *2012 N.E. Alberta St., Alberta Arts District* ☎ *503/208–3475* ⊕ *www.proudmary-coffee.com* ⊗ *No dinner.*

★ Salt & Straw Ice Cream

$ | Café. This artisan ice cream shop began here with this still always-packed cafe in the Alberta Arts District and continues to wow the public with its wildly inventive classics as well as seasonal flavors (freckled-chocolate zucchini bread and green fennel and maple are a couple of recent examples). Locally produced Woodblock chocolate bars and house-made salted-caramel sauce are among the toppings, and the related Wiz Bang Bar in Old Town's Pine Street Market offers delicious softserve. **Known for:** strawberry-honey-balsamic ice cream with black pepper; monthly rotating specialty flavors; flavor collaborations with local chefs and restaurants. *Average main: $5* ✉ *2035 N.E. Alberta St., Alberta Arts District* ☎ *971/208–3867* ⊕ *www. saltandstraw.com.*

Seastar Bakery

$ | Bakery. Devoted to sourcing grains from local organic farms— and serving chocolate, coffee, and tea from some of the city's best purveyors—and baking all of its products in a wood-fired oven, Seastar produces heavenly breads, including seeded whole-grain challah, nutty dark rye, and rosemary cornbread. You can order any toast with a variety of toppings (tahini, bacon, chevre, raw honey), or try one of the savory breakfast and lunch dishes. **Known for:** artisan toasts with unusual toppings; sweet and savory baked goods; house-made hot chocolate. *Average main: $7* ✉ *1603 N.E. Killingsworth St., Woodlawn/Concordia* ☎ *503/247–7499* ⊕ *www.seastarbakery.com* ☙ *Closed Tues. No dinner.*

¶¶ Dining

Acadia

$$$ | Creole. For all of its barbecue restaurants, Portland is surprisingly lacking when it comes to New Orleans fare, but this Cajun and Creole bistro in Irvington serves well-seasoned and authentic food along with a great cocktail list. Along with classic crawfish étouffée,

jambalaya, and seafood gumbo, you'll find some Pacific Northwest variations like cornmeal-fried Willapa Bay oysters with miso remoulade, and local peaches with hazelnuts and chevrè. **Known for:** Creole and Cajun seafood; bargain-priced three-course prix-fixe menu (Mondays only); vanilla bread pudding with salted-caramel sauce. *Average main: $26* ✉ *1303 N.E. Fremont St., Irvington* ☎ *503/249–5001* ⊕ *www.acadiapdx.com* ☙ *Closed Sun. No lunch Thurs.–Tues.*

Akadi PDX

$$ | African. This casual but colorful West African restaurant owned by a Portland State University grad who originally hails originally from the Ivory Coast serves an impressive array of dishes from throughout West Africa. Grilled tilapia with sweet plantains, fermented cassava couscous with Dijon-marinated chicken, and slow-cooked goat in a rich tomato stew are among the standouts, and *gbofloto* (fried beignets with powdered sugar) make for a sweet ending. **Known for:** hearty West African stews; live music Friday–Sunday; full bar and Kenyan beer (but no craft brew options). *Average main: $17* ✉ *3601 N.E. Martin Luther King Jr. Blvd., North Williams Ave.* ☎ *503/477–7138* ⊕ *www.akadipdx.com* ☙ *Closed Mon.*

Aviary

$$$ | Asian Fusion. Eschewing many culinary conventions, this visionary Alberta Street eatery serves up innovative dishes that sometimes push boundaries but consistently succeed in flavor and execution.

The simple menu of small plates (order two to three per person) is influenced by Asian flavors and uses European cooking techniques, combining unusual ingredients that offer pleasing contrasts in flavor and texture, such as crispy pig ears over mildly sweet coconut rice, and hoisin-glazed beef brisket with a macaroni salad croquette and sour mango powder. **Known for:** vegetarian tasting menu option; knowledgeable, helpful service; artfully presented food. *Average main: $27 ⊠ 1733 N.E. Alberta St., Alberta Arts District ☎ 503/287–2400 ⊕ www.aviarypdx.com ⊗ Closed Sun. No lunch.*

Beast

$$$$ | Pacific Northwest. This meat-centric exemplar of Portland's cutting-edge culinary scene is the domain of James Beard Award–winning chef-owner Naomi Pomeroy, who oversees a six-course prix-fixe dinner (and three-course brunch on Sunday) that changes weekly, depending on the meat at the market. Most dishes are prepared right before your eyes in the open kitchen: there might be an ahi crudo with smoked pine nuts and pickled ginger, or wagyu coulottte with pink pepper-corn–cognac sauce. **Known for:** communal seating overlooking open kitchen; some of the most creative meat-centric food in the city; sublime Sunday brunch. *Average main: $118 ⊠ 5425 N.E. 30th Ave., Woodlawn/Concordia ☎ 503/841–6968 ⊕ www.beastpdx.com ⊗ Closed Mon. No lunch except Sun. brunch.*

Dame

$$$ | European. In Concordia's mini dining hub around 30th and Killingsworth, this snug bistro with French doors, soft lighting, and an endearing mishmash of antiques and old paintings feels European in its sensibility and focus on simple, seasonal fare. A typical meal might feature peach-tomato gazpacho, followed by a rabbit cavatelli pasta with guanciale, ricotta, and chile flakes. **Known for:** handmade pastas tossed with seasonal ingredients; friendly and knowledgeable service; an extensive and international list of natural wines. *Average main: $25 ⊠ 2930 N.E. Killingsworth St., Woodlawn/Concordia ☎ 503/227–2669 ⊕ www.damerestaurant.com ⊗ Closed Mon.–Tues. No lunch.*

DOC

$$$ | Italian. With red-checked curtains and candlelit tables draped in white linens, cozy DOC is an authentic nod to casual Italian neighborhood trattorias, but the gorgeously presented cuisine here borrows heavily from the Pacific Northwest. Although you're free to order everything à la carte, most guests opt for the tasting menu, which comprises six courses for $75 (it's an additional $60 for wine pair-ings) and might feature halibut with a romesco sauce, Pacific oysters on the half shell with a hibiscus vinaigrette, and olive oil cake with strawberry, pine nuts, and tarragon. **Known for:** family-style suppers offered on Sundays; extraordinary selection of natural and difficult-to-procure wines; local seafood prepared with Italian-inspired recipes. *Average main: $27* ✉ *5519 N.E. 30th Ave., Woodlawn/Concordia* ☎ *503/946–8592* ⊕ *www.docpdx.com* ✆ *Closed Mon. No lunch.*

Firehouse Restaurant

$$ | Italian. Occupying a stately, redbrick, former firehouse, this inviting neighborhood spot in Woodlawn is warmed by a wood-fire oven, rustic redbrick-and-wood decor, and sunlight streaming through a glass garage door that's open in nice weather. Although justly well-known for the delicious thin-crust pizzas (try the one with chanterelles, garlic, mozzarella, and thyme), the restaurant receives deserved kudos for its appetizers, salads, and grills, from lightly battered and perfectly fried cauliflower with crème fraîche to meatballs with tomato, rosemary, and kale. **Known for:** affordable three-course prix fixe that includes appetizer, salad, and pizza; well-curated list of after-dinner drinks; wood-fired pizzas. *Average main: $20* ✉ *711 N.E. Dekum St., Woodlawn/Concordia* ☎ *503/954–1702* ⊕ *www.firehousepdx.com* ✆ *No lunch.*

Grain & Gristle

$$$ | Modern American. At this rustic gastropub with timber-beam ceilings and polished wood floors and tables, the kitchen embraces a tail-to-snout approach to food, which includes a great burger, perfectly grilled honey-roasted pork chops, and a beautifully plated meat-and-cheese board. You'll find several excellent seafood options as well, and on weekends, the restaurant presents a popular brunch. **Known for:** prodigious burgers; blueberry waffles with blueberry-lime-thyme syrup at brunch; easy walk from Alberta Arts District. *Average main: $24* ✉ *1473 N.E. Prescott St., Alberta Arts District* ☎ *503/288–4740* ⊕ *www.grainand-gristle.com* ✆ *No lunch Tues.–Thurs.*

★ Hat Yai

$ | Thai. Operated by the acclaimed chef behind Langbaan and Eem, this cozy and casual counter-service eatery takes its name from a small Thai city near the Malaysian border and its concept from that region's spicy and delicious fried chicken with sticky rice and rich Malayu-style curries with panfried roti bread. Other treats here uncommon to Thai restaurant culture in the States include fiery turmeric curry with mussels and heady lemon-grass oxtail soup. **Known for:** the roti dessert with condensed milk; perfectly crunchy free-range fried chicken; good selection of Asian beers. *Average main: $14* ✉ *1605 N.E. Killingsworth St., Woodlawn/Concordia* ☎ *503/764–9701* ⊕ *www.hatyaipdx.com.*

Kargi Gogo

$ | European. Two former Peace Corps workers run this cute and cozy café devoted to the food and wine of the Republic of Georgia, where they lived for nearly three years. The menu provides a delicious introduction to this culinarily blessed nation, serving up hearty *khachapuri* (breads stuffed with pepper bacon, cheese, and vegetables), lamb dumplings, and cold cucumber-yogurt soup, and stocking an extensive list of Georgian wines, to enjoy on site or for purchase to go. **Known for:** khinkali soup dumplings; a 100% Georgian wine list; sampler appetizer platters of cheese, bread, and fermented vegetables. *Average main: $11* ⊠ *3039 N.E. Alberta St., Alberta Arts District* ☎ *503/764–9552* ⊕ *www.kargigogo.com* ☽ *Closed Mon. No lunch Tues.–Thurs.*

★ Ned Ludd

$$$ | Pacific Northwest. Named for the founder of the Luddites, the group that resisted the technological advances of the Industrial Revolution, this Northwest-inspired kitchen prepares its food the most low-tech way possible: in a wood-burning brick oven, over an open flame. Sourcing most of its ingredients locally (or carefully, if they come from afar), Ned Ludd's menu varies completely depending on the season and weather, and the from-the-earth theme continues through to the decor, which incorporates salvaged wood, dried flowers, and small succulent plants under glass domes. **Known for:** whole roasted trout with charred leeks; nice selection of craft ciders; a $60 per person family-style dinner option that features some of the kitchen's most interesting food. *Average main: $27* ⊠ *3925 N.E. Martin Luther King Blvd., North Williams Ave.* ☎ *503/288–6900* ⊕ *www.nedluddpdx.com* ☽ *No lunch.*

★ Pine State Biscuits

$ | Southern. Loosen your belt a notch or two before venturing inside this down-home Southern restaurant that's especially beloved for its over-the-top breakfast biscuit fare. Pat yourself on the back, or belly, if you can polish off the Reggie Deluxe (a fluffy house-baked biscuit topped with fried chicken, bacon, cheese, an egg, and sage gravy), a masterful mélange of calorie-laden ingredients, or the gut-busting smoked-brisket-club biscuit sandwich, shrimp and grits, and andouille corn dog featuring locally made Otto's sausage. **Known for:** made-from-scratch seasonal fruit pies; arguably the best food stall at the Portland Farmers Market; the massive Reggie Deluxe sandwich. *Average main: $9* ⊠ *2204 N.E. Alberta St., Alberta Arts District* ☎ *503/477–6605* ⊕ *www.pinestatebiscuits.com* ☽ *No dinner.*

Podnah's Pit BBQ

$$ | Barbecue. Firing up the smoker at 5 every morning, the pit crew at Podnah's spends the day slow cooking some of the best Texas- and Carolina-style barbecue in the Northwest, including melt-in-your-mouth, oak-smoked brisket, ribs, pulled pork, chicken, whole trout, and lamb, all served up in a sassy vinegar-based sauce. Some sides, like the delicious green-chili mac and cheese, rotate on and off the menu, but the collard greens, barbecue baked beans, and the iceberg wedge, topped with blue cheese and a punchy Thousand Island dressing, are excellent mainstays. **Known for:** green-chili mac and cheese (when available); daily specials (fried catfish on Friday, smoked lamb on Thursday);

casual and lively vibe. *Average main: $18* ⊠ *1625 N.E. Killingsworth St., Woodlawn/Concordia* ☎ *503/281-3700* ⊕ *www.podnahspit.com.*

Ranch Pizza

$ | Pizza. If you love your pizza with a thick crust that's crunchy on the bottom and chewy on top, head to this purveyor of square-cut Detroit-style pies. On warm days, try to snag one of the wooden booths out on the sidewalk. **Known for:** Detroit-meets-Sicilian-style pizzas; house-made ranch sauce served on the side; focaccia bread sticks with garlicky red dipping sauce. *Average main: $13* ⊠ *1760 N.E. Dekum St., Woodlawn/Concordia* ☎ *971/288-5187* ⊕ *www.ranchpdx.com.*

★ Tamale Boy

$ | Mexican. While the cooks at this lively counter-service restaurant are adept at preparing tamales—both the Oaxacan style wrapped in banana leaves and the more conventional style wrapped in corn husks (try the version filled with roasted pasilla peppers, onions, corn kernels, and queso fresco)—the kitchen also turns out fabulous ceviche and *alambre de camarones* (adobo shrimp with bacon and Oaxacan cheese over flat corn tortillas). Be sure to check out the colorful murals that decorate the space and don't miss the chance to dine on the spacious side patio. **Known for:** the El Diablo margarita with roasted-habanero-infused tequila and mango puree; tableside gaucamole; hearty and filling tamales. *Average main: $11* ⊠ *1764 N.E. Dekum St., Woodlawn/Concordia*

☎ *503/206-8022* ⊕ *www.tamaleboy. com.*

Tiffin Asha

$ | South Indian. Set in an urbane high-ceilinged space with tall windows and wood-bench tables, this contemporary Indian restaurant focuses on the country's southern states, offering a half-dozen crispy, crepe-like dosas filled with both traditional spices and vegetables and Western ingredients (like Rogue Creamery smoky blue cheese with honey and fleur de sel). The free-wheeling culinary approach leads to some unexpected and unusual dishes, with *idli* (fermented rice cakes), *uttapams* (reminiscent of croquettes), and savory dal donut holes rounding out the menu. **Known for:** house-made gunpowders (flavor-packed powdered spice mixes), chutneys, and pickles; big portions; Sunday brunch. *Average main: $12* ⊠ *1670 N.E. Killingsworth St., Woodlawn/Concordia* ☎ *503/936-7663* ⊕ *www.tiffinasha.com* ⊙ *Closed Mon.–Fri. No dinner.*

Tin Shed Garden Cafe

$ | Café. This busy, informal restaurant on Alberta Street is known for its hearty breakfasts—namely, its biscuits and gravy, shredded-potato cakes, egg and tofu scrambles, and breakfast burritos—but the lunch menu offers plenty of creative choices as well, like a creamy artichoke sandwich and a mac and cheese of the day. With a large stone fireplace and chimney, the covered, comfortable outdoor area doubles as a beer garden on warm spring and summer days, and the adjacent garden rounds off the property with a peaceful sitting area. **Known for:** dog-friendly patio (and special menu); cozy ambience with stone fireplace; picturesque and cheerful outdoor seating. *Average main: $15* ✉ *1438 N.E. Alberta St., Alberta Arts District* ☎ *503/288–6966* ⊕ *www.tinshedgardencafe.com* ☾ *No dinner.*

Urdaneta

$$ | Tapas. One of the most sophisticated restaurants on generally funky Alberta, this romantic spot with an open kitchen produces out-of-this-world Basque-inspired tapas and pinxtos (or pinchos) and stocks an encyclopedic selection of Spanish wines and sherries. Northwestern ingredients figure prominently in these Iberian dishes—consider the Oregon albacore crudo with ground cherries, and grilled spare ribs with pickled peaches and sherry caramel. **Known for:** weeknight pinxtos hour, featuring great deals on bar snacks and house wines; house-made ice cream and other exceptional desserts; four-year-aged Jamón ibérico. *Average main: $20* ✉ *3033 N.E. Alberta St., Alberta Arts District* ☎ *503/288–1990* ⊕ *www.urdanetapdx.com* ☾ *Closed Mon. No lunch.*

Verdigris

$$$ | French. On a small strip of laudable restaurants and bars between Irvington and Alberta, this elegantly contemporary space with wrought-iron chandeliers offers market-driven French cuisine that bridges traditional and contemporary approaches. Consider starting off your repast with a duck confit salad or smoked-pork rillettes, before graduating to local coho salmon with white beans and fennel oil or classic beef Bourguignon. **Known for:** bargain-priced three-course prix-fixe option; weekend brunch; fallen chocolate soufflé. *Average main: $28* ✉ *1315 N.E. Fremont St., Irvington* ☎ *503/477–8106* ⊕ *www.verdigrisrestaurant.com* ☾ *No lunch weekdays.*

🍸 Bars and Nightlife

The Bye and Bye

An Alberta go-to specializing in creative drinks (sample the house favorite, the Bye and Bye, a refreshing concoction of peach vodka, peach bourbon, lemon, cranberry juice, and soda served in a Mason jar) and vegan fare, Bye and Bye has a big covered patio and a festive dining room. The owners also operate several other similarly trendy bars around town, including Century Bar, Dig a Pony, Sweet Hereafter, and Jackknife. ✉ *1011 N.E. Alberta St., Alberta Arts District* ☎ *503/281–0537* ⊕ *www.thebyeandbye.com.*

★ Expatriate

Operated by Kyle Webster and his wife, celeb-chef partner Naomi Pomeroy of Beast (across the street), this intimate, candlelit spot has a devoted following for its balanced, boozy cocktails and addictively delicious Asian bar snacks, like Burmese curried noodles. Each of the eight nightly cocktails are meticulously crafted. ✉ *5424*

N.E. 30th Ave., Woodlawn/Concordia ☏ *503/805-3750* ⊕ *www.expatri-atepdx.com.*

Free House

Look to this rustic-chic urban pub with a snug heated back patio for sophisticated cocktails and carefully selected beer and wine lists. Friendly and in a quiet area a bit south of Alberta, it's a great venue for dates and conversation, and there's first-rate bar fare on offer—think creatively prepared burgers, sausage plates, and salads. ⊠ *1325 N.E. Fremont St., Irvington* ☏ *503/946-8161* ⊕ *www.freehousepdx.com.*

Jinx

A welcome rarity in Portland, Jinx works hard to be a family-friendly spot for food yet still grown-up-enough in personality to be a nice option for drinking adults (kids are welcome here daily until 8 pm, and there's a nice kids menu, too). It's in a handsome corner space amid the cluster of buzzy restaurants at Killingsworth and 30th, and the entertaining diversions include a slew of pinball machines and satisfyingly good pub fare. ⊠ *3000 N.E. Killingsworth St., Woodlawn/Concordia* ☏ *503/288-8075* ⊕ *www.jinxpdx.com.*

The Knock Back

A highly popular lounge in the heart of Alberta, the Knock Back does several things well: there's a good-value happy hour, live music some evenings, two different outdoor spaces as well as a warmly lighted interior, and an impressively varied and affordable selection of food and drink. ⊠ *2315 N.E. Alberta St., Alberta Arts District* ☏ *503/284-4090* ⊕ *www.theknockback.com.*

Local Lounge

Welcoming to all but especially popular with LGBTQ folks, this unpretentious spot on MLK keeps things interesting with a slew of events and theme nights, including Ru Paul's Drag Race viewing parties, jazz shows, reggae parties, and bear beer busts. ⊠ *3536 N.E. Martin Luther King Jr Blvd., Irvington* ☏ *503/282-1833* ⊕ *www.locallounge.wordpress.com.*

Radio Room

A big, rambling tavern set inside a converted art deco Texaco station, Radio Room offers two levels of heated outdoor space as well as a couple of roomy inside areas, one warmed by a fireplace. It's a popular destination for coffee and pecking away on your laptop during the day, and dining on eclectic comfort food at any time, but it's especially lively at night as a neighborhood drinkery that boasts a lengthy cocktail and beer menu. ⊠ *1101 N.E. Alberta St., Alberta Arts District* ☏ *503/287-2346* ⊕ *www.radioroompdx.com.*

Retro Game Bar

The name says it all at this gamer-inspired hangout whose bar is backlit with bright video game lights and framed by a bunch of vintage game consoles. Order drinks and pub grub, grab a seat at a table or sofa, and play Mario Kart, Donkey Kong, and countless other video and board games from your childhood to your heart's content. There's even video game–themed art for sale on the walls. ✉ *6720 N.E. Martin Luther King Jr. Blvd., Woodlawn/Concordia* ☎ *971/271–8079* ⊕ *www.rgbpdx.com.*

 Performing Arts

Alberta Rose Theatre
This 300-seat theater began life in the 1920s as a movie house, but today you can catch a mix of pop and jazz concerts, plays, burlesque shows, arts festivals, lectures, and tapings of the public radio show *Live Wire.* This handsome venue in the Alberta Arts District has exceptional acoustics. ✉ *3000 N.E. Alberta St., Alberta Arts District* ☎ *503/719–6055* ⊕ *www.albertarosetheatre.com.*

Curious Comedy Theater
Improv shows are the bread and butter of this popular comedy venue, which also offers classes and occasionally brings in regional and national talents. ✉ *5225 N.E. Martin Luther King Jr. Blvd., Alberta Arts District* ☎ *503/477–9477* ⊕ *www.curiouscomedy.org.*

★ Kennedy School Theater
Furnished with couches and end tables, the Kennedy School theater, which is located in a renovated elementary school that also contains a hotel, a restaurant, several bars, and a soaking pool, screens second-run and occasional indie movies. ✉ *5736 N.E. 33rd Ave., Woodlawn/Concordia* ☎ *503/249–3983* ⊕ *www.mcmenamins.com/kennedy-school.*

Portland Playhouse
This volunteer-driven nonprofit community theater near the Alberta Arts District uses the performing arts to bring together people of all ages and backgrounds—community engagement and creating empathy and understanding through story-telling are key objectives of this terrific grassroots organization. The theater, which occupies a handsome old wood-frame church, presents a wide range of shows throughout the year. ✉ *602 N.E. Prescott St., Alberta Arts District* ☎ *503/488–5822* ⊕ *www.portlandplayhouse.org.*

Hollywood and Beaumont

 Sights

Beaumont Village
This attractive 20-block commercial strip of Northeast Fremont Street has long served the surrounding Beaumont-Wilshire neighborhood as well as the adjoining districts of Alameda, Cully, and Grant Park. Commonly referred to as Beaumont, the stretch of neatly maintained one- and two-story storefronts contains mostly independently owned businesses, including a fairly new spate of attention-getting eateries and bars, such as Hi-Top Tavern, Prince Coffee, Wonderly, and the more well-established doughnut destination, Pip's. It's much more low-key and less-touristy than Alberta or Division, making it an enjoyable spot for a relaxing stroll and a bite to eat. Just up the hill from the Hollywood District, the neighborhood was named (it means

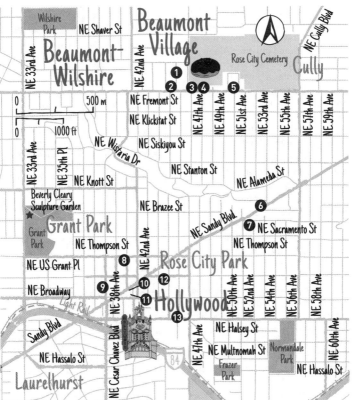

SIGHTS
Beaumont Village 1
Hollywood District 13
Hollywood
Public Library................ 8

SHOPPING
Hollywood
Farmers Market........... 12

COFFEE & QUICK BITES
Bakeshop...................... 6
Pip's Doughnuts............. 4
Prince Coffee 2

DINING
Gado Gado 9
Hogan's Goat Pizza........ 7
Vivienne Kitchen &
Pantry 10

BARS & NIGHTLIFE
Hi-Top Tavern 5
Wonderly 3

PERFORMING ARTS
Hollywood Theatre....... 11

"beautiful mountain" in French) by its original real estate developers in 1910 as a way to promote its slightly elevated position. Along the adjoining residential streets you'll encounter a pleasing mix of early-20th-century Colonial Revival, Tudor, and Arts and Crafts homes. ⊠ *N.E. Fremont St. between N.E. 38th and 57th Aves., Beaumont* ⊕ *www.beaumontvillagepdx.com.*

Hollywood District

A bustling hub of small indie and larger franchise businesses surrounded by apartment buildings and blocks of early 20th-century homes, Hollywood is named for the iconic 1926 Spanish Colonial movie theater at its center. One of Northeast Portland's key transportation hubs, it contains both a stop on the MAX light rail red, blue, and yellow lines and an exit off Interstate 84; it's also bisected by the major commercial thoroughfares of Sandy Boulevard, Cesar E. Chavez Boulevard, and Broadway Street. More established and less cutting edge than some of the East Side's buzzier sections, it nonetheless contains several notable draws, including the aforementioned movie theater, one of the city's best farmers markets, and a growing number of cool places to shop and eat. ⊠ *From N.E. 37th Ave. east to N.E. 47th Ave., between Interstate 84 and N.E. Thompson St., Hollywood/Rose City Park.*

Hollywood Public Library

Fans of celebrated children's and young-adult novelist Beverly Cleary might want to stop by this

WORTH A TRIP

On the eastern edge of metro Portland (about a 20-minute drive from the Hollywood District), Troutdale has a cute downtown and is the gateway to the 75-mile-long Historic Columbia River Highway. Stop for lunch or gourmet softserve at the hip Sugarpine Drive-In, which adjoins a wooded park on the Sandy River, or explore the decidedly offbeat McMenamins Edgefield resort, which has a winery, brewery, distillery, concert venue, spa, and 74 acres of gardens and orchards.

library branch, which occupies a modern building at 40th Avenue and Tillamook Street. The author lived in the neighborhood and worked for a time at a previous location of the library, and she based her Ramona and Henry books on her life here. You can view displays about her at the library and pick up a walking tour of Cleary-related neighborhood sites, which include the Grant Park Beverly Cleary Statue Garden, home to life-size statues of Ramona, Henry, and—of course—Ribsy. Note that many businesses in the adjoining Grant Park (to the west) and Rose City Park (to the east) neighborhoods identify as being part of Hollywood, which is more prominently known around the city. ⊠ *4040 N.E. Tillamook St., Hollywood/Rose City Park* ☎ *503/988–5123* ⊕ *www.multcolib.org/library-location/hollywood.*

Shopping

Hollywood Farmers Market

One of the best of the many farmers' markets in this city with more than a dozen good ones, this popular gathering takes place on Saturday mornings (every other Saturday in winter) and carries a bounty array of seasonal Oregon goods: fresh berries in summer, asparagus in spring, apples and pears in fall. You'll also find several food stalls selling tasty breakfast fare, from Suzette Creperie to Fleur de Lis Bakery, as well as artisan products from 503 Distilling, Central City Coffee, Fraga Farmstead Creamery, Mt. Tabor Bread, and Hot Mama Salsa. ⊠ *4420 N.E. Hancock St., Hollywood/Rose City Park* ☎ *503/709-7403* ⊕ *www. hollywoodfarmersmarket.org.*

 Coffee and Quick Bites

★ **Bakeshop**

$ | Bakery. A James Beard award-winning cookbook author who's trained with some of America's most celebrated bakers runs this beautiful little shop that doles out ethereal whole-grain strawberry-barley scones, corn-and-Gruyère muffins, marionberry jam shortbread cookies, brown-butter-apple handpies, and—well, the list goes on and on. **Known for:** baguette sandwiches; house-made granola; stunning cakes and pies with seasonal ingredients. *Average main: $7* ⊠ *5351 N.E. Sandy Blvd., Hollywood/Rose City Park* ☎ *503/946-8884* ⊕ *www.bakeshoppdx. com* ☉ *Closed Mon.-Tues. No dinner.*

★ **Pip's Doughnuts**

$ | Bakery. More than a few aficionados of these classic American sweets claim Pip's has the best doughnuts in a town that's pretty serious about them. These miniature made-to-order confections are just a little crispy on the outside and moist within, and they come in flavors such as honey-sea salt, candied-bacon-maple, and several other delectable flavors. **Known for:** house-made chai in several unusual flavors; sometimes long lines, especially on weekends; seasonal flavors like strawberry-rhubarb and Meyer lemon-pear. *Average main: $5* ⊠ *4759 N.E. Fremont St., Beaumont* ☎ *503/206-8692* ☉ *No dinner.*

Prince Coffee

$ | Café. Head to this airy, minimalist-chic Beaumont café with Dutch provenance for top-grade coffee drinks, but also to sample a famous treat from the Netherlands: *stroopwafel* (caramel-filled wafer cookies), which are baked fresh here daily. They also serve sandwiches and other goodies from the nearby Bakeshop bakery. **Known for:** stroopwafel cookies; sandwiches and other baked goods; coffee from some of the city's best purveyors. *Average main: $5* ⊠ *4523 NE Fremont St., Beaumont* ⊕ *www.princecoffeepdx.com* ☉ *No dinner.*

🍴 **Dining**

★ **Gado Gado**

$$ | Indonesian. Bold colors play a central role in the look and culinary approach of this trendy restaurant, from the tropical-print wallpaper to the ornately ornamented tableware, and above all else in the consistently delicious Indonesian fare. Roti with coconut-cream corn, braised-beef Rendang with kumquats, and Coca Cola clams steamed with chilies and lemongrass reflect the kitchen's creative and sometimes surprising interpretation of a cuisine that's gotten very little play in Portland until recently. **Known for:** family-style ($55 per person) "rice table" featuring a wide selection of chef favorites; whole wok-fried Dungeness crabs; weekend brunch with mimosas. *Average main: $17 ⊠ 1801 N.E. Cesar E. Chavez Blvd., Hollywood/Rose City Park ☎ 503/206-8778 ⊕ www.gadogadopdx.com ⊙ Closed Tues. No lunch weekdays.*

Hogan's Goat Pizza

$ | Pizza. This friendly little pizza joint on the edge of the Hollywood District doubles as a wine shop with an excellent, affordable selection that's available to drink in-house or to go. The reasonably priced pizzas are excellent, particularly the Unami, with a garlic-olive oil base, crimini mushrooms, truffle oil, sheep feta, and spinach. **Known for:** outstanding wine selection; gluten-free crust options; creative pie-of-the-week specials. *Average main: $15 ⊠ 5222 N.E. Sacramento St., Hollywood/Rose City Park ☎ 503/281-9008 ⊕ www.hogansgoatpizza.com ⊙ Closed Mon.–Tues. No lunch.*

Vivienne Kitchen + Pantry

$ | Café. Fresh flowers grace the tables of this refreshingly sweet and simple storefront in Hollywood that's built a devoted following for rustic breakfast and lunch fare that showcases produce from local farms and biscuits and toasts baked in-house. Egg sandwiches with brie and duck confit, and vegetable tians topped crispy potatoes and a poached egg reflect the kitchen's proclivity for recipes you might find in a Provençal farmhouse. **Known for:** a rotating selection of seasonal cakes and sweets; house-made granolas and porridge; an extensive collection of antique tea cups. *Average main: $11 ⊠ 4128 N.E. Sandy Blvd., Hollywood/Rose City Park ☎ 503/3842473 ⊕ www.viviennepdx.com ⊙ Closed Mon. No dinner.*

Bars and Nightlife

★ Hi-Top Tavern

A fun neighborhood bar in Beaumont with a lovely, cloistered, tree-shaded back patio, the Hi-Top pours a nice Manhattan and offers beers in a can "dressed" with sea salt, tajin, and grapefruit. Also note the menu of tasty bar bites, including harissa cauliflower and Cuban sandwiches. *⊠ 5015 N.E. Fremont St., Beaumont ☎ 503/206-4308 ⊕ www.hitoptavern.com.*

Wonderly

This dapper yet unpretentious neighborhood lounge anchored by a horseshoe-shaped bar is known for its generously poured "martini-and-a-half" and "Manhattan-and-a-half" cocktails, which are sure to calm your nerves after a long day. Folks also pile in for arguably the best bar food in Beaumont—the seared scallop with an egg, beet puree, and capers is a standout. ✉ *4727 N.E. Fremont St., Beaumont* ☎ *503/288–4520* ⊕ *www.wonderlypdx.com.*

 Performing Arts

★ **Hollywood Theatre**
A landmark movie theater that showed silent films when it opened in 1926, the not-for-profit Hollywood Theatre screens everything from obscure foreign art films to old American classics and second-run Hollywood hits, and hosts an annual Academy Awards viewing party. It also hosts a slew of film series and festivals, including the QDoc LGBTQ documentary film festival, the Grindhouse Film Festival, the Northwest Animation Festival, the Portland Latin American Film Festival, and POW, which showcases top women directors. ✉ *4122 N.E. Sandy Blvd., Hollywood/Rose City Park* ☎ *503/281–4215* ⊕ *www.hollywood-theatre.org.*

Outer Northeast

 Sights

The Grotto
Owned by the Catholic Church, the National Sanctuary of Our Sorrowful Mother, as it's officially known, displays more than 100 statues and shrines in 62 acres of woods that adjoin Rocky Butte Natural Area. The grotto was carved into the base of a 110-foot cliff, and has a replica of Michelangelo's *Pietà*. The real treat is found after ascending the cliff face via elevator, as you enter a wonderland of gardens, sculptures, and shrines, and a glass-walled cathedral with an awe-inspiring view of the Columbia River and the Cascades. There's a dazzling Christmas Festival of Lights (late November and December, $12.50), with 500,000 lights and more than 160 holiday concerts in the 500-seat chapel, and an indoor petting zoo. Daily masses are held here, too.
■ **TIP→** Hours can vary seasonally so call ahead if visiting late in the day. ✉ *8840 N.E. Skidmore St., Northeast* ✛ *Main entrance: N.E. Sandy Blvd. at N.E. 85th Ave.* ☎ *503/254–7371* ⊕ *www.thegrotto.org* ▧ *Plaza level free; upper level $8.*

Rocky Butte Natural Area
Although it's easy to view this forested, extinct cinder cone from the junction of the Interstate 205 and 5 freeways, relatively few visitors explore the scenic 18-acre park that covers a good portion of it. Rising about 600 feet above northeast Portland and adjoining

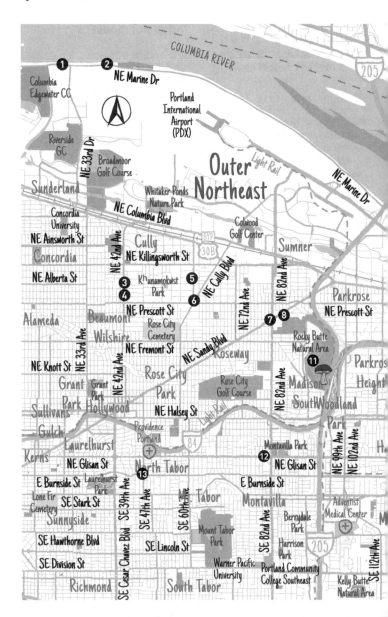

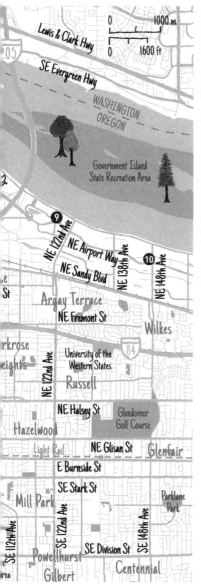

the area's other distinctive attraction, the Grotto, the scenic summit is reached—by car or bike—via a steep, twisting road and tunnel, and then a curving staircase, ornate lampposts, and stonewalls all constructed in the 1930s by the WPA in the distinctive style typical of similar projects in the area, like Timberline Lodge and Historic Columbia River Highway. From this 2.4-acre section of the butte, known officially as Joseph Wood Hill Park, you can see Mt. Hood and the other major volcanic peaks in the region as well as the Downtown skyline and planes taking off and landing nearby at Portland International Airport. There's a grassy lawn and picnic tables. Rocky Butte is a popular destination with experienced climbers, but even casual urban hikers can trek to the summit by way of a 1.2-mile trail that begins at the intersection of Northeast Skidmore Street and 92nd Avenue, and it's easy to combine a hike here with exploring the Grotto. ⊠ *3102 N.E. Rocky Butte Rd., Northeast* ☎ *503/823–7529* ⊕ *www. portlandoregon.gov/parks.*

 Shopping

Danner Factory Store

Since 1932, this Portland footwear company has been producing sturdy yet stylish boots for hiking and the outdoors. At their factory store near the airport, you can score terrific prices on seconds and discontinued items. ⊠ *12021 N.E. Airport Way, Northeast* ☎ *503/251–1111* ⊕ *www. stores.danner.com/factory-store.*

🍴 Dining

Angel Food & Fun

$ | Mexican. The specialty of this casual Mexican restaurant is the tropical—and relatively less spicy—cuisine food of the Yucatán Peninsula, with tender *cochinita pibil*, hearty *chocolomo* (beef soup with cilantro, radishes, and habanero) and *menudo* (beef tripe in a red chile broth), and flavorful *relleno negro* and *relleno blanco* (with turkey smothered in rich black or white sauces). The location is a bit out of the way, and the simple space is decorated with vibrantly colored tapestries and Yucateco artwork. **Known for:** cochinita pibil; cash only; pool tables in the adjoining lounge. *Average main: $10* ⊠ *5135 N.E. 60th Ave., Woodlawn/Concordia* ☎ *503/287–7909* ▭ *No credit cards.*

Cameo Cafe

$ | American. The folksy knick-knacks and floral wallpaper in this homey diner-style café on a nondescript stretch of Sandy Boulevard are a refreshing callback to Portland's pre-hipster past, but it's the Korean-inflected home-style cooking that makes Cameo special. Both classic blueberry and Korean pancakes are available, along with an array of egg dishes and burgers, bulgogi, Monte Cristo sandwiches, and kimchee beef soup later in the day. **Known for:** unusual mix of Korean and diner-style American dishes; big portions of waffles and pancakes; entrée-size soups. *Average main: $9* ⊠ *8111 N.E. Sandy Blvd., Northeast* ☎ *503/284–0401*

⊕ www.cameocafe.com ⊘ No dinner Sun.–Mon.

Cully Central

$ | Lao. This modest-looking roadhouse seems like your typical neighborhood bar with its undeniably genial milieu for beer and conversation, except there's a dramatic butterfly mural on the exterior and it's one of the only restaurants in Portland that specializes in Lao food. Flavorful specialties include beef brisket with sticky rice, rice noodles with shredded chicken and quail eggs, and grilled lemongrass-pork sausage. **Known for:** a pretty patio with ample seating; short menu of excellent Lao street food; good rotation of craft beer on tap. *Average main: $10* ⊠ *4579 N.E. Cully Blvd., Woodlawn/Concordia* ☎ *503/206-8911* ⊘ *No lunch weekdays.*

The Deck

$$ | Seafood. At this seasonal (spring–fall) floating restaurant set amid pleasure craft and houseboats on the Columbia River, the water views and relaxing pace feel a world away from Downtown Portland (although low-flying planes from nearby Portland International Airport may remind you that civilization is near). Expect straightforward but competently batter-fried coconut shrimp, halibut fish-and-chips, steamer clams, and burgers, plus cocktails and beer by the pitcher, but what you're here for is the view. **Known for:** enchanting waterfront setting; fish-and-chips; dog-friendly seating. *Average*

main: $17 ⊠ *McCuddy's Marina, 2901 N.E. Marine Dr., Northeast* ☎ *503/283-6444* ⊕ *www.thedeckpdx.com* ⊘ *Closed Oct.–Mar.*

East Glisan Pizza Lounge

$ | Pizza. This unimposing spot on the edge of Montavilla turns heads with its ambitiously creative daily specials (rabbit lasagna, duck pizza), but the more conventional offerings from the regular menu are always deftly prepared, too. Pizzas are available classic style, with a gluten-free cornmeal crust, or—twice a week—Detroit-style with a thick crust and brick cheese. **Known for:** oversized sweet-ricotta cannoli; excellent happy hour; well-curated and affordable beer, wine, and cocktail list. *Average main: $14* ⊠ *8001 N.E. Glisan St., Montavilla/82nd Ave.* ☎ *971/279-4273* ⊕ *www.eastglisan.com* ⊘ *No lunch.*

★ Pizza Jerk

$$ | Pizza. The red-checked tablecloths, Tiffany-style lamps, and simple decor of this pizza joint might not inspire high expectations, but just wait until you taste the blistered-crust East Coast–style pies and slices. You can build your own pizza selecting from a long list of ingredients, or choose one of the signature favorites, like the white pie with ricotta and garlic, or the dan dan with sweet pork, chili paste, and mustard greens. **Known for:** thin-crust and cast-iron deep-crust pizzas; adult "slushies"; soft-serve ice cream. *Average main: $18* ⊠ *5028 N.E. 42nd Ave., Woodlawn/Concordia* ☎ *503/284-9333* ⊕ *www.pizzajerkpdx.com.*

Salty's on the Columbia

$$$$ | Seafood. Both a heated, covered deck and an open-air, uncovered deck offer views of boats plying the Columbia River at this bustling seafood restaurant, which is an especially lovely setting during the day for lunch or weekend brunch. Friends might want to share the huge seafood sample platter, which is loaded with prawns, oysters, crab, shrimp and scallops. **Known for:** Pacific Northwest salmon and steelhead; 2-lb. Dungeness crab and live lobster feasts; Columbia River and Mt. Hood views. *Average main: $36* ✉ *3839 N.E. Marine Dr., Northeast* ☎ *503/288-4444* ⊕ *www.saltys.com.*

Wajan

$ | Indonesian. The Indonesian-raised owner of this friendly and affordable restaurant bases the menu on both family recipes and traditional Jakarta street food, with coconut-rice, banana, and corn fritters, and stir-fried pork belly-and-potato dishes leading the way. A woven-mat ceiling and detailed murals of Indonesian city and nature landscapes contribute to the cheerful, informal mood. **Known for:** shareable street-food snacks; spicy yellow and green curry stews; shaved-ice dessert. *Average main: $14* ✉ *4611 E. Burnside St., Laurelhurst* ☎ *503/206-5916* ⊕ *www.wajanpdx.com* ☾ *Closed Tues. No lunch weekdays.*

Yonder

$ | Southern. Gifted and much celebrated chef Maya Lovelace opened this homage to Southern cuisine in a rather snazzy space in the Cully neighborhood in 2019, with this casual "meat and three" themed eatery occupying the main dining room and specializing in fried chicken, wings, catfish, and a wealth of glorious side dishes. In back, a slightly dressier space called Mae bills itself a "secret Southern kitchen" and rotates artfully plated dishes with fanciful ingredients like sorghum-brined pork chops and lavender grits with confit chicken hearts. **Known for:** the spiced tea and moonshine cocktail (it serves two); fried Southern specialties done right; weekend brunch. *Average main: $12* ✉ *4636 N.E. 42nd Ave., Woodlawn/Concordia* ☎ *503/444-7947* ⊕ *www.yonderpdx. com* ☾ *Closed Mon.–Tues. No lunch Wed.–Fri.*

🍸 Bars and Nightlife

Level Beer

It's a bit out of the way, in far northeast Portland, and yet Level Beer draws ale enthusiasts from all over. Why? This ale aficionado's playground with a greenhouse-style beer garden, games, food carts, and its very own crop of hops is fun to visit, and it turns out delicious, interesting brews: fresh hop saisons, nitro stouts, sours, barrel-aged Belgians, and more. ✉ *5211 N.E. 148th Ave., Northeast* ☎ *503/714-1222* ⊕ *www. levelbeer.com.*

GO FOR

Verdant nature parks

Diverse ethnic restaurants

Funky shops

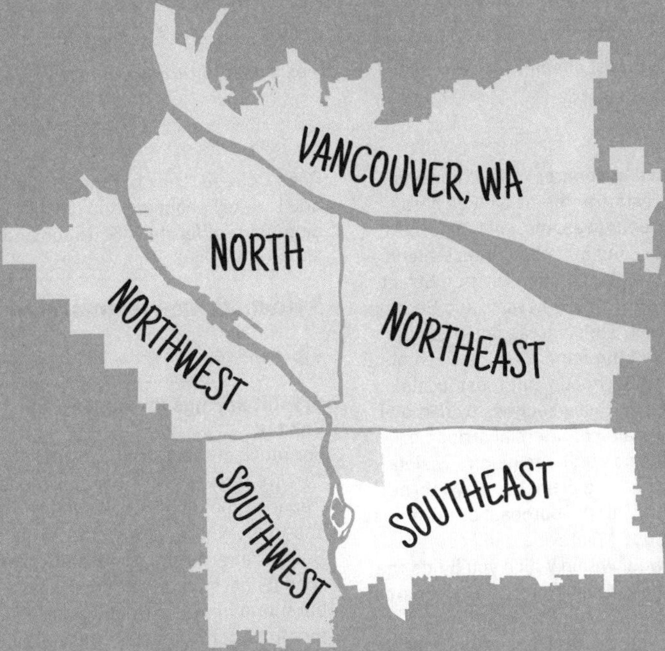

VANCOUVER, WA

NORTH

NORTHWEST

NORTHEAST

SOUTHWEST

SOUTHEAST

Sightseeing ★★★☆☆ | Shopping ★★★★☆ | Dining ★★★★★ | Nightlife ★★★★☆

The less-central—and remarkably vast—outer portion of the city's Southeast quadrant takes in an economically and ethnically diverse collection of neighborhoods, from trendy retail and dining strips to gracious residential areas to internationally inflected business districts. In this book, we've divided Southeast Portland into two sections—this "outer" chapter takes everything south of Burnside Street and east of 30th Avenue, as well as everything south of Powell Boulevard and east of the Willamette River. Officially, Southeast extends to the city border with Gresham, but few points of interest to visitors lie east of Interstate 205. See the Inner Southeast chapter for coverage of the areas closer to Downtown.—*by Andrew Collins*

You'll encounter vibrant pockets of restaurants—as well as bars, coffeehouses, markets, food-cart pods, and indie boutiques—along east–west running Division Street, Hawthorne Boulevard, and Belmont Street. These areas fall officially within the Sunnyside and Richmond neighborhoods, but most locals refer to these sections by name of the main commercial strip (e.g., "let's go bar-hopping on Division" or "I'm having brunch in Hawthorne"). Other Outer Southeast areas of note include Montavilla and Foster-Powell, within which you'll find the largely Asian-American commercial hub known as the Jade District as well as some booming pockets of affordable dining and nightlife. A bit south, Woodstock, Creston-Kenilworth, and Brooklyn contain a mix of modest but historic residential blocks along with a smattering of cool pubs, shops, and eateries. And to the extreme south, attractive homes, the beautiful campus of Reed College, and charming parks and low-key shopping and dining districts proliferate in Sellwood and Moreland.

Sellwood and Westmoreland

◉ Sights

Crystal Springs Rhododendron Garden

For much of the year, this nearly 10-acre retreat near Reed College is frequented mainly by bird-watchers and those who want a restful stroll. But starting in April, thousands of rhododendron bushes and azaleas burst into flower, attracting visitors in larger numbers. The peak blooming season for these woody shrubs is May; by late June the show is over. ✉ *5801 S.E. 28th Ave., Sellwood/Moreland* ☎ *503/771-8386* ⊕ *www.portlandoregon.gov/parks* ⊠ *$5 Apr.–Sept., Tues.–Sun.; otherwise free.*

Oaks Amusement Park

There's a small-town charm to this park that has bumper cars, thrill rides, miniature golf, and roller-skating. A 360-degree-loop roller coaster and other high-velocity, gravity-defying contraptions border the midway, along with a carousel and Ferris wheel. The wooden skating rink, built in 1905, is the oldest continuously operating one in the United States, and it features a working Wurlitzer organ. To help protect it from Willamette River flooding, the rink floats on airtight iron barrels. There are outdoor concerts in summer. ⊠ *7805 S.E. Oaks Park Way, Sellwood/Moreland* ☎ *503/233-5777* ⊕ *www.oakspark. com* 🖾 *Park free; multiride bracelets $19 and up; individual-ride tickets $4.95* ⊘ *Closed Oct.–mid-Mar.*

Oaks Bottom Wildlife Refuge

Bring your binoculars, because birds are plentiful at this 163-acre refuge situated in a flood-plain wetland near Sellwood. More than 175 species reside here seasonally, including hawks, quail, pintails, mallards, coots, woodpeckers, kestrels, widgeons, hummingbirds, and the sedately beautiful blue heron. The hiking is easy and relatively flat, but wear sturdy shoes, as it can get muddy; part of the park is on top of a landfill layered with soil. Southeast Portland's Springwater biking and pedestrian trail connects Oaks Bottom with Downtown. ⊠ *S.E. 7th Ave. and S.E. Sellwood Ave., Sellwood/Moreland* ☎ *503/729-0318* ⊕ *www.portlandoregon.gov/parks.*

GETTING HERE

It's pretty easy to reach most of the neighborhoods highlighted in this chapter by bus, but a car gives you more flexibility, and free street parking is easy to find throughout the Outer Southeast area. MAX light rail's Orange line can get you to Sellwood and Westmoreland.

Sellwood District

The pleasant, historic neighborhood that begins east of the Sellwood Bridge was once a separate town. Annexed by Portland in the 1890s, it retains a modest charm, with stores and restaurants along 13th Avenue carrying an interesting mix of goods and edibles. Just north is the Westmoreland neighborhood, another cluster of mostly indie retail and dining centered around the intersection of S.E. Milwaukee Avenue and S.E. Bybee Boulevard. ⊠ *S.E. 13th Ave. between S.E. Malden and S.E. Clatsop Sts., Sellwood/Moreland* ⊹ *TriMet's MAX light rail Orange line stops in Sellwood (the SE Tacoma/Johnson Creek stop) and Westmoreland (the SE Bybee stop).*

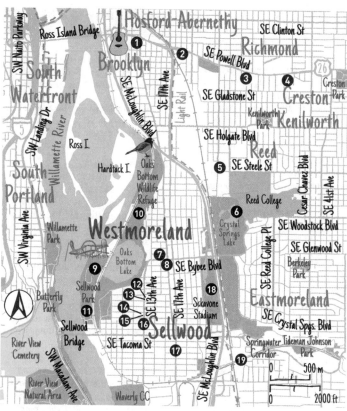

SIGHTS

Crystal Springs
Rhododendron Garden .. 6

Oaks Amusement
Park 9

Oaks Bottom
Wildlife Refuge.............. 10

Sellwood District 17

Sellwood Park.............. 11

Springwater
Corridor 19

Westmoreland Nature
Park 18

SHOPPING

Cloud Cap Games 14

Stars Antique Mall......... 8

Tilde 15

COFFEE & QUICK BITES

Tea Chai Té.................... 16

DINING

A Cena............................ 13

Holy Trinity Barbecue.... 4

Reverend's BBQ........... 12

BARS & NIGHTLIFE

Aladdin Theater 1

Bible Club....................... 7

Gigantic Brewing 5

Hopworks Urban
Brewery 3

Teutonic
Wine Company 2

Sellwood Park

Nearly 17 acres of tall old pines and grassy lawns overlooking the Willamette River make a visit here purely relaxing. A paved path circles the park and most of the action—ballpark, ball fields, playground, and tennis court. Sellwood also sports a terrific location—Oaks Bottom Refuge and Oaks Amusement Park are nearby, and the easy-going Sellwood neighborhood has charming shops and restaurants, convenient for a takeout picnic. ⊠ *S.E. 7th Ave. and S.E. Miller St., Sellwood/Moreland* ☎ *503/823–2525* ⊕ *www.portlandoregon.gov/parks.*

Springwater Corridor

A paved 21-mile multiuse trail built atop a former railroad track, this picturesque route passes through the heart of Southeast Portland, connecting the Willamette River near OMSI and the Tilikum Bridge (at S.E. 4th Ave. and S.E. Ivon St.) with Oak Bottoms Wildlife Refuge, Sellwood, Powell Butte Nature Park, and eventually the suburb of Boring. The Springwater is popular for jogging, walking, cycling, and even horseback rides. It passes through historic residential areas, wildlife-rich wetlands, and and farm fields, and alongside portions of one of the city's only remaining free-flowing streams, Johnson Creek. It's a wonderfully scenic way to make your way through this part of the city. ⊠ *Southeast* ✛ *Accessed at many points, but begins at S.E. 4th Ave. and S.E. Ivon St.* ☎ *503/823–7529* ⊕ *www.portlandoregon.gov/parks.*

WORTH A TRIP

It's a 20-minute drive south of Sellwood to visit the first incorporated U.S. city west of the Mississippi. The Hudson Bay Company settled Oregon City in 1829, and it briefly served as the territorial capital. The historic downtown overlooks dramatic Willamette Falls and has enjoyed a resurgence of late, with several worthy dining and drinking options, and the End of the Oregon Trail Interpretive Center has interesting history exhibits. Don't miss the Jetsonesque 130-foot Municipal Elevator, built in 1955 to connect a pair of downtown neighborhoods.

Westmoreland Nature Park

One of Portland's best outdoor kids' destinations is actually a lot of fun for visitors of any age. Anchoring a 42-acre park in a pretty residential area that's an easy stroll from the commercial districts of Sellwood and Westmoreland, the nature playground opened in 2014 as an initiative to make it easier and more enjoyable for kids to connect with nature. Features include boardwalk trails through wetlands and around an evergreen-lined duck pond, picnic areas, and an imaginatively designed playground situated among boulders and logs that feels almost like a touch-friendly outdoor art installation. Westmoreland Park also contains sports fields, tennis courts, and restrooms, and is adjacent to MAX light rail's SE Bybee Blvd. station. ⊠ *7530 S.E. 22nd Ave., Sellwood/Moreland* ☎ *503/823–7529* ⊕ *www.portlandoregon.gov/parks.*

Shopping

★ Cloud Cap Games

There's more than just run-of-the-mill board games at Cloud Cap. For children and grown-ups alike, the games here challenge the mind and provide hours of entertainment. There's a room with tables to play or try out a game, and game nights some evenings. The knowledge-able owners and staff may sit down and join in the fun and are always happy to answer questions and offer suggestions. ✉ 1226 S.E. Lexington St., Sellwood/Moreland ☎ 503/505–9344 ⊕ www.cloudcapgames.com.

Stars Antique Mall

Portland's largest antiques mall, Stars has two stores across the street from each other in the Sellwood-Moreland neighborhood. Since it rents its space to about 200 antiques dealers, you might find anything from low-end 1950s kitsch to high-end treasures. ✉ 7027 S.E. Milwaukie Ave., Sellwood/Moreland ☎ 503/235–5990 ⊕ www.starsantique.com.

Tilde

With wares that could work just as well in an urban loft as in a cozy country cottage, this compact storefront space is filled with a mix of eye-catching lifestyle goods and functional artwork, including Mrs. Fortune Cookie bags, lacy steel-and-silver earrings, ceramic bowls and vases, and stylish Nixon watches in bright colors. ✉ 7919 S.E. 13th Ave., Sellwood/Moreland ☎ 503/234–9600 ⊕ www.tildeshop.com.

Coffee and Quick Bites

★ Tea Chai Té

$ | Café. One of the city's most outstanding purveyors of loose-leaf teas has two larger cafes in Nob Hill and the Central East Side, but the Sellwood branch—inside a historic quirky red caboose—is perhaps the most fun. More than 130 types of tea are displayed in the colorful sipping room, and there's a cute side garden that's perfect for savoring a rich chai tea or a bubbly kombucha, along with a slice of pie. **Known for:** an eye-popping selection of chai and milk teas; locally made pastries and baked goods; cool seating inside a vintage caboose. *Average main: $5* ✉ 7983 S.E. 13th Ave., Sellwood/Moreland ☎ 503/432–8747 ⊕ www.teachaite.com.

Dining

a Cena

$$$ | Italian. A cozy and relaxed trattoria serving exceptionally well-prepared Italian food, a Cena is one of the more romantic spots in Sellwood for dinner. The beautifully presented cuisine showcases plenty of local ingredients—open the meal with house-made meatballs and rosemary focaccia or a plate of grilled octopus with local Mama Lil's marinated peppers, before venturing on to one of the hearty pasta dishes or grills. **Known for:** braised beef short rib with gnocchi; antipasti platters; an excellent, predominantly Italian, wine list. *Average main: $27 ⊠ 7742 S.E. 13th Ave., Sellwood/Moreland ☎ 503/206-3291 ⊕ www.acenapdx.com ⊙ Closed Mon. No lunch Sun.*

Holy Trinity Barbecue
$ | Barbecue. Texas transplant and pitmaster Kyle Rensmeyer helms this justly beloved bright-blue food cart in a parking lot on Powell Boulevard, doling out hefty platters of tender, slow-cooked brisket, pulled pork, pork ribs, and Czech sausage. Loosen your belt and add on a couple of side orders of cheesy grits, and unusual coleslaw with vinegar and ramen noodles. **Known for:** 14-hour-smoked beef brisket; homemade banana pudding; outdoor seating. *Average main: $9 ⊠ 3582 S.E. Powell Blvd., Division/Clinton ☎ 469/964-9256 ⊕ www.holytrinitybarbecue.com ⊙ Closed Mon.–Wed. No dinner.*

Reverend's BBQ
$$ | Barbecue. It seems appropriate that you'll find some of the city's best barbecue in Sellwood, one of its southernmost neighborhoods, where the owners of the celebrated meat-centric Laurelhurst Market dole out slow-smoked pork shoulder, tempeh, and sausage, plus burgers, crispy fried chicken, and banana pudding. You can eat in the nostalgia-tinged dining room hung with old advertising signs and—conveniently—paper towel dispensers, or take your bounty to go and picnic at nearby Sellwood Park. **Known for:** St. Louis-style pork ribs; cold-smoked oyster shooters; a nice selection of craft cocktails. *Average main: $17 ⊠ 7712 S.E. 13th Ave., Sellwood/Moreland ☎ 503/327-8755 ⊕ www.reverendsbbq.com.*

🍸 Bars and Nightlife

Aladdin Theater
Housed in a vintage former movie theater, this music venue specializes in indie and alternative acts, many with national followings. The adjacent Lamp pub offers microbrews, pizza, and pub fare, too. *⊠ 3017 S.E. Milwaukie Ave., Division/Clinton ☎ 503/234-9694 ⊕ www.aladdin-theater.com.*

★ Bible Club
There's a speakeasy-like quality to this hip, vintage-style bar with signs referencing Prohibition and the 18th Amendment. The Bible Club serves up some of the most creative cocktails in the Sellwood and Westmoreland area, as well as a good mix of Oregon beers. Out back there's an expansive seating area with picnic tables and an additional outdoor bar. *⊠ 6716 S.E. 16th Ave., Sellwood/Moreland ☎ 971/279-2198 ⊕ www.bibleclubpdx.com ⊙ Closed Mon.–Tues.*

⭐ **Gigantic Brewing**

This well-respected craft brewer is in a slightly off-the-beaten-path industrial area that doesn't have a whole lot going on, but this in no way keeps it from pulling in a consistently big crowd most days, and especially on weekend afternoons, when folks sip Gigantic's first-rate beer on the front patio. In addition to conventional Northwest-style IPAs and some terrific German ales, the brewery produces interesting seasonal and barrel-aged varieties. ⊠ *5224 S.E. 26th Ave., Southeast* ☎ *503/208–3416* ⊕ *www. giganticbrewing.com.*

Hopworks Urban Brewery

A bicycle-themed microbrewery with deftly crafted beer, sandwiches, and pizzas, Hopworks Urban Brewery (HUB for short) occupies an industrial lodge-inspired building that's 100% renewably powered and water neutral. Hopworks BikeBar, located on the cycling-friendly North Williams corridor, offers similar fare with the same bikey, eco-conscious vibe. ⊠ *2944 S.E. Powell Blvd., Division/Clinton* ☎ *503/232–4677* ⊕ *www.hopworksbeer.com.*

Teutonic Wine Company

Fans of minerally Rieslings, berry-forward Gamays, and peachy Alsace-style Pinot Gris should seek out this slightly out-of-the-way winemaker that specializes in German-style grapes sourced from throughout Oregon's primarily cooler-climate vineyards. This urban winery's charmingly intimate tavern serves wines by the glass or bottle along with cheeses, charcuterie, and other small-plate fare, and there's live jazz some evenings. ⊠ *3303 S.E. 20th Ave., Division/Clinton* ☎ *503/235–5053* ⊕ *www.teutonic-wines.com.*

Outer Division, Hawthorne, and Belmont

👁 Sights

⭐ **Division Street**

Back in the early 1970s, Division Street (aka "Southeast Division") was earmarked for condemnation as part of a proposed—and thankfully never built—freeway that would have connected Downtown to Mt. Hood. For many years, this street sat forlornly, just a long stretch of modest buildings and empty lots. These days, Southeast Division—no longer threatened with condemnation—is one of the hottest restaurant rows on the West Coast, and sleek three- and four-story contemporary condos and apartments are popping up like dandelions. If culinary tourism is your thing, head to the 10 blocks of Southeast Division from about 30th to 39th avenues, where you'll find such darlings of the culinary scene as Pok Pok, Ava Gene's, Bollywood Theater, Olympia Provisions Public House, an outpost of Salt & Straw ice cream, Little T bakery, Lauretta Jean's, and several others. The main draw here is mostly food-and-drink related; there are several great bars, and the excellent Oui! Wine Bar at SE Wine Collective urban winery. You'll also find a growing number of other noteworthy restaurants and bars extending all the way to 12th Avenue to the west, and 50th Avenue to the east (note that businesses west of 30th Avenue are covered in the Inner Southeast chapter). As well as "Division" and "Southeast Division," you may hear some locals refer to the western end of the neighborhood as "Division/Clinton" referring to Clinton Street, a block south of Division, where you will find lovely early- to mid-20th-century bungalows and houses and a few noteworthy eateries (Broder, La Moule, Magna Kusina, Jaqueline), mostly from 27th to 20th Avenue. ⊠ *S.E. Division St., and parts of S.E. Clinton St., from 12th to 50th Aves., Division/Clinton* ⊹ *Bus 2 crosses the Hawthorne Bridge from Downtown and continues along Division Street; there's also free street parking, although increased development has made it a bit harder to find* ⊕ *www. divisionstreetportland.com.*

★ Hawthorne District

Stretching from the foot of Mt. Tabor to S.E. 12th Avenue (where you'll find a terrific little food-cart pod), with some blocks far livelier than others, this eclectic commercial thoroughfare was at the forefront of Portland's hippie and LGBTQ scenes in the 1960s and 1970s. As the rest of Portland's East Side has become more urbane and popular among hipsters, young families, students, and the so-called creative class over the years, Hawthorne has retained an arty, homegrown flavor. An influx of trendy eateries and retailers opening alongside the still-colorful

and decidedly low-frills thrift shops and old-school taverns and cafés make for a hodgepodge of styles and personalities—you could easily spend an afternoon popping in and out of boutiques, and then stay for happy hour at a local nightspot or even later for dinner. Highlights include a small (but still impressive) branch of Powell's Books, House of Vintage emporium, Bagdad Theater, Farmhouse Kitchen Thai, Apizza Scholls, OK Omens wine bar, and the Sapphire Hotel lounge. ▓ **TIP** → Note that Hawthorne businesses west of SE 30th Avenue are covered in the Inner Southeast chapter. ⊠ *S.E. Hawthorne Blvd., between S.E. 12th and S.E. 50th Aves., Hawthorne* ⊹ *Bus 14 runs from Downtown along the length of Hawthorne, and there's plenty of free street parking* ⊕ *www.thinkhawthorne.com.*

Laurelhurst Park

Manicured lawns, stately trees, and a wildfowl pond make this 31-acre southeast Portland park a favorite urban hangout since 1912. **Laurelhurst,** one of the city's most beautiful neighborhoods, surrounds the park. It was the first city park to be named on the National Register of Historic Places. ⊠ *SE 39th Ave. between SE Ankeny and SE Oak Sts., Laurelhurst* ⊕ *www.portlandoregon. gov/parks.*

Peacock Lane

This quiet four-block street, added to the national historic register in 2017, brims with attractive and neatly kept examples of the early 20th century residential

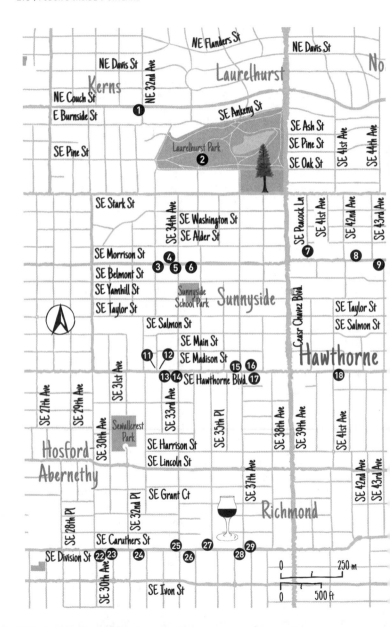

SIGHTS

SHOPPING

COFFEE & QUICK BITES

DINING

BARS & NIGHTLIFE

PERFORMING ARTS

THE JADE DISTRICT

Nearly 8% of Portland's population is Asian-American, and a significant segment of this community lives or works in the Jade District. Officially recognized and named in 2011 as part of the city's Neighborhood Prosperity Initiative (NPI) program, this neighborhood centered around the intersection of S.E. 82nd and S.E. Division is one of the most ethnically diverse census tracts in all of Oregon.

With especially large Chinese and Vietnamese populations (as well as many Russian, African American, and Hispanic residents), the Jade District has become the city's top destination for Asian dining. You'll find several shopping centers filled with noodle houses, banh mi shops, hot pot restaurants, and other enticing eateries as well as sprawling Asian supermarkets, such as Fubonn and Hong Phat Food Center.

One of the best ways to acquaint yourself with the neighborhood is to attend the annual **Jade International Night Market** (⊕ *www.jadedistrictnight-market.org*), which takes places the final two Saturdays of August at Portland Community College's Southeast Campus (✉ *2305 S.E. 82nd Ave.*). More than 25,000 people attend this dynamic celebration of international food, crafts, and music.

architecture—Dutch Colonials, Tudor Revivals, Arts and Crafts bungalows, and the like—that proliferates throughout Portland, especially on the East Side. But the neighborhood's true claim to fame is its colorful holiday lights display in December. During this time, the peaked gables, bay windows, and front porches of these homes are strung with white and colored lights, and trees, snowmen, candy canes, and other illuminated decorations glow in the front yards. The streets are closed to car traffic in the evenings. Parking can be challenging—consider taking the bus or parking a few blocks away on Belmont or Hawthorne and combining your stroll with dinner at one of the area's many excellent restaurants. ✉ *S.E. Peacock La.,* *between S.E. Stark and S.E. Belmont Sts., Belmont* ⊕ *www.facebook.com/peacockln.*

 Shopping

★ Altar

A tiny but impressively stocked boutique in a charming, old, Craftsman-style house that also houses the excellent Hazel Room café, Altar is devoted to decorative items, fashion, jewelry, and crafts made by Portlanders. The selection is eclectic and fun—everything from handcrafted soaps made with local beer to geometric-shaped brass necklaces. Clothing at Altar is geared mostly to women. ✉ *3279 S.E. Hawthorne Blvd., Hawthorne* ☎ *503/236–6120* ⊕ *www.altarpdx.com.*

Artifact: Creative Recycle

You never know what sort of special treasure you might discover while rummaging the aisles of this boho-chic vintage shop with a carefully curated collection of mid-century housewares, 1970s fashion, wicker patio furniture, funky jewelry, and Asian and African bedding and rugs. Artifact is also one of Portland's best places to upcycle your own goods. ✉ *3630 S.E. Division St., Division/Clinton* ☎ *503/230–4831* ⊕ *www.artifactpdx.com.*

House of Vintage

This mammoth 13,000-square-foot shop, just down the street from one of the better Goodwill shops in the city, is de rigueur among vintage aficionados. Inside, you can rifle through the wares of some 60 dealers; bell-bottom jeans and plaid blazers are a big draw, but this time capsule also brims with kitschy ceramic ashtrays, Naugahyde couches, 1950s magazines, old-school lunchboxes, and pretty much anything else you might recall from your childhood. ✉ *3315 S.E. Hawthorne Blvd., Hawthorne* ☎ *503/236–1991* ⊕ *www.houseofvintagenw.com.*

★ Movie Madness Video

Although at this point you could probably count the country's video rental shops on one hand, Movie Madness continues to thrive, albeit thanks to a successful 2018 crowd-funding campaign that enabled Portland's historic and nonprofit Hollywood Theatre to buy the beloved business. Meander through its several rooms to peruse more than 80,000 titles, including hard-to-find indie, foreign, LGBTQ, and cult flicks, and to admire a fun and fascinating collection of movie memorabilia, including dozens of props from classic films like *Psycho* and *Citizen Kane*. ✉ *4320 S.E. Belmont St., Belmont* ☎ *503/234–4363* ⊕ *www.moviemadness.org.*

★ Music Millennium

The oldest record store in the Pacific Northwest, Music Millennium stocks a huge selection of new and used music in every possible category, including local punk groups. The store also hosts a number of in-store performances, often by top-name artists, which have included Lucinda Williams, Richard Thompson, Sheryl Crow, and Randy Newman. ✉ *3158 E. Burnside St., Laurelhurst* ☎ *503/231–8926* ⊕ *www.musicmillennium.com.*

Noun

This quirky Belmont Street boutique carries discerning home accessories and oddities—stylish Edison bulb lamps, nested bowls, arty journals and planners—along with a smattering of well-chosen vintage items and a nice range of jewelry. Be sure to peek inside the old phone booth inside. ✉ *3300 S.E. Belmont St., Belmont* ☎ *503/235-0078* ⊕ *www.shopnoun.com.*

Perfume House

A trip to the perfume counter at a large department store is for amateurs. If you're seeking an olfactory experience and a signature scent, you'll find it at this emporium to fragrance. Hundreds of big-name fragrances for women and men are sold here under the guidance of a trained and knowledgeable staff. ✉ *3328 S.E. Hawthorne Blvd., Hawthorne* ☎ *503/234-5375* ⊕ *www.theperfumehouse.com* ☾ *Closed Mon.*

Powell's Books for Home and Garden

The inventory at this Powell's location, a couple of doors down from a general outpost on Hawthorne, focuses on cooking and gardening books, with a sizable selection of crafting books and unique gift items. ✉ *3747 S.E. Hawthorne Blvd., Hawthorne* ☎ *503/228-4651* ⊕ *www.powells.com.*

Presents of Mind

It happens all the time. You pop into this animated Hawthorne boutique to buy a card or gift for a friend, and you emerge an hour later with knit logo'd socks, a "Gay AF" rainbow coffee mug, a roll of pastel-animal stickers, and a tin of beard balm all for yourself. The owners of this terrific little shop make a strong effort to support local and sustainable makers and designers. ✉ *3633 S.E. Hawthorne Blvd., Hawthorne* ☎ *503/230-7740* ⊕ *www.presentsofmind.tv.*

🍵 Coffee and Quick Bites

★ **Lauretta Jean's**

$ | Café. This pie-focused operation began as a stall at Portland's Saturday farmers' market at PSU and now comprises a couple of charming, homey, brick-and-mortar cafés, one Downtown, but the most atmospheric along Division Street in Southeast. While it's the delicious pies—with feathery-light crusts and delicious fillings like tart cherry, salted pecan, and chocolate-banana cream—that have made Lauretta Jean's a foodie icon in Portland, these cheerful eateries also serve exceptional brunch fare, including the LJ Classic, a fluffy biscuit topped with an over-easy egg, Jack cheese, bacon, and strawberry jam. **Known for:** salted-caramel apple pie; short but well-curated cocktail list; breakfast sandwich that features the bakery's fluffy biscuits. *Average main: $8* ✉ *3402 S.E. Division St., Division/Clinton* ☎ *503/235-3119* ⊕ *www.laurettajeans.com* ☾ *No dinner.*

Never Coffee Lab

$ | Café. At this hip third wave coffeehouse on Belmont Street, enjoy mochas, macchiatos, cold brews, and pour-overs that feature carefully sourced, house-roasted beans. It's also a good source for buying specialty coffee-making gear. **Known for:** specialty flavored lattes; knowledgeable but friendly baristas; delicious vegan and non-vegan pastries. *Average main: $5* ⊠ *4243 S.E. Belmont St., Suite 200, Belmont* ☎ *541/223-3580* ⊕ *www. nevercoffeelab.com* ⊗ *No dinner.*

Pinolo Gelato

$ | **Café.** Portland's ongoing love affair with artisanal frozen desserts extends to this gelateria on the ground floor of one of Division Street's many modern apartment blocks. Pinolo makes every scoop of creamy gelato from scratch, using local ingredients as much as possible, and featuring intriguing flavors like almond-fig and cassata (a ricotta-flavored cake from Sicily). **Known for:** both creamy and dairy-free gelatos; espresso drinks using acclaimed Caffè Umbria beans; seasonal fresh-fruit flavors. *Average main: $5* ⊠ *3707 S.E. Division St., Division/Clinton* ☎ *503/719-8686* ⊕ *www.pinologelato.com* ⊗ *Closed Sun. and Mon.*

Tao of Tea

$ | **Café.** With soft music and the sound of running water in the background, the Tao of Tea serves more than 100 loose-leaf teas as well as vegetarian snacks and sweets. The company also operates the serene tearoom inside Old Town's Lan Su Chinese Garden. **Known for:** tranquil ambience; especially good variety of chai and oolong teas; Asian-influenced veggie and noodle

bowls. *Average main: $7* ⊠ *3430 S.E. Belmont St., Division/Clinton* ☎ *503/736-0119* ⊕ *www.taooftea.com.*

🍴 Dining

★ Apizza Scholls

$$ | **Pizza.** The pies at Apizza Scholls, which have been lauded by Anthony Bourdain, Rachael Ray, and thousands of everyday pizza lovers, deserve the first-class reputation they enjoy. The greatness of the pies rests not in innovation or complexity, but in the simple quality of the ingredients, such as dough made by hand in small batches and baked to crispy-outside, tender-inside perfection and toppings—including basil, pecorino romano, and house-cured bacon—that are fresh and delicious. **Known for:** interesting beer list; the bacon bianca pizza (white, with no sauce); occasionally long waits for a table (reservations are a good idea). *Average main: $18* ⊠ *4741 S.E. Hawthorne Blvd., Hawthorne* ☎ *503/233-1286* ⊕ *www.apizzascholls.com* ⊗ *No lunch weekdays.*

★ Ava Gene's

$$$$ | **Modern Italian.** This highly acclaimed Roman-inspired Italian eatery—with a buzzy dining room with a vaulted ceiling and two long rows of banquette seats—ranks among the top tables in town both in popularity and quality. The menu emphasizes regional, home-style recipes from throughout Italy, but focuses on local produce—you could make an impressive feast of three or four *giardini* (gardens) sides, such

as melon with tomatillos, ground cherries, and prosciutto, while the satisfyingly hearty mains might include tagliatelle with chicken ragu or lamb grilled with artichokes and celery root. **Known for:** flatbreads with creative toppings; a top-notch cocktail and wine program; $85 per person family-style "chef's selection" option. *Average main: $32* ⊠ *3377 S.E. Division St., Division/Clinton* ☎ *971/229–0571* ⊕ *www.avagenes.com* ☉ *No lunch weekdays.*

★ Bollywood Theater

$ | Indian. Set beneath a soaring beamed ceiling, and with a welcoming mix of worn wooden seating, kitschy decor, bright fabrics, and intoxicating smells, this lively restaurant along Division Street's hoppin' restaurant row specializes in Indian street food. Order at the counter, and your food—perhaps *vada pav* (spicy potato dumplings with chutney), *gobi* Manchurian (Indo-Chinese fried cauliflower with lemon, curry leaves, and sweet-and-sour sauce), or Goan-style shrimp served with a full complement of chutneys, paratha bread, and dal—will be brought out to you. **Known for:** delicious breads and vegetable side dishes; small Indian gourmet market with spices and curries; mango lassi. *Average main: $14* ⊠ *3010 S.E. Division St., Division/Clinton* ☎ *503/477–6699* ⊕ *www.bollywoodtheaterpdx.com.*

Farmhouse Kitchen Thai Cuisine

$$ | Thai. At this Bay Area import, the rambling old Hawthorne house setting does feel a touch country-chic, but all's forgotten when friendly servers deliver platters of almost gorgeous, colorful Thai food—mounds of florid jasmine blue rice, spicy Esan-style tuna larb, wagyu beef lettuce rolls, and crispy pork belly with garden veggies. Locally sourced and often organic produce and meats are favored, and quite a few of the dishes pack serious heat (but can be tamed a bit on request). **Known for:** anything with jasmin blue rice; homemade crispy pork belly (which can be added to any dish); Thai micheladas. *Average main: $18* ⊠ *3354 S.E. Hawthorne Blvd., Central East Side* ☎ *503/432–8115* ⊕ *www.farmhous-ethai.com/portland.*

★ Pok Pok

$$ | Thai. Andy Ricker, the owner of one of Portland's most talked-about restaurants, regularly travels to Southeast Asia to research street food and home-style recipes to include on the menu of this always-hopping spot. Diners have the option of sitting outside under tents, or in the funky, cavelike interior, while they enjoy enticing dishes like green papaya salad, charcoal-roasted game hen, and Ike's Vietnamese chicken wings, which are deep-fried in caramelized fish sauce and garlic. **Known for:** Ike's Vietnamese chicken wings; charcoal-roasted game hen and other meaty fare; fiery-hot food (although there are plenty of milder dishes—you just have to ask). *Average main: $19* ⊠ *3226 S.E. Division St., Division/Clinton* ☎ *503/232–1387* ⊕ *www.pokpokdivision.com.*

Por Que No?

$ | Mexican. This often jam-packed Hawthorne taqueria with a second location on North Mississippi makes a strong effort to support sustainable practices, both with its decor—in which recycled wood and other materials are favored—and its commitment to line-caught fish and organic local meats. Of course, it's the flavorful fare that keeps regulars coming back, especially the soft tacos with fillings based on the owners' travels throughout Mexico, such as carne asada with fiery arbol-chili salsa, the braised-brisket barbacoa with cilantro and crema, and cornmeal-crusted cod with escabeche crema. **Known for:** plentiful outdoor seating; an extensive salsa and condiments bar; all-evening happy hour on Tuesdays (and 3 to 6 on other days). *Average main: $12* ⊠ *4635 S.E. Hawthorne Blvd., Hawthorne* ☎ *503/954-3138* ⊕ *www.porquenotacos.com.*

★ Tasty n Daughters

$$ | Contemporary. This is the latest outpost of the amazing restaurant empire of Portland chef-restaurateur John Gorham, and it's essentially a revival of his original but now defunct Tasty n Sons, serving a similar menu of wonderfully inventive daily brunch and dinner fare. In this handsome redbrick spot with tile walls and leather banquettes, you'll discover a globally inspired menu of flavorful dishes, from French toast with peach-maple syrup to Moroccan chicken hash with harissa cream to Ghanaian-style kebabs with suya spice and pineapple jam. **Known for:** $1 oysters on the half shell at happy hour; ambitious bar and wine program (with especially interesting brunch cocktails); lemon curd beignets with berry jam. *Average main: $21* ⊠ *4537 S.E. Division St., Division/ Clinton* ☎ *503/621-1400* ⊕ *www. tastyndaughters.com.*

🍸 Bars and Nightlife

Aalto Lounge

Artsy, hip East Siders hang and drink martinis and wine at this minimalist, bubble-lamped bar along a buzzy stretch of Belmont Street. ⊠ *3356 S.E. Belmont St., Belmont* ☎ *503/235-6041* ⊕ *www.aaltolounge. com.*

Horse Brass Pub

A laid-back beer-drinking crowd fills the venerable, dark-wood Horse Brass Pub, an English-style tavern with more than 50 beers on tap (including some cask-conditioned varieties) and pretty tasty fish-and-chips and other British classics. ⊠ *4534 S.E. Belmont St., Belmont* ☎ *503/232-2202* ⊕ *www.horsebrass. com.*

Imperial Bottle Shop & Taproom

Occupying a sleek, contemporary corner space on Division Street, Imperial carries a regularly changing rotation of about a dozen connoisseur-worthy microbrews and has shelves filled with hundreds of additional bottles of craft beers. While you ponder your beer options, you can order in takeout from any of the several restaurants on the same block. ✉ *3090 S.E. Division St., Division/Clinton* ☎ *971/302–6899* ⊕ *www.imperialbottleshop.com.*

The Liquor Store

To be clear, this darkly lit drinking and live music venue with both ground-floor and basement spaces is not an actual liquor store. But it does stock one of the more impressive selections of booze along this youthful stretch of Belmont bars and eateries, and there's a reliably good selection of bar food. ✉ *3341 S.E. Belmont St., Belmont* ☎ *503/754–7782* ⊕ *www.theliquorstorepdx.com.*

★ Oui! Wine Bar at SE Wine Collective

This hive of boutique wine-making has an inviting tasting room–cum–wine bar in which you can sample the vinos of several up-and-coming producers. You could carve out a full meal from the extensive menu's tapas, salads, baguette sandwiches, and cheese and meats plates. Although Oregon is chiefly known for Pinot Noir, Pinot Gris, and Chardonnay, the wineries at the collective produce a richly varied assortment of varietals, from racy Sauvignon Blancs to peppery Cabernet Francs. ✉ *2425 S.E. 35th Pl., Division/Clinton* ☎ *503/208–2061* ⊕ *www.sewinecollective.com.*

The Sapphire Hotel

In the lobby of a former brothel in lively Hawthorne, the deep-red, candlelit Sapphire Hotel serves cocktails, beer, and wine with an intimate, sultry atmosphere. There's a terrific food menu, too, served late and at bargain prices during happy hour. ✉ *5008 S.E. Hawthorne Blvd., Hawthorne* ☎ *503/232–6333* ⊕ *www.thesapphirehotel.com.*

 Performing Arts

★ Bagdad Theater

Built in 1927, the stunningly restored, eminently quirky Bagdad Theater shows first-run Hollywood films on a huge screen and serves pizza, burgers, sandwiches, and McMenamins ales. The Bagdad is a local favorite. ✉ *3702 S.E. Hawthorne Blvd., Hawthorne* ☎ *503/249–7474* ⊕ *www.mcmenamins.com/bagdad-theater-pub.*

Mt. Tabor and Montavilla

 Sights

Montavilla

Anchored by an eight-block commercial strip of Southeast Stark Street extending from the eastern slope of Mt. Tabor to busy Southeast 82nd Avenue, Montavilla is a sizable middle-class neighborhood on the city's East Side. Its name is shorthand for "Mount Tabor Village," and it officially covers everything from Southeast Division north to Interstate 84 and from Mt. Tabor east to Interstate 205. The neighborhood developed as a streetcar suburb in the late 19th century, and over time it's become one of the city's most ethnically diverse areas (the Jade District, with its myriad international restaurants and shopping centers, lies within a significant portion of it). But when locals refer to Montavilla, they usually mean just this bustling little Stark Street corridor of funky cafés and retailers, including a popular co-op natural foods grocery and some excellent happy hour venues (The Observatory and Redwood, in particular). It's a perfectly charming neighborhood destination for brunch or dinner—and maybe a movie at the historic Academy Theater—after a stroll through Mt. Tabor. Every Sunday morning from 10 to 2, from June through October, there's a great little farmers' market held at Stark and 77th. The annual Montavilla Street Fair in late July features live music, kids' activities, arts and crafts vendors, and great food and is a fun time for a visit. ✉ *S.E. Division St. north to I-84 between Mt. Tabor/N.E. 68th Ave. and I-205, Montavilla/82nd Ave.* ⊕ *www. montavillapdx.org.*

⭐ Mt. Tabor Park

A playground on top of a volcano cinder cone? Yup, that's here. The cinders, or glassy rock fragments, unearthed in this 190-acre park's construction were used to surface the respite's roads; the ones leading to the very top are closed to cars, but popular with cyclists. They're also popular with cruisers—each August there's an old-fashioned soapbox derby. Picnic tables and tennis, basketball, and volleyball courts make Mt. Tabor Park a popular spot for outdoor recreation, but plenty of quiet, shaded trails and wide-open grassy lawns with panoramic views of the Downtown skyline appeal to sunbathers, hikers, and nature lovers. The whole park is closed to cars on Wednesday. ■TIP→ Just down the hill on the west side of Mt. Tabor, you'll find the lively cafés and restaurants of the hip Hawthorne District. ✉ *S.E. 60th Ave. and S.E. Salmon St., Mt. Tabor* ⊕ *www.port-landoregon.gov/parks.*

Powell Butte Nature Park

One of the four extinct cinder cones in the city, Powell Butte rises 614 feet over far southeastern Portland. Its grassy and forested slopes contain a 611-acre city park laced with relatively easy hiking, horseback, and mountain-biking trails and scenic panoramas of the surrounding mountains. You can access trails at several points (download PDFs of the park brochure and the trail map at the official website), but the main visitor center, which has ample parking, is a good place to start. The strikingly contemporary, eco-designed building opened in 2016 and contains excellent exhibits about the park's flora and fauna, and a short interpretive trail sheds further light on both the natural habitat and the indigenous tribes that thrived here over the centuries. ✉ *16160 S.E. Powell Blvd., Southeast* ☎ *503/823-6131* ⊕ *www.friendsofpowellbutte.org.*

 Shopping

Union Rose

For distinctive women's fashion and accessories designed and made in Portland, check out this boutique in up-and-coming Montavilla. Though there are scores of dresses for any

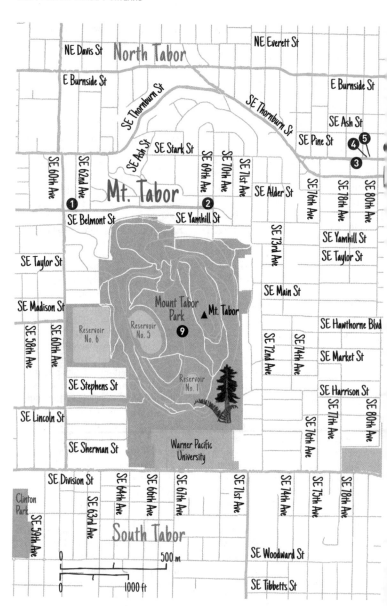

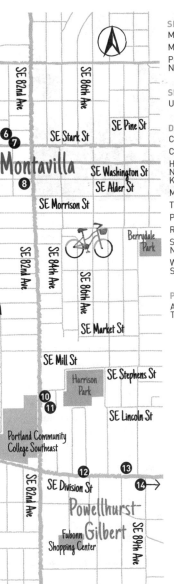

season, including a very good selection of dresses and skirts in plus sizes, there's also plenty of everyday wear, like hoodies and hats. ✉ *7909 S.E. Stark St., Montavilla/82nd Ave.* ☎ *503/287–4242* ⊕ *www.union-rosepdx.com* ⊗ *Closed Tues.*

🍴 Dining

★ Cheese Bar

$ | Café. For years, many of Portland's top restaurateurs have sourced their cheese from nationally renowned cheesemonger Steve Jones, who operates this casual fromagerie near Mt. Tabor Park that functions both as a specialty cheese market and neighborhood bistro. Try the "stinky board" to sample two strong cheeses of the day with crostini. **Known for:** hard-to-find imported and local cheeses (to go or dine-in); an extensive selection of beers, wines, and aperitifs; cheese and charcuterie boards. *Average main: $10* ✉ *6031 S.E. Belmont St., Mt. Tabor* ☎ *503/222–6014* ⊕ *www.cheese-bar.com* ⊗ *Closed Mon.*

★ Coquine

$$$ | French. A sunny neighborhood café serving brunch daily, Coquine blossoms into a romantic, sophisticated French–Pacific Northwest bistro in the evening. Early in the day, sup on sourdough pancakes with huckleberry compote, or black cod–based fisherman's stew with garlic toast, while in the evening, you might encounter pappardelle noodles with pork ragu or roasted whole chicken padron peppers, sungold tomatoes, pole beans, and

pickled red onion. **Known for:** four- and seven-course tasting menus (with optional wine pairings); a dim sum–style candy tray offered during the dessert course; cheerful setting near Mt. Tabor. *Average main: $27* ✉ *6839 S.E. Belmont St., Mt. Tabor* ☎ *503/384–2483* ⊕ *www.coquinepdx.com* ⊗ *No dinner Mon. and Tues.*

Heartbreaker Neighborhood Kitchen

$ | Contemporary. Just off Montavilla's bustling commercial strip, this vegan-friendly Southern cafe serves up wonderfully tasty lunch, dinner, and weekend brunch options. In addition to generously portioned sandwiches, Heartbreaker carries a rotating selection of house-made small-batch ice creams and sorbets in flavors like red velvet, spiced peach, and sweet honeydew. **Known for:** vegan options for nearly every dish and several vegan ice cream flavors; Mexican Coke ice cream floats; creamy grits with pimento cheese, candied bacon, and fried egg. *Average main: $9 ⊠ 411 S.E. 81st Ave., Montavilla/82nd Ave.* ☎ *503/253–3344* ⊕ *www.heartbreakerpdx.com* ⊗ *Closed Mon.–Thurs.*

Master Kong

$ | Chinese. When it comes to authentic, robustly seasoned Chinese noodle soups—the versions with tender beef brisket or mustard pork are both sublime—Master Kong rises to the top among its many Asian neighbors. In a cozy wood-accented dining room, the friendly staff delivers colorful plates and bamboo steamer baskets filled with well-prepared clam congee, potstickers, baos, and steamed veggies. **Known for:** jianbing (Chinese-style crepes); braised pork belly rice; handmade meat and veggie dumplings. *Average main: $8 ⊠ 8435 S.E. Division St., Montavilla/82nd Ave.* ☎ *971/373–8248* ⊗ *Closed Mon.*

The Observatory

$ | American. This convivial neighborhood bistro and its adjoining side bar Over and Out have developed a devoted following over the years for friendly service, well-crafted and affordable contemporary American food, and a long, impressive list of local beers and creative cocktails. Start things off with one of the starter platters (smoked fish, Mediterranean, and charcuterie are all options), before graduating to one of the larger plates, such as the lamb burger with local goat cheese, or blackened catfish with remoulade. **Known for:** fantastic happy hour deals; popular weekend brunch; pinball and games in adjoining bar. *Average main: $15 ⊠ 8115 S.E. Stark St., Montavilla/82nd Ave.* ☎ *503/445–6284* ⊕ *www.theobservatorypdx.com.*

Pot & Spicy

$ | Chinese. This no-frills Szechuan eatery is in a small but popular strip mall of Asian restaurants near 82nd Avenue and succeeds with a clever concept (and, of course, a cute name): skewers and soups. You can order full-on hot pot feasts (veggie, intestines, beef, or seafood), or a wide variety of palatable skewers, which can be served deep-fried or accompanying a soup or noodle bowl of your choosing—the mix-and-match possibilities are endless, and the quality top-notch. **Known for:** Taiwanese popcorn chicken appetizer; huge selection of meat, seafood, and veggie skewers; seafood hot pot with shrimp, mussels, fish, and crab cakes. *Average main: $13 ⊠ 8230 S.E. Harrison St., Montavilla/82nd Ave.* ☎ *503/788–7267* ⊗ *Closed Tues.*

Redwood

$$ | Modern American. This neighborhood café with a redwood-panel bar, red-painted walls, and varnished-wood tables is casual enough for brunch (served weekdays and weekends) or happy hour with friends but charming enough for an intimate date night. Whatever the occasion, you can count on stellar, reasonably priced modern American fare, including smoked-trout hash with pickled veggies at brunch and tender tri-tip steak with bacon-fried red potatoes at dinner. **Known for:** one of the best happy hours in Southeast; Swedish lemon pancakes with powdered sugar and bacon; the Redwood Original cocktail: aged bourbon, sweet vermouth, bitters, muddled orange, cherry, and lime. *Average main: $16 ⊠ 7915 S.E. Stark St., Montavilla/82nd Ave.* ☎ *503/841-5118 ⊕ www.redwoodpdx. com* ⊙ *Closed Mon.–Tues.*

So Good Taste Noodle House

$ | Chinese. This reliably excellent if not especially atmospheric source of Chinese comfort food excels in particular with flat egg noodle bowls and dumpling soups. Glass cases displaying freshly prepared meat on hooks serve both as decoration and enticement in the otherwise plain dining room of formica tables and unflattering lighting. **Known for:** salt-and-pepper squid; anything with duck, from whole barbecue-roasted to congee or wonton noodle soup; bargain-priced big portions. *Average main: $8 ⊠ 8220 S.E.*

Harrison St., Montavilla/82nd Ave. ☎ *503/788-6909 ⊕ www.sogoodtaste-noodle.com.*

Wong's King Seafood

$$ | Chinese. Portland's top neighborhood for Asian fare is S.E. 82nd Avenue (and the blocks near it), and this Cantonese seafood restaurant with an expansive dining room that looks a bit like a hotel banquet hall is one of the area's most authentic venues. The lengthy menu of delicious fare includes a number of fresh seafood specialties like braised abalone in oyster sauce and tamarind-stir-fried Dungeness crab. **Known for:** daily dim sum; Cantonese seafood; a good variety of pork, beef, veggie, and other non-seafood items. *Average main: $21 ⊠ 8733 S.E. Division St., Suite 101, Montavilla/82nd Ave.* ☎ *503/788-8883 ⊕ www.wongsking.com.*

 Performing Arts

Academy Theater

This art deco movie theater in Montavilla shows second-run and classic films and serves tasty pizzas from neighboring Flying Pie Pizzeria, along with craft beers. Ticket prices are cheap, and the building's dramatic neon sign is a fun landmark for the neighborhood. ⊠ *7818 S.E. Stark St., Montavilla/82nd Ave.* ☎ *503/252-0500 ⊕ www.academytheaterpdx.com.*

Foster-Powell and Woodstock

◎ Sights

Foster-Powell

One of the city's fastest-growing areas, Foster-Powell encompasses a triangular swath of Outdoor Southeast and is lined with ethnic restaurants, arty dive bars, food carts, tattoo parlors, colorful murals, and offbeat businesses—plus plenty of more prosaic enterprises—along the two main thoroughfares for which the district is named (they intersect, diagonally, about 5 miles east of downtown). The district extends as far east as 82nd Avenue and is one of the city's most diverse, with large Chinese, Vietnamese, Russian, and Hispanic populations. It's also still fairly affordable, hence the more recent influx of younger entrepreneurs as well as artists and students. ⊠ Bounded by S.E. Powell Blvd., S.E. Foster Rd., and S.E. 82nd Ave., Foster/Powell ⊕ www.fosterpowell.com.

★ Portland Mercado

This colorful and community-driven complex of indoor and outdoor food stalls and markets, flanked by a row of picnic tables, is Portland's own little Latin America with business owners from Mexico, Brazil, Cuba, Venezuela, and elsewhere throughout Central and South America. A great destination for eating and socializing, the colorfully painted Mercado is also a business incubator that helps Latin American entrepreneurs thrive both here

and throughout Portland, and it's a thriving anchor of the diverse Foster Powell neighborhood. Be sure to step inside the central interior space to view displays with facts and historic photos about the city's and region's Latin American community. Vendor highlights include Sandino Coffee Roasters, Kaah Neighborhood Market, Tierra del Sol (Oaxacan), Que Bola (Cuban), and Barrio neighborhood bar. ⊠ 7238 S.E. Foster Rd., Foster/Powell ☎ 971/200–0581 ⊕ www.portlandmercado.org.

Shopping

Fubonn Shopping Center

The elder statesman among a growing number of international markets around Southeast 82nd Avenue, Fubonn consists of independent vendors carrying sushi, bubble tea, pho, and more. The biggest draw is the ginormous Asian grocery, where you'll encounter a seemingly endless array of imported fruit and veggies, meat and seafood, and packaged goods. The candy section itself is larger than some grocery stores. ⊠ 2850 S.E. 82nd Ave., Montavilla/82nd Ave. ☎ 503/517–8877 ⊕ www.fubonn.com.

💻 Coffee and Quick Bites

Bella's Italian Bakery

$ | Bakery. The heavenly baked goods—ricotta cheesecake, pear tartines, anise biscotti, and savory pepperoni rolls—are reason enough to venture out to this Lents neighborhood bakery-cafe, but don't overlook the delicious breakfast and lunch fare (and pizza dinners, on Thursdays only). Bella's is also a gourmet Italian food and wine market. **Known for:** Sunday baked lasagna and Thursday-night pizza; Italian cold-cut sandwiches; fresh local-fruit tartines and cakes. *Average main: $8* ✉ *9119 S.E. Woodstock Blvd., Foster/Powell* ☎ *971/255–1212* ⊕ *www.bellasitalian-bakery.com* ☽ *Closed Mon. No dinner (except Thurs. pizza night).*

Doe Donuts

$ | Bakery. On the eastern edge of Foster-Powell, this cute and tiny shop offers a menu of both year-round and seasonal vegan dough-nuts in such tantalizing flavors as pink lemonade (tart-lemon glaze with pink sprinkles) and zucchini-chocolate chip. There's also vegan ice cream. **Known for:** completely vegan menu; a retail space with no seating; Heart coffee and Numi tea drinks. *Average main: $5* ✉ *8201 S.E. Powell Blvd., Foster/Powell* ☎ *503/333–4404* ⊕ *www.doedonuts. com* ☽ *Closed Tues. No dinner.*

★ Heart Coffee

$ | Café. Inside this sleek Woodstock café, with additional locations Downtown and on East Burnside, patrons sip fine coffees sourced from Central America, South America, and Africa, and indulge in breakfast and lunch fare, such as savory and sweet porridges, granola, toasts, and salads. Finnish owner Wille Yli-Luoma brings a modern, minimalist aesthetic to this striking space with plenty of tables for working and socializing. **Known for:** well-crafted lattes; deca-dent pastries; toasts using local Tabor River Bread. *Average main: $8* ✉ *5181 S.E. Woodstock Blvd., Southeast* ☎ *503/208–2710* ⊕ *www. heartroasters.com* ☽ *No dinner.*

🍴 Dining

Arleta Library Bakery Cafe

$ | American. Steps from tree-shaded Mt. Scott Park and just a few blocks from the up-and-coming Foster Road corridor, this cozy family-owned café has been a favorite for affordable and tasty breakfast and lunch fare—using mostly organic ingredients—for years. The semolina-wheat griddle-cakes are topped with organic maple syrup and seasonal fruit, and the "gooey grilled cheese" with avocado and bacon hits the spot on a cool rainy day. **Known for:** flaky scones and biscuits with house-made jam and parmesan eggs; Sicilian hash (weekends only) with braised beef; rotating quiche of the day. *Average main: $9* ✉ *5513 S.E. 72nd Ave., Foster/Powell* ☎ *503/774–4470* ⊕ *www.arletalibrary.com* ☽ *No dinner.*

Assembly Brewing

$ | Pizza. Detroit-style pizza with thick, crunchy crusts are the specialty of this handsome craft brewery in increasingly hip Foster-Powell. It's open until 2 am, and there's ample seating inside and on the adjacent patio. **Known for:** diverse list of house-brewed craft beers; gorgeous murals on both inside and exterior walls; plenty of salad, appetizer, and sandwich options. *Average main: $15* ✉ *6112 S.E. Foster Rd., Sellwood/Moreland* ☎ *971/888-5973* ⊕ *www.assembly-brewingco.com.*

Ate-O-Ate

$ | Hawaiian. This laid-back counter-service restaurant in Woodstock, with a second location at East Burnside and 24th, specializes in classic Hawaiian fare, such as kalbi beef shortrib and kalua pig plate lunches with creamy macaroni salad, and ahi poke bowls with kimchee. There's also a noteworthy selection of sandwiches, including a huge teriyaki burger. **Known for:** frozen tropical cocktails; Spam musubi; coconut rice pudding. *Average main: $14* ✉ *5200 S.E. Woodstock Blvd., Woodstock* ☎ *971/865-5984* ⊕ *www.ate-oh-ate.com.*

Char

$ | Pizza. This quintessential neighborhood pizza joint in Foster-Powell has a number of features that set it apart from the usual, including interesting toppings on the pizzas (each are named for the owners' cats), a row of old-school arcade games in section called the "Charcade," and a worthy selection of well-crafted cocktails. Picnic tables and a bar facing the pizza-making kitchen impart a convivial vibe. **Known for:** interesting pizza topping combinations; arcade games; chocolate cannoli. *Average main: $12* ✉ *4144 S.E. 60th Ave., Foster/Powell* ☎ *503/477-5942* ⊕ *www.charpizza.com* ⊗ *No lunch weekdays.*

★ Ha & VL

$ | Vietnamese. This humble, no-frills banh mi shop amid the many cheap and authentic Asian restaurants on S.E. 82nd stands out not just for its filling sandwiches (these crispy-bread creations come with fillings like spicy Chinese sausage, pork meat loaf, or sardines) but also for the daily featured soup, such as peppery pork-ball noodle soup on Wednesday and Vietnamese turmeric soup, with shrimp cake and sliced pork, on Sunday. There's also a diverse selection of thick milkshakes—top flavors include avocado, mango, and durian. **Known for:** milkshakes in unusual flavors; pork-ball noodle soup (on Wednesday only); barbecue pork loin banh mi sandwiches. *Average main: $9* ✉ *2738 S.E. 82nd Ave., No. 102, Montavilla/82nd Ave.* ☎ *503/772-0103* ⊗ *Closed Tues. No dinner.*

Off the Griddle
$ | Vegetarian. With bar-top and wooden table and booth seating, fresh-baked pies on display, and a super-relaxed counter-service ambience, Off the Griddle feels like a pretty typical—if extra cute—diner, but this Foster Road standby is entirely vegetarian (and mostly vegan). Indeed, the menu reflects the greasy-spoon sensibility, with jackfruit brisket hash, biscuits and gravy with braised kale, walnut-meatloaf Benedicts, and veggie burgers with tempeh bacon among the standouts. **Known for:** full liquor bar plus vegan milkshakes; delicious vegan fruit pies; outdoor picnic table seating on the sidewalk. *Average main: $12* ✉ *6526 S.E. Foster Rd., Foster/Powell* ☎ *503/764-9160* ⊕ *www.offthegriddle.com* ⊘ *Closed Tues.*

SuperDeluxe
$ | Burger. With a catchy colorful burger logo, this fast-food joint aims to be Portland's answer to In-N-Out Burger and other trendy burger spots. Don't overlook the English muffin breakfast sandwiches, including a delicious avocado and egg version, but the big star here are the juicy burgers. **Known for:** Stumptown Cold Brew milkshakes; really good veggie burgers; fast-food ambience, including a drive-thru window. *Average main: $6* ✉ *5009 SE Powell Blvd., Foster/Powell* ⊕ *www.eatsuperdeluxe.com.*

Tierra del Sol
$ | Mexican. If you had to choose a star among the several outstanding Latin American food carts at the Portland Mercado, you could make a strong argument for this cheap and friendly purveyor of authentic Oaxacan fare. The owners turn out flavorful renditions of their own long-treasured family recipes, including chicken with *chochoyotes* (masa dumplings) in a complex yellow mole sauce, and *tlayudas* (prodigious corn tortillas) topped with chich-arrón, black beans, and Oaxacan cheese. **Known for:** authentic Oaxacan moles; lots of other food and beverage options in the same complex; outdoor (but covered) communal seating. *Average main: $11* ✉ *Portland Mercado, 7238 S.E. Foster Rd., Foster/Powell* ☎ *503/975-4805* ⊕ *www.tierradelsolpdx.com.*

Toast
$ | American. A worth-the-trip breakfast spot in the upbeat Woodstock neighborhood, Toast serves up hearty fare—goat cheese, bacon, and egg breakfast sand-wiches, seared pork belly over pota-toes with a duck egg—using fresh and local ingredients. It's a casual spot with a friendly staff—it feels decidedly Old Portland and unpre-tentious, and there's a pleasant side patio. **Known for:** French toast with apple and pear compote; full beer, wine, and cocktail menu; griddled coffee cakes. *Average main: $10* ✉ *5222 S.E. 52nd Ave., Woodstock* ☎ *503/774-1020* ⊕ *www.toastpdx.com* ⊘ *No dinner.*

Bars and Nightlife

Bar Maven
This popular Foster-Powell standby has a couple of key strengths: lots of outdoor seating, both on the sidewalk and in a large covered patio area with lush landscaping, and excellent Mediterranean-influenced bar food. Best of all, perhaps, is the enticing list of aged whiskeys, bourbons, and aperitifs. ✉ *6219 S.E. Foster Rd., Foster/Powell* ☎ *503/384–2079* ⊕ *www.barmaven-pdx.com.*

5 and Dime
A stylish retro-inspired cocktail bar that's a touch swankier than many of the dive bars on Foster Road, this lively spot turns out well-made drinks—both craft creations and classics, most of them under $10. There's also tasty bar food, such as brussels sprouts and scallop skewers and smoked-fish boards. The bar also shares its kitchen with the casual Atlas Pizza, next door. ✉ *6535 S.E. Foster Rd., Foster/Powell* ⊕ *www.5anddimepdx.com.*

VANCOUVER, WA

NORTH

NORTHWEST

NORTHEAST

SOUTHWEST

SOUTHEAST

Sightseeing ★★★☆☆ | Shopping ★★☆☆☆ | Dining ★★★★☆ | Nightlife ★★★★☆

Although it's located in a different state and is very much its own city—with a population of 175,000—Vancouver is also an important part of greater Portland. Historically, it's also been unfairly overshadowed, both by Portland and because it shares a name with the largest city in western Canada. It's often the case that when you're in Portland, and you mention going to a great restaurant or checking out the new Waterfront in Vancouver, the person you're talking to assumes you're referring to the city 300 miles north, in B.C. (they're both, by the way, named for British explorer George Vancouver, but Washington's settlement is actually older by nearly 30 years). To add insult to injury, the U.S. Vancouver is sometimes disparagingly called "Vantucky," although as the city's "it" factor has lately begun to rise, more than a few locals have begun embracing this nickname positively.—by Andrew Collins

Indeed, residents and visitors to Portland have begun finding plenty of reasons to trek across the Columbia River, most of them in Vancouver's core neighborhoods, which include Downtown and adjacent Uptown Village, and perhaps most significantly, the city's dramatic Waterfront, which underwent a dazzling transformation in 2018. These three areas, along with nearby Fort Vancouver National Historic Site, can easily be visited from Portland in the span of a few hours, and they make up the bulk of this chapter. Downtown and Uptown Village stand out for their impressive array of excellent—and reasonably priced—restaurants as well as a cluster of craft breweries that rank right up there with the best ones in Portland. Shopping is a less compelling reason to visit, in part because Vancouver retailers have trouble competing with Oregon's lack of a sales tax, but the farmers' market in Downtown Vancouver is one of the best in the region. If you're wanting to spend a bit more time in Vancouver, keep in mind that there's a big, pleasant Hilton Hotel in the heart of Downtown, new hotels planned for the Waterfront, and a few other notable accommodations in the area, including the Heathman Lodge. Approach Vancouver with an open mind—were it not adjacent to one of the country's most buzzed-about urban destinations, you'd probably have already heard far more about it by now.

◉ Sights

Clark County Historical Museum

This impressive regional history museum occupies Downtown Vancouver's 1909 Carnegie Library building and contains artifacts and materials related to the region's early indigenous tribes and the later settlements by Europeans. Rotating exhibits tell the continuing story of Vancouver's development, and the museum offers historic walking tours of Downtown and other neighborhoods throughout the year. The museum also operates the Marshall House, adjacent to Fort Vancouver National Historic Site and open to the public daily except Tuesdays. ⊠ *1511 Main St., Vancouver* ☎ *360/993–5683* ⊕ *www.cchmuseum. org* 🖃 *$5* 🕙 *Closed Sun.–Mon.*

Downtown Vancouver

The focal point of Vancouver's steady renaissance into a destination well worth crossing the Columbia River for has been the relatively recent boom in buzzworthy restaurants and brewpubs in the Downtown core. Here you'll find a mix of century-old storefronts and modern buildings, and a beautifully landscaped main square, Esther Short Park, which hosts a popular farmers' market on weekends. The primary thoroughfares, Main and Broadway Streets, abound with eateries and bars along with a growing number of boutiques and galleries. The most festive time for a stroll is during Downtown's monthly First Friday Art Walks, during which galleries and other businesses stay open later than usual and present music, art, pop-ups, and food and drink specials. ⊠ *Vancouver* ✛ *Between 6th St. and Mill Plain Blvd., from Franklin St. to I-5* ⊕ *www. vdausa.org.*

GETTING HERE

Vancouver is most easily reached and explored by car, and you'll find inexpensive metered or free parking in its key neighborhoods. It's about a 20-minute drive from Downtown Portland or a 10-minute drive from Kenton, Woodlawn, or other North Portland neighborhoods, but traffic delays on the Interstate 5 bridge are notorious, so check your favorite navigation app before going. Using public transit, you can take Vancouver's C-Tran Bus 60, which connects with the Delta Park/Vanport yellow line MAX stop in Portland.

Esther Short Park

Vancouver's own little green lung is a compact but beautifully landscaped main square with tall evergreens, a fountain, a picnic shelter, and plenty of park benches. There's also a cute playground, with a clever design inspired by Fort Vancouver, and swings and slides. The park hosts a popular farmers' market on weekends from spring through fall. ⊠ *W. 8th and Columbia Sts., Vancouver* ☎ *360/487–8177* ⊕ *www. cityofvancouver.us.*

★ Fort Vancouver National Historic Site

The earliest permanent settlement on either side of the Columbia River was established as a trading post in 1824 by Hudson's Bay Company. When Washington fell under complete control of the United States through the 1846 Oregon Treaty, Fort Vancouver became the nation's foremost military post in the Pacific Northwest. This 207-acre site in the middle of present-day Vancouver tells the story of the settlement's early days, and how it's been the home of such renowned military leaders as Ulysses S. Grant, George McClellan, and George Marshall (of Marshall Plan fame). In this impressive and somewhat overlooked component of the National Park System, orient yourself at the park visitor center, where you can watch a film about its history. Then tour the reconstructed fort stockade and barracks, and visit the 22 stately Victorian homes of Officer's Row (including the Queen Anne–style Marshall House, which is actually operated by the Clark County Historical Museum). The Pearson Air Museum is also part of the park. ⊠ *1501 E. Evergreen Blvd., Vancouver* ☎ *360/816–6230* ⊕ *www.nps.gov/ fova* 🎟 *Park free; reconstructed Fort Vancouver $10* ⊗ *Closed Sun.–Mon.*

Pearson Air Museum

Located on the campus of Fort Vancouver National Historic Site, Pearson Airfield was established in the 1920s and remains one of the oldest continuously operating airports in the country. The museum, set inside a vintage hangar, contains vintage planes, photos, and related memorabilia. ⊠ *1115 E. 5th St., Vancouver*

WORTH A TRIP: CAMAS, WA

With its all-American downtown of narrow tree-lined streets, boutiques, and cafes, this gateway to the Columbia Gorge is 15 miles east of Downtown Vancouver and makes for a fun afternoon getaway. Sample an IPA on the patio of Grains of Wrath Brewery, browse the vintage goods at Camas Antiques, and catch a movie at the restored 1927 Liberty Theatre. You can even overnight in one of the 23 warmly appointed rooms in the historic Camas Hotel, which also boasts the excellent Pacific fusion restaurant, Tommy O's.

☎ *360/816–6232* ⊕ *www.nps.gov/fova* ⊗ *Closed Sun.–Mon.*

Uptown Village

Just north of Downtown Vancouver, Uptown Village is concentrated mostly along north-south–running Main and Broadway Streets and is home to a clutch of noteworthy restaurants, boutiques, and craft breweries. A good time is during the annual Sip & Stroll in mid-August, during which more than 30 area businesses offer up food and drink throughout the neighborhood. ⊠ *Vancouver* ✛ *Between 15th St. and 4th Plain Blvd., from Franklin St. to I-5* ⊕ *www.uptownvillage.com.*

Vancouver Lake Regional Park

In a city with a remarkable number of parks and green spaces, this 190-acre tract that flanks the western shore of Vancouver Lake stands out for its attractive beach, picnic shelters and barbecue grills, and volleyball courts. Swimming, kayaking, and windsurfing are popular activities on the lake. Bikers, runners, and strollers enjoy making their way along the 2.5-mile paved trail that connects the lake with Frenchman's Bar Regional Park, on the Columbia River. ⊠ *6801 N.W. Lower River Rd., Vancouver* ☎ *360/397–2285* ⊕ *www.clark.wa.gov/ public-works* 🅟 *$3 parking fee for cars.*

★ Vancouver Waterfront

Just a five-minute walk south of Downtown's Esther Short Park, Vancouver's formerly industrial waterfront has been transformed into a handsome, contemporary mixed-use development flanked by a beautifully landscaped promenade and V-shape, cantilevered Grant Street Pier, which is suspended over the Columbia River by cable stays. The $1.5 billion project opened in 2018 and will be expanded over the years—potentially to include a public market. Its other key features include a 7.3-acre Waterfront Park with dramatic public art installations, a sweeping grassy area that's perfect for picnics, a small urban beach, and direct access to the Columbia River Renaissance Trail, an existing 5-mile paved multiuse track that connects additional parks, restaurants, and public art along the north shore of the Columbia River. The waterfront's new mixed-used development houses low- and mid-rise residences and offices, a growing crop of prominent Washington winery tasting rooms (Maryhill, Brian Carter Cellars, Amavi, Pepper Bridge, and Naked

The visual showpiece of the Vancouver Waterfront district is strikingly contemporary Grant Street Pier—pose for a selfie on the edge, which seems to float over the Columbia River. But this is also a prime photo op for planes ascending from or descending into, depending on which way the wind is blowing, Portland International Airport, which is less than 4 miles upstream.

 Share your photo with us!
@FodorsTravel #FodorsOnTheGo

Winery among them), several restaurants, and a brand-new Indigo Hotel (expected to open in early 2020, followed by an AC Hotel by Marriott in 2021). Especially when the sun is out, dynamic new development's restaurant terraces, pathways, and pier fill up with friends, families, and onlookers of all ages. ⊠ *Waterfront Way at Esther St., Vancouver* ⊕ *www.thewaterfront-vancouverusa.com.*

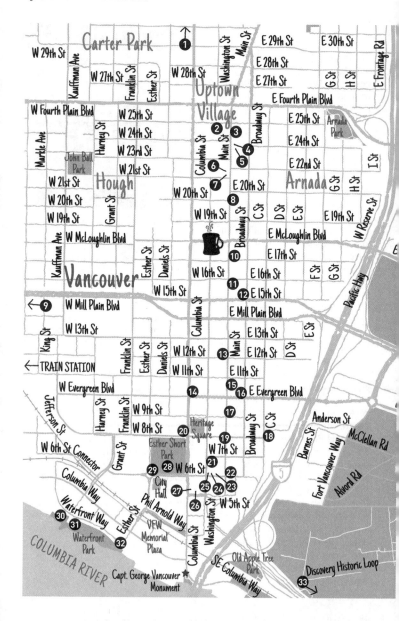

K St
L St
M St
N St
E 29th St

Leach Park
St. James Cemetery
E 27th St
P St
Q St

Vancouver Barracks Post Cemetery
St. Johns Blvd

E Fourth Plain Blvd

Portland VA Medical Center

E McLoughlin Blvd
Fort Vancouver Way
Clark College

Marshall Park

0   250 m

0   1000 ft

E Mill Plain Blvd

Officers Row
E Evergreen Blvd
Memory/Mill Plain Park

Hudson's Bay
E 5th St
Davis Ave

Fort Vancouver National Historic Site
E 4th St
E Reserve St

Pearson Field

SIGHTS

Clark County
Historical Museum .. 11

Downtown
Vancouver 19

Esther Short Park.... 28

Fort Vancouver
National
Historic Site.............. 34

Pearson
Air Museum 35

Uptown Village 2

Vancouver Lake
Regional Park 9

Vancouver
Waterfront 32

SHOPPING

Doppelgänger........... 20

Urban Eccentric 5

Vancouver Farmers
Market 29

Wild Fern
Boutique 7

**COFFEE & QUICK
BITES**

Ice Cream
Renaissance 8

Relevant Coffee........ 10

Treat Bakery 14

DINING

Amaro's Table 13

Bleu Door Bakery 3

Brewed Cafe
& Pub 22

Elements
Restaurant 17

Lapellah.................... 33

Little Conejo 25

Marcell's Pie House .. 1

Nom Nom
Restaurant 18

Nonavo Pizza............ 24

Rally Pizza 36

Smokin' Oak Pit 26

Wildfin
American Grill.......... 31

BARS & NIGHTLIFE

Beerded Brothers
Brewing 23

Burnt Bridge
Cellars Winery
& Bar......................... 12

Grocery
Cocktail & Social 21

Loowit Brewing 27

Maryhill Winery
Tasting Room
& Wine Bar 30

Thirsty
Sasquatch................... 6

Trap Door
Brewing 4

Trusty Brewing 16

PERFORMING ARTS

Kiggins Theatre........ 15

Shopping

Doppelgänger

This petite boutique overlooking Esther Short Park is stocked with smartly curated women's and men's clothing—think oversized sweaters, flannel shirts, denim from Silver Jeans, and practical but fashionable shoes and boots. ⊠ *302 W. 8th St., Vancouver* ☎ *360/328–1084.*

Urban Eccentric

This endearingly funky vintage shop in Uptown Village and impressive—and very reasonably priced—assortment of high-quality pre-owned men's and women's clothing and accessories, including hats, shoes, and jewelry. ⊠ *2311 Main St., Vancouver* ☎ *360/694–2934.*

★ Vancouver Farmers Market

One of the largest farmers' markets in the Northwest, this wildly popular event (held Saturdays and Sundays from mid-March through late October) in leafy Esther Short Park features some 250 vendors offering up everything from crafts and gifts to produce, baked goods, artisan coffee, and a wide range of short-order snacks and foods. There's always live music and great people-watching. Additional related events include a Harvest Market held the Saturday before Thanksgiving and a Holiday Market, which takes place across the street at the Hilton Vancouver the Saturday and Sunday after Thanksgiving. ⊠ *Esther Short Park, W. 6th and Esther Sts., Vancouver* ☎ *360/737–8298* ⊕ *www.vancouverfarmersmarket.com.*

Wild Fern Boutique

This hip little Uptown Village clothier carries both men's and women's attire, with brands like Free People and Brixton leading the charge. You'll also find locally made skincare products and jewelry. ⊠ *2106 Main St., Vancouver* ☎ *360/823–8600* ⊕ *www.wildfernboutique.com.*

 Coffee and Quick Bites

Ice Cream Renaissance

$ | Café. This friendly little ice cream parlor in Uptown Village specializes in rather elaborate ice cream sundaes—such as the Bellini banana split with strawberries 'n' cream, honey vanilla, and milk chocolate ice creams—as well as ice cream sodas with cherry or vanilla syrup and old-fashioned s'mores. Flavors range from conventional to offbeat, with honey-lavender and bittersweet chocolate among the favorites. **Known for:** over-the-top ice cream sundaes; malted milkshakes; affogato. *Average main: $5* ⊠ *1925 Main St., Vancouver* ☎ *360/694–3892* ⊕ *www.icecreamrenaissance.com.*

★ Relevant Coffee

$ | Café. This spacious, contemporary coffeehouse turns out some of the best third-wave, single-origin coffees and espresso drinks, including nitro cold brew and mochas made with Portland's Ranger Chocolates. **Known for:** a rotating list of pour-over coffees; turmeric tea with coconut and almond milk and cracked black pepper; an attractive, airy dining room with ample seating. *Average main: $5 ✉ 1703 Main St., Vancouver ☎ 971/319–5773 ⊕ www.relevant-coffee.com ☉ No dinner.*

Treat Bakery

$ | Bakery. This slick and stylish little dessert café is perfect for a midday sweet or an after-dinner (it's open later on Friday and Saturday evenings) bowl of "ooeygooey buttercake" or seasonal bramble-berry-crisp ice cream. Chocolate chip cookies with locally sourced Freddy Guys hazelnuts, home-made ding dongs, rhubarb-jam doughnuts, and apple hand-pies are among the decadent offerings. **Known for:** heavenly frosted sugar cookies; house-made hard and soft-serve ice cream; open until 9 pm on Friday and Saturday. *Average main: $5 ✉ 210 W. Evergreen Blvd., Vancouver ☎ 360/750–0811 ⊕ www.facebook.com/treatvancouver ☉ Closed Sun. No dinner.*

🍴 Dining

Amaro's Table

$$ | Modern American. One of the more sophisticated contemporary dining spaces in Downtown Vancouver, this locally focused modern American bistro offers a surprisingly affordable menu, with many dinner entrées clocking in under $20, including a daily-changing risotto and a wild-salmon nicoise salad. Other highlights include one of the best cheeseburgers in town, ricotta doughnuts with caramel sauce for dessert,

and a well-chosen wine list with a mix of international and Northwest bottles. **Known for:** crispy, classic fried chicken with honey butter; a vast selection of amaro and related cocktails; pleasant and peaceful side patio with umbrellas. *Average main: $18 ✉ 1220 Main St., Vancouver ☎ 360/718–2942 ⊕ www.amarostable.com.*

Bleu Door Bakery

$ | Bakery. Breakfast is the biggest draw at this Uptown Village bakery, with bacon-cheddar biscuits with sausage gravy, and ham and Swiss over waffles with syrup being especially popular. But don't overlook the tasty Cobb salad, tuna-avocado sandwiches, and made-from-scratch soups at lunch. **Known for:** crab Benedicts and mimosas at brunch; breakfast and lunch quiches; croissants, lemon bars, cookies, and other pastries. *Average main: $12 ✉ 2411 Main St., Vancouver ☎ 360/693–2538 ⊕ www.bleudoorbakery.com ☉ Closed Mon. No dinner.*

Brewed Cafe & Pub

$ | Café. A favorite venue for hobnobbing with friends and people-watching, this two-level lounge and café is a great place to dine, snack, drink, or work away on your laptop. Kickstart your day with a breakfast sandwich or everything bagel, or opt for a mango-ham melt or BLT with avocado later in the day, washing down your meal with cold brew, flavored lattes, or a pint of beer. **Known for:** well-prepared coffee drinks along with beer and wine; hearty lunch and breakfast sandwiches; excellent desserts.

Average main: $8 ✉ *603 Main St., Vancouver* ☎ *360/597–3386* ⊕ *www. brewedcafepub.com* ☾ *No dinner Sun.*

★ **Elements Restaurant**

$$$ | **Pacific Northwest.** This romantic bistro in Downtown Vancouver is one of the city's most esteemed sources of deftly prepared, European-influenced Northwestern cuisine, such as Spanish-style octopus a la plancha with harissa and kalamata olive oil emulsion, and cocoa-and-chile-rubbed New York strip steak with red wine honey. Elements is also one of the best brunch spots in town—consider the shrimp and grits with Cajun gravy. **Known for:** decadent steak and seafood grills; great happy hour prices; bread pudding French toast with stone-fruit chutney. *Average main: $29* ✉ *907 Main St., Portland* ☎ *360/258–0989* ⊕ *www.elementsvancouver.com* ☾ *Closed Mon. No dinner Sun.*

Lapellah

$$$ | **Pacific Northwest.** A stylish, contemporary space with dim lighting and views of a wood-fired oven, this upscale Pacific Northwest bistro is in a shopping center a couple of miles east of Downtown. It's worth the trip for seasonally sourced fare like confit pork belly with peach emulsion and shishito peppers, and fire-roasted chicken with coq au vin ragout, and there's a noteworthy happy hour with smart food and drink deals. **Known for:** coal-grilled steaks with interesting seasonal preparations; excellent desserts, some featuring house-made ice cream; popular,

boozy weekend brunches. *Average main: $24* ✉ *Grand Central Retail Center, 2520 Columbia House Blvd., Vancouver* ☎ *360/828–7911* ⊕ *www. lapellah.com.*

★ **Little Conejo**

$ | **Modern Mexican.** The brick-and-mortar home base of one of the best purveyors of authentic Mexico City-style tacos in the region (they also operate a food truck in North Portland), this hip little counter-service cantina also boasts an impressive mezcal and margarita cocktails. About 10 reasonably priced tacos are offered, including Modelo beer–battered fish, carrots *al pastor* with crema and avocado salsa, and chorizo and gooey melted cheese. **Known for:** chilaquiles and eggs at Sunday brunch; extensive mezcal selection; outstanding street-food-style tacos. *Average main: $12* ✉ *114 W. 6th St., Vancouver* ☎ *360/718–2633* ⊕ *www.littleconejo. com* ☾ *Closed Mon. No dinner Sun.*

Marcell's Pie House

$ | **American.** Well-versed in the art of baking rich savory pies and fresh-fruit dessert pies, this charming little café also offers live music, an arts and ceramic gallery, and a charming garden patio. Brunches are a highlight at Marcell's (consider the eggs Benedict), and there's a noteworthy wine and beer list. **Known for:** chicken potpie; a cozy sitting room with a fireplace and a lending library; a daily-changing selection of fresh fruit pies. *Average main: $12* ✉ *3100 Columbia St., Portland* ☎ *360/258–1583* ⊕ *www.*

marcellspiehouse.com ⊙ *Closed Mon. No dinner.*

Nom Nom Restaurant

$ | Vietnamese. Plenty of Portlanders know this popular modern Asian restaurant from the delicious food it doles out in the PSU farmers' market in Portland, but at the brick-and-mortar location in Downtown Vancouver you can sample a far more extensive menu of Vietnamese and Thai delights, including sweet-and-sour tamarind tom yum soup, wok-fried shrimp with ginger and green beans, pineapple-fried rice, and beef green curry. The contemporary dining room has soaring floor-to-ceiling windows—it can get a little loud in here on busier nights. **Known for:** a variety of fried-rice (pineapple, basil, crab) dishes; satisfying pho, noodle, and curry bowls; extensive cocktail list. *Average main: $11* ⊠ *801 C St., Vancouver* ☎ *360/718-7360* ⊕ *www.nomnomnw.com.*

Nonavo Pizza

$ | Pizza. This hip, contemporary pizzeria—set along a strip of trendy little Downtown eateries—serves up delectable personal pies with both classic (crushed tomatoes, pepperoni, wild mushrooms) and less-common (Bolognese sauce, herbed almond ricotta cheese, chorizo) toppings. There are always a few bountiful salads on hand, the components of which change according to what's in season, and ice cream and root-beer floats are on offer for dessert. **Known for:** a margherita pizza and a draft beer

for $10 during daily happy hour; hazelnut pizza with red onion, garlic, mozzarella, and greens; cheerful, high-ceilinged storefront dining room with counter service. *Average main: $13* ⊠ *110 W. 6th St.* ☎ *360/843-9696* ⊕ *www.nonavopizza. com* ⊙ *Closed Sun.–Mon.*

★ Rally Pizza

$ | Pizza. Make your way to this spacious, contemporary spot in a small shopping center 6 miles east of Downtown to devour some of the metro area's best hearth-baked pizzas—the fennel sausage pie with sweet-and-sour onions and smoked mozzarella is a standout. Also worth trying are sides of seasonal vegetables roasted in the pizza oven, along with generous salads and house-made frozen custard "concretes" and sundaes for dessert. **Known for:** blistered, perfectly crispy pizza crusts; the campfire frozen-custard sundae with Graham cracker crumbles, fudge sauce and smoked marshmallow; boozy milkshakes. *Average main: $15* ⊠ *8070 E. Mill Plain Blvd., Vancouver* ☎ *360/524-9000* ⊕ *www.rallypizza.com.*

Smokin' Oak Pit

$$ | Barbecue. Head to this stylish joint next to Loowit Brewing with brick walls, high ceilings, and a massive whiskey bottle chandelier for seriously delicious Texas barbecue. The Texas Trinity platter of sliced brisket, spare ribs, and sausage is a crowd pleaser, but you'll also find tender pulled-pork sandwiches, smoked beet salads, buffalo-style fried cauliflower, and sides of moist corn bread. **Known**

for: Guiness-braised smoked pork belly (Tuesday only); wallet-friendly happy hour deals; cheesecake with seasonally rotating flavors. *Average main: $20* ✉ *501 Columbia St., Vancouver* ☎ *360/433–2755* ⊕ *www. thesmokinoakpit.com* ☉ *Closed Mon.*

Wildfin American Grill

$$$ | **Seafood.** The wall of tall windows and spacious terrace overlooking Grant Street Pier and the beautiful Vancouver Waterfront account for part of this cavernous restaurant's popularity, but the well-priced, Northwest-sourced seafood also earns high marks. Consider sharing a Wildfin appetizer tower (garlic prawns, calamari, smoked salmon spread) among friends, before graduating to Alaskan crab-stuffed cod with chive beurre blanc, or the local seafood fettuccini Alfredo with clams, wild salmon, white fish, and prawns. **Known for:** sweeping views of the Columbia River; "barrel to bar" Northwest wines on tap; excellent steaks and burgers. *Average main: $23* ✉ *777 Waterfront Way, Portland* ☎ *360/718–7701* ⊕ *www.wildfinameri-cangrill.com.*

☕ Bars and Nightlife

Beerded Brothers Brewing

This hole-in-the-wall Downtown tap room gives new meaning to the term "nano-brewery," but despite its tiny dimensions, Beerded Brothers turns out big-flavored craft ales, including a heady black IPA and a crisp pale ale. Sugarfoots BBQ provides tasty bar food on week-ends, including Frito pies and bourbon bread pudding. ■**TIP**➜ This is a 21+ only establishment. ✉ *106 W. 6th St., Vancouver* ☎ *360/606–5806* ⊕ *www.beerdedbrothers.net* ☉ *Closed Mon.*

★ **Burnt Bridge Cellars Winery & Bar**

When wine publications single out the best of Vancouver and surrounding Clark County's increasingly well-respected producers, this Downtown winemaker with a handsome art-filled tasting room usually makes—and sometimes tops—the list. Stop for a flight or a full pour—standouts include the well-balanced Tempranillo, the Bordeaux-style Merlot-forward Blend X, and the inky, food-friendly Pont Brûlé Grenache-Syrah-Mourvedre. ✉ *1500 Broadway St., Vancouver* ☎ *360/695–3363* ⊕ *www.burntbridgecellars.com* ☉ *Closed Mon.–Wed.*

Grocery Cocktail & Social

Satisfyingly tasty pub fare, including massive burgers, and an eclectic menu of cocktails, wines, ciders, and beers with a decidedly local slant are the highlights of this oft-packed Downtown lounge with exposed rafters and a cozy upstairs conversation nook. ✉ *115 W. 7th St., Vancouver* ☎ *360/258–1324* ⊕ *www. thegrocerycocktailsocial.com.*

★ **Loowit Brewing**

This well-respected craft brewer on the south edge of Downtown offers some of the better pub grub (try the bone marrow elk burger) of any taproom in town plus live music many evenings, darts and video games, and a dog-friendly patio. The extensive tap list includes some guest brews and ciders, and you can also order Maryhill Wines. ✉ *507 Columbia St., Vancouver* ☎ *360/566–2323* ⊕ *www.loowitbrewing.com.*

★ Maryhill Winery Tasting Room & Wine Bar

Enjoy a full tasting, or sit back with a glass or bottle over a plate of Olympia Provisions charcuterie or a Dungeness crab roll at this big, rambling tasting room and bistro on Vancouver's scenic waterfront. At this outpost of the famous winery in the eastern Columbia gorge, both the indoor and outdoor tables offer great views of Grant Street Pier and the Columbia River. ✉ *801 Waterfront Way, Vancouver* ☎ *360/450–6211* ⊕ *www.maryhill-winery.com.*

Thirsty Sasquatch

This warmly lit, timber-walled bar in a vintage brick building in Uptown Village stands out for two specialties: a superb list of nearly 30 Oregon and Washington drafts (some of them quite hard to find), and an equally estimable list of local artisan ryes and whiskeys. Flights are a good way to acquaint yourself with a few types of each. ■**TIP**➔ This is a 21+ only establishment. ✉ *2110 Main St., Vancouver* ☎ *360/597–3223* ⊕ *www.thirstysasquatch.com.*

Trap Door Brewing

A convivial tap room with a large side patio and food carts, Trap Door was started in 2015 by a fourth-generation family of brewers and has quickly become one of the most vaunted microbreweries in the metro area. It's a favorite of hop lovers, with several IPAs (including New England–style hazy and a tart wild-yeast collaboration with Portland's Cascade Brewing). ✉ *2315 Main St., Vancouver* ☎ *360/314–6966* ⊕ *www.trapdoor-brewing.com.*

Trusty Brewing

This corner craft brew pub with tall windows and ample sidewalk seating turns out some of the best IPAs in the metro Portland–Vancouver region, plus a roasty brown ale and a coriander-inflected Belgian-style Grand Cru. If you're feeling a bit peckish, the pickled-veggie board and potato taco with jalapeño-avocado sauce are reliable bets. ✉ *114 E. Evergreen Blvd., Vancouver* ☎ *360/258–0413* ⊕ *www.trustybrewing.com.*

 Performing Arts

★ Kiggins Theatre

With its striking red-and-gold vertical marquee and art deco Streamline Moderne design, this 1930s single-screen cinema—which received a painstaking restoration in 2006—is one of Vancouver's most prominent buildings. It's also a fun place to catch a film, with indies, classics, and other offbeat fare presented. The cozy Marquee Lounge upstairs serves craft beer and local wine along with pizza by the slice. ✉ *1011 Main St., Vancouver* ☎ *360/816–0352* ⊕ *www.kigginstheatre.com.*

RESOURCES

Car: Although traffic has increased dramatically in recent years (Portland ranks as the 10th worst city in the country in traffic congestion), the city is fairly easy to navigate by car, and if you're planning to explore neighboring regions—such as the coast, Willamette Wine Country, and Columbia Gorge—it's best to do so by car, as public transportation options to these areas, especially the coast, are very limited. That said, parking Downtown can get expensive and a car isn't necessary for getting around the city itself. If you plan to rent a car, most major rental agencies have Downtown offices, and renting Downtown can save you plenty of money, as you avoid paying the hefty taxes and surcharges that you must pay at the airport agencies.

Public Transportation: TriMet (⊕ *www.trimet.org*) operates an extensive system of buses, streetcars, and light-rail trains. The North–South streetcar line runs from Nob Hill through the Pearl District, Downtown, and Portland State University campus to South Waterfront. The A and B Loop streetcar lines cross the Willamette River to the East Side via Broadway Bridge and the Tilikum Crossing Bridge.

MAX light rail links the city's eastern, southern, and western suburbs as well as North Portland with Downtown, Washington Park and the Oregon Zoo, the Lloyd Center District, and the Hollywood District and the airport. From Downtown, trains operate daily about 5 am–1 am, with a fare of $2.50 for up to 2½ hours of travel (transfers to other MAX trains, buses, and streetcars are free within this time period), and $5 for an unlimited all-day ticket, which is also good system-wide. A one-month pass costs $100. The ticket for riding without a fare is stiff.

You can pay your fare by purchasing a reloadable Hop Fastpass card at a number of grocery and convenience stores around town, downloading Hop Fastpass app and paying with your phone, or paying in cash on buses (exact change required) or at ticket vending machines at streetcar and MAX light rail stops. If you buy a physical ticket, hold onto it whether you're transferring or not; it also serves as proof that you have paid your fare. The most central bus routes operate every 10 to 15 minutes throughout the day. Bikes are allowed in designated areas of MAX trains, and there are bike racks on the front of all buses.

VISITOR INFORMATION

Up to date information can be found on Portland's tourism website, ⊕ *www.travelportland.com*. Several local magazines, papers, and websites provide information on the city's culture and entertainment. "A&E, The Arts and Entertainment Guide," published each Friday in the *Oregonian* (⊕ *www.oregonlive.com*), contains listings of events. *Willamette Week* (⊕ *www.wweek.com*), published free each Wednesday, is available throughout the metropolitan area with hipper listings. The *Portland Mercury* (⊕ *www.portlandmercury.com*), also free, is an even edgier entertainment publication distributed each Wednesday. The glossy newsstand magazine *Portland Monthly* (⊕ *www.pdxmonthly.com*) covers Portland culture and lifestyle and provides great nightlife, entertainment, and dining coverage.

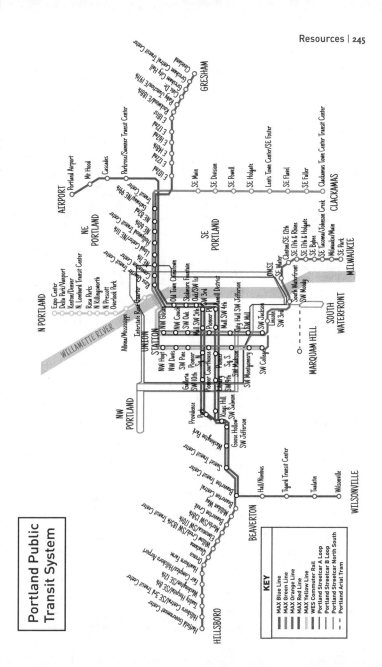

Portland Public Transit System

INDEX

Photo Credits

Chapter 4: ARTYOORAN/Shutterstock (96). Chapter 5: Hotel Eastland (114). Chapter 9: Nicholas Steven/Shutterstock (222). Chapter 10: Van Rossen/Shutterstock (235).

NOTES

NOTES

Fodor's INSIDE PORTLAND

Publisher: Stephen Horowitz, *General Manager*

Editorial: Douglas Stallings, *Editorial Director;* Jill Fergus, Jacinta O'Halloran, Amanda Sadlowski, *Senior Editors;* Kayla Becker, Alexis Kelly, Rachael Roth, *Editors*

Design: Tina Malaney, *Director of Design and Production;* Jessica Gonzalez, *Graphic Designer;* Mariana Tabares, *Design & Production Intern*

Production: Jennifer DePrima, *Editorial Production Manager;* Carrie Parker, *Senior Production Editor;* Elyse Rozelle, *Production Editor;* Jackson Pranica, *Editorial Production Assistant*

Maps: Rebecca Baer, Senior *Map Editor;* Andrew Murphy, *Cartographer*

Photography: Viviane Teles, *Senior Photo Editor;* Namrata Aggarwal, Ashok Kumar, Carl Yu, *Photo Editors;* Rebecca Rimmer, *Photo Intern*

Business & Operations: Chuck Hoover, *Chief Marketing Officer;* Robert Ames, *Group General Manager;* Devin Duckworth, *Director of Print Publishing;* Victor Bernal, *Business Analyst*

Public Relations and Marketing: Joe Ewaskiw, *Senior Director Communications & Public Relations;* Esther Su, *Senior Marketing Manager*

Fodors.com: Jeremy Tarr, *Editorial Director;* Rachael Levitt, *Managing Editor;* Teddy Minford, *Editor*

Technology: Jon Atkinson, *Director of Technology;* Rudresh Teotia, *Lead Developer;* Jacob Ashpis, *Content Operations Manager*

Illustrator: Jennifer Reynolds

Writers: Andrew Collins, Jon Shadel

Editor: Alexis Kelly

Production Editor: Carrie Parker

Designers: Tina Malaney, Chie Ushio

1st Edition
ISBN 978-1-64097-250-6
ISSN 2688-9749

All details in this book are based on information supplied to us at press time. Always confirm information when it matters, especially if you're making a detour to visit a specific place. Fodor's expressly disclaims any liability, loss, or risk, personal or otherwise, that is incurred as a consequence of the use of any of the contents of this book.

SPECIAL SALES
This book is available at special discounts for bulk purchases for sales promotions or premiums. For more information, e-mail SpecialMarkets@fodors.com.

PRINTED IN CANADA

10 9 8 7 6 5 4 3 2 1

ABOUT OUR WRITERS

Former Fodor's staff editor **Andrew Collins** is based in Mexico City but resides part-time in Portland, where he's the editor of *The Pearl* magazine (which focuses on the city's trendy Pearl District). A long-time contributor to more than 200 Fodor's guidebooks, including *Pacific Northwest, Santa Fe, New England, Inside Mexico City,* and *National Parks of the West,* he's also written for dozens of mainstream and LGBTQ publications—*Travel + Leisure, New Mexico Magazine, AAA Living, The Advocate,* and *Canadian Traveller* among them. Additionally, Collins teaches travel writing and food writing for New York City's Gotham Writers Workshop. You can find more of his work at AndrewsTraveling.com. He authored the following chapters: Experience Portland, Pearl District and Old Town/Chinatown, Inner North and Northeast Portland, Inner Southeast Portland, Outer North Portland, Outer Northeast Portland, Outer Southeast Portland, and Vancouver, Washington. You can find more of his work at ⊕ *AndrewsTraveling.com.*

Jon Shadel is a Portland-based writer, editor, and multimedia journalist, whose work appears in the *Washington Post, VICE,* Condé Nast's *them., Atlantic CityLab,* and many other outlets. Prior to embarking on a career as a roving freelancer, they worked as the top editor at MEDIAmerica, a publisher of Pacific Northwest magazines and travel guides. They authored the Nob Hill and Downtown chapters in this book. Learn more about their work covering culture, travel, and technology at ⊕ *www.jdshadel.com.*

As an Army brat living overseas, **Jennifer Reynolds** used to thumb through Fodor's guidebooks in the back seat of the family car on road trips to find all the places she wanted to see. Today she is an illustrator and graphic designer living in Portland, Oregon. She has a BFA in Painting and Drawing from UNT and attended PNCA for Communication Design. Her work include branding for many of Portland's belo food establishments, illustrated maps for travel and airline magazines and an Oregon themed coloring book, published by West Margin Press. She can be found in one of Portland's many parks or coffee shops when she isn't in her North Portland studio. She illustrated all of *Inside Portland.* You can follow her Instagram adventures @jennyreynoldspdx.